THE NEW
INTERNATIONAL
WILDLIFE
ENCYCLOPEDIA

Volume 7

THE NEW INTERNATIONAL
WILDLIFE ENCYCLOPEDIA

GENERAL EDITORS
Dr. Maurice Burton
Robert Burton

Purnell Reference Books
Milwaukee • Toronto • Melbourne • London

Contents

Library of Congress Cataloging in Publication Data

Main entry under title:

The New international wildlife encyclopedia.

Previous ed. by M. Burton and R. Burton published in 1969-70 under title: The international wildlife encyclopedia.
SUMMARY: A 21-volume encyclopedia devoted to the physical characteristics, behavior, and natural environment of animals, birds, and fishes of the world.
1. Animals — Dictionaries. [1. Animals — Dictionaries] I. Burton, Maurice, 1898- II. Burton, Robert, 1941- III. Burton, Maurice, 1898- The international wildlife encyclopedia.
QL9.B8 1979 591'.03 79-9181
ISBN 0-8393-6178-5

Gall wasp

The familiar oak apples and marble galls on oak, and 'robin's pin-cushion' on wild roses are made by insect larvae. Some of these are made by the gall wasps, minute insects belonging to the order Hymenoptera and forming a superfamily, the Cynipoidea. They are closely related to the chalcid wasps (p 408). Over 80% of cynipid wasps make their galls on oak and about 7% of them affect roses. There are 228 species of cynipid wasps in Britain alone. Other gall-forming insects include certain saw-flies (also Hymenoptera), the gall flies and gall midges (Diptera) and some of the aphids (Hemiptera). In most cases, as in gall wasps, particular species confine their attentions to one species or genus of plant.

Food and shelter for the larvae

All gall wasps lay their eggs in the tissues of some particular part of the plant, a flower-bud, a leaf-bud, the blade of a leaf or even the root. No effect is seen until the minute larva hatches from the egg, but from this time on, the tissue of the plant surrounding the larva develops abnormally, usually swelling up and providing the insect with both shelter and food. It is believed that the plant tissues are stimulated to grow in this irregular way by some secretion given out by the larva. The swelling size, colour and shape of the gall depend on the species of wasp that laid the egg. In some cases a number of eggs are laid and the larvae grow up together enclosed in the same gall. The activities of the mature insects, as far as they are known, seem to be concerned almost solely with completing the complicated life cycles typical of gall wasps.

Types of gall

There are many different types of gall only a few of which can be described here.

Oak apple. When fully formed the oak apple is a round, spongy, fruit-like object, 1–2 in. diameter and coloured light brown or pink. If opened in June and July when mature it will be found to contain a number of larvae, usually about 30, each enclosed in a little chamber in the gall tissue. The oak apple represents a stage in the life history of the gall wasp *Biorhiza pallida*, whose life cycle will be described later.

Marble gall. Caused by the gall wasp *Andricus kollari*, this is the most familiar of all the oak galls and is often mis-named 'oak apple'. It is green when it reaches full growth—rather less than 1 in. diameter—in August and then turns brown and woody and remains on the twig after the leaves fall, when it is very conspicuous. It harbours only one larva of the gall wasp, whose exit hole can be seen in an old gall. Often there is more than one exit hole, and this means that the gall has harboured other parasites or 'inquilines'. Males of this gall wasp are quite unknown. In an attempt to find them 1½ bushels of the galls were once collected and the wasps bred out, but among over 12 000 females that hatched not one male was found.

Common spangle gall. In July numbers of little round button-like objects can often be seen on the undersides of oak leaves, attached by a central stalk, so they look like tiny, very short-stemmed mushrooms. This is one of the two kinds of gall formed by *Neuroterus quercus-baccarum*. Each contains a single larva, and in September the stems break, and the galls fall to the ground where the insects inside them pass the winter. The wasps that hatch in April (females only) climb the trees again and give rise to currant galls, which look like bunches of red currants and in no way resemble the spangle galls, which the next generation of wasps will again produce. This alternation of generations is more fully described below.

Bedeguar gall. Also known as the moss gall or robin's pin-cushion this spectacular gall of wild rose bushes is almost as familiar as the marble gall. The part containing the larvae is surrounded by a tangled mass of branched fibres, green at first, turning to bright red in July and August. Inside it are 50 or more cells, each containing a larva of the gall wasp *Diplolepis rosae*.

Unusual life history

In many gall wasps there is an 'alternation

Top left: Spangle galls on underside of leaf. Top right: Marble gall showing exit hole, with oak apple sectioned to show grub. Above: Ready to face the world, a wasp leaves its gall.

of generations', already mentioned in connection with the spangle and currant galls. The rather similar life cycle of the oak apple gall wasp *Biorhiza pallida* shows this.

When the oak apple is mature, the larvae in it pupate; the wasps hatch in July and eat their way out. They include both males and females, the former being winged, the latter wingless. After mating, the females crawl down the trunk of the tree and enter the soil, making their way to the small fibrous roots, in which they lay their eggs. When the larvae hatch, galls develop on the roots, round, dark brown and of ½ in. diameter, wholly unlike an oak apple. The wasps which emerge from these are all wingless females. They must find the tree trunk, crawl up it and seek the ends of the shoots, where they lay their eggs (without mating) in the terminal buds. When these hatch the larvae form a new generation of oak apples.

In the case of the spangle gall and currant gall wasp *Neuroterus quercus-baccarum* the female-only generation appears in April,

having overwintered in the fallen spangle galls among dead leaves under the tree. These wasps lay unfertilised eggs which form the larvae, giving rise to the currant galls and causing a bi-sexual generation.

The life history of the marble gall wasp *Andricus kollari* is something of a mystery. We have mentioned that males of this gall wasp are quite unknown, but as long ago as 1882 an entomologist claimed that the species known as *Andricus circulans*, which makes galls on Turkey oak, is really the bi-sexual generation of *Andricus kollari*. This was confirmed in 1953.

Food always to hand

The sole food of the larva of any gall wasp is the substance of the gall which forms round it. The mature insects probably do little more than take a drink when needed.

Woodpeckers are known to peck open marble galls to get at the larva and currant galls are sometimes eaten by birds, which probably mistake them for fruit. By far the most serious enemies of gall wasps, however, are other insects which lay eggs in the gall. The larvae of some of these are parasites or predators on the 'legitimate' larva, the parasites slowly eating it alive, the predators

killing it and eating it outright. Others are inquilines, which feed on the substance of the gall, and so rob the primary inmate but do not otherwise harm it except sometimes to starve it enough to stunt its growth. The inquilines do not have it all their own way, for they too are preyed upon by predators and parasites, and these in their turn have parasites specially adapted to afflict them, known as hyperparasites. The inquilines are usually other species of gall wasp and the parasites chalcid wasps or ichneumons.

If bedeguar galls are collected in late winter and kept in jars over damp sand, a remarkable assembly of tiny wasps will emerge. In one such experiment only a quarter of the insects were *Diplolepis rosae*, the makers of the gall, and of these (which numbered over 16 000) less than 1% were males. No alternation of generations is known in *D. rosae*, and it looks as if males are on the way to disappearing altogether.

Make your own ink

The very common and familiar marble gall has been a feature of the British countryside only since 1834, when it was found in a nursery garden in Devon. The gall, with its

△ *Sliced-open gall shows a mature wasp and the chamber in which it has developed.*

wasp *Andricus kollari*, had been brought into the country for use in the dyeing industry and for making ink, the tannic acid in the galls being the chemical agent involved. In fact, anyone can make ink from marble galls. All you have to do is to bruise 4 oz of galls with a hammer, put them in a quart of boiling water and leave for 24 hours. Then take $1\frac{1}{2}$ oz of ferrous sulphate and dissolve rather less than an ounce of gum arabic in a little water. Filter the infusion of galls through cloth and add the other ingredients together with a few drops of carbolic acid. But perhaps it is better to buy a bottle of ink!

phylum	**Arthropoda**
class	**Insecta**
order	**Hymenoptera**
super-family	**Cynipoidea**

Gannet

Gannets are goose-sized relatives of the boobies (p 264) that live in temperate regions of the world. The three kinds are considered by some ornithologists to be separate species and by others to be varieties of one species. There is little difference between the three.

Gannets are oceanic birds coming ashore only for the breeding season. They are strong fliers and cover vast distances, especially during the first year of life. Ringing has shown that New Zealand gannets migrate to Australian waters, setting out shortly after they have left the nest and crossing the intervening sea at an average of up to 240 miles a day. The northern gannet migrates south to the Gulf of Mexico and the Canaries.

The gannet of the North Atlantic, known in parts of northern Britain as the solan goose, breeds on both sides of the ocean. In America, there are half a dozen colonies around Newfoundland and the Gulf of St Lawrence. It also breeds off Iceland, the Faeroes and the British Isles, with small colonies in Norway, Brittany and the Channel Islands. The largest colony is on the island of St Kilda. The Cape gannet breeds off South Africa and the Australian or Pacific gannet in the Bass Strait between Australia and Tasmania and North Island, New Zealand.

Gannet pugnacity

Gannets live by feeding on fish and squid, plunging in from a height or diving from the surface. Fish are caught as the birds surface rather than being impaled on the beaks of the gannets as they penetrate the water. The gannets do not dive very deep and will chase their prey, propelling themselves with both feet and wings.

The main food of the northern gannet is haddock, herring, mackerel, saithe, sprat, and whiting. These are important commercially but it is very unlikely that the gannets affect the numbers caught by fishermen. In fact, the commercial catches of herring and other fish around the British Isles are going down, probably because of overfishing, yet the gannet population is steadily rising. So there are almost certainly no direct links between numbers of either the gannets or their prey. The Australian gannet feeds mainly on anchovies although it will take a variety of fish.

Gannet colonies are usually perched on small offshore islands or rocks, often no more than steep-sided towers rearing out of the sea, like Bass Rock on the Firth of Forth or Bird Rock in the Gulf of St Lawrence. The nests are closely packed together, perhaps $2-2\frac{1}{2}$ ft between each, so the cliff ledges and the tops of the rocks or islands are white with birds.

In February, when the rocks are still being

Top: A gannet colony carpets a cliff-top.
Right: Like a diver on a high board, a gannet goes through its take-off procedure.

Eric Hosking

John Barrie

lashed by winter gales, the male gannets appear in the colonies to re-establish ownership of last year's nest or if breeding for the first time they fly low over the colonies looking for abandoned nests. Fights are frequent as gannets defend their nests or seek to oust interlopers. They are not sham fights as often is the case among birds that nest in dense colonies. The gannets grapple each other's bills or grab their opponent's head or neck, shaking, twisting and lunging for up to 2 hours.

chalky white. As the egg is being laid, the gannet bends its tail under its body, directing the egg into the nest. This is probably another adaptation from their original cliff-nesting habit, where it is essential that the egg should not be allowed to roll away. Gannets have no brood patch where the egg is held to keep it warm. Instead the egg is held between the webbed feet. The gannet holds the egg lengthwise under its body and wraps a web around each side of the egg, overlapping underneath. Both parents in-

tors, except on St Kilda and a few other places where man has taken the sitting birds or their young. On Bird Rock, the building of a lighthouse gave access to the gannet colony which was nearly wiped out because the birds were killed for use as fish bait.

The main enemies of the colonies are herring gulls or black-backed gulls that steal eggs. Skuas chase the adults, forcing them to disgorge the food they are carrying back to their chicks.

John Warham

Furious fights in courtship

Bryan Nelson, who spent several years studying gannets on Bass Rock, has suggested that gannets originally nested on cliff ledges and the nesting on the flat spaces on top is relatively recent. This would explain several of the gannets' habits. When cliff-nesting birds fight, one of them is sure to be pushed over the edge within a short time, automatically cutting short the fight. Gannets, on the other hand, grapple with their beaks and wrestle to and fro, neither bird appearing to be able to disengage. The fierceness of the gannets' behaviour is continued in their courtship. The females are pecked during mating and whenever the males return to the nests after feeding.

The nests are large, compacted piles of seaweed, grass, earth and all sorts of rubbish including fish nets and tin cans. One list of materials included a gold watch and a set of false teeth. The pile is cemented by droppings and is useful as a jumping-off point for takeoff, as gannets have difficulty taking off from flat ground.

Feet make a hotwater bottle

The single egg, about 3 in. long, is a translucent pale blue at first, later turning to a

cubate, working in shifts of 1—2 days apiece.

Incubation lasts about 44 days. The chick hatches naked but quickly acquires a coat of down. At first it is brooded on top of the parents' feet then later sits by itself in the nest while the parents collect food for it. At Bass Rock the chicks are fed mainly on mackerel which they take by thrusting their heads into the parent's mouth.

When they have fledged at the age of 2 months the young gannets are abandoned by their parents and left to fend for themselves. They leap out of their nests and if they are lucky they immediately become airborne. Otherwise each has to struggle through the colony to the cliff edge, being attacked on the way and perhaps killed by the other gannets. Once airborne, the young gannets can fly quite well, but after they have settled on the sea they cannot rise again. On leaving the nest they are very fat and they spend some time losing weight until they become airborne again and learn to catch their own food.

Violated sanctuary

On their inaccessible stacks and rocks gannets are immune to mammalian preda-

△ *Open wide: mealtime for a gannet chick.*

Dive-bombing technique

A flock of gannets feeding is a most spectacular sight. Like boobies, they plunge vertically into the sea, with wings half-closed, from a height of 100 ft or more. There is a continual rain of gannets diving down and disappearing with a spurt of spray. Later they emerge and climb again to rejoin their companions flying around above them before repeating the descent.

Hitting the water at perhaps 100 mph could result in severe injury. But gannets and boobies have very much strengthened skulls that protect the brain. An intricate system of air sacs in the head cushions the impact, and the nostrils open inside the bill so preventing water from entering the air passages.

class	**Aves**
order	**Pelecaniformes**
family	**Sulidae**
genus & species	***Sula bassana*** *common gannet* ***S. capensis*** *cape gannet* ***S. serrator*** *Australian gannet*

Gaper

*Normally a bivalve mollusc lives within two shells or valves which can be closed tight or allowed to gape when the animal feeds—but a gaper is a bivalve mollusc which cannot close its shell. The two siphons of a gaper are connected throughout their length and although they may sometimes be withdrawn into the shell they are usually held fully extended. This causes the shell at the hinder end to gape widely. In Britain closely related species of **Mya** and **Lutraria** are given the name. Off the coasts of North America there are two species.*

The three British species are the sand gaper, or old maid, with a shell nearly 8 in. long, the similar blunt gaper, with a narrower shell, and the small gaper. The sand gaper is also found on the coast of North America. The North American gaper of the Pacific shores from Alaska to San Diego is similar to but slightly smaller than the sand gaper.

Fountains on the shore

Found along the seashore or in shallow water down to 150 ft, the gaper burrows slowly into the mud, using the small foot at its lower end. It normally digs in vertically at 8–12 in. depth, with its long, fringed valve openings at its top end flush with the surface of the mud. A small depression in the mud shows where it lies buried.

When the tide is out, the North American gaper—which rejoices in the alternative names of summer clam, rubber-neck clam, high-neck clam, horse clam, otter-shell clam, and great Washington clam—gives more spectacular evidence of its presence. At fairly regular intervals, its siphons shoot a jet of water to a height of 2–3 ft. These jets are even more powerful when someone walks over the sand. Another water-squirting clam which looks and behaves like a gaper is the geoduck (pronounced go-ee-duck). Both geoduck and gaper are dug out for food, and so—occasionally—are the sand and blunt gapers in Britain.

How the siphon works

These water jets give a good clue to the gaper's methods of feeding and breathing. Water is drawn in through one siphon and passes across the gills, as explained under clam (see clam on page 449). Fine particles of food are extracted and oxygen is taken from the water for breathing. The water is then ejected through the other siphon, carrying with it waste products from the body. The way food is dealt with by the ciliated gills has been described for the cockle (p 470).

Losing its beard

The sexes are separate, the eggs and milt are shed into the sea through the exhalant siphon. The fertilised egg is developed into the usual veliger larva (see cockle, p 470). When the larva changes into the gaper, it is only 1/10 in. across, and at first is quite different from the adult. The very small gaper has a relatively large foot and short siphons, and it has a small bunch of byssus threads (see clam, p 449) for fastening itself to a solid support. Gapers are known to live 17 years.

Food for walruses

Gapers are attacked by different enemies according to where they grow. Everywhere they are eaten by carnivorous sea-snails, such as whelks, which are collectively known as drills, from their habit of drilling holes in the shells with their radulae, or file-like tongues. On the shore, gapers are attacked by seabirds and in some places foxes visit the shore at low-tide and dig out gapers. Fishes with stout jaws for crushing shellfish may take them, and in northern latitudes the blunt gaper forms the main food of the walrus.

Cutting off their feet

Although the double siphon of a gaper is protected by a tough brown skin with two horny valves at the tip, part of it, apparently, is often sacrificed, because these tips are commonly found in the stomachs of halibuts. Nevertheless, these lost portions can be regrown.

Another natural hazard of clams in general is that when violently disturbed they contract the muscles closing their shells so forcibly that a slight blow on the outside will cause their shells to break. A gull seizing one and flying up to 50 ft or so to drop it onto the beach is on to a good thing. The shell will then break as certainly as if dropped onto rock.

Some clams are their own enemies. When suddenly disturbed they may snap their shells so rapidly that they cut off the end of the siphons or the tip of their own foot. Professors GE and Nettie MacGinitie, American marine biologists, report how they found small living animals on the shore which puzzled them. Even with the aid of zoologist colleagues they were unable to classify them. Finally, these 'animals' turned out to be pieces of clam siphon, still capable of muscular contraction and with cilia still beating, hours after they had been cut off by their former owners.

Heather Angel

Common otter-shell. When relaxed and undisturbed, the gaper's siphon protrudes from its shell, taking in food and water and discharging body wastes and water. Some gapers are valuable: **Mya arenaria,** *the sand gaper, is well-known to Americans as the soft-shelled clam, and forms the basis of East Coast clam-bakes and chowders.*

phylum	**Mollusca**
class	**Bivalvia**
subclass	**Lamellibranchia**
order	**Heterodonta**
family	**Lutraridae**
genus & species	*Lutraria lutraria* common otter-shell
order	**Adapedonta**
family	**Myidae**
genera & species	*Mya arenaria sand gaper* *M. binghami small gaper* *M. truncata blunt gaper* *Schizothaerus nuttallii* N American gaper others

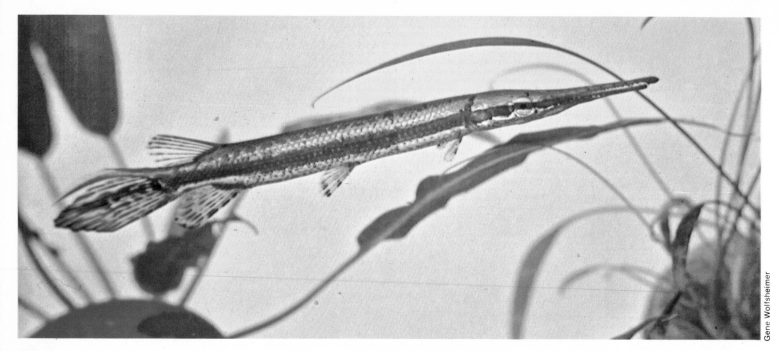

Gene Wolfsheimer

Gar

These slender pike-like fishes are living fossils of a family that reached its peak in the Mesozoic period 70—220 million years ago. There are seven species living in the rivers and lakes of North and Central America.

The commonest is the longnose gar, or billfish, which lives from the Great Lakes southwards. It is up to 5 ft long, its slim body covered with a tough armour of close-set diamond-shaped or rhombic enamelled (ganoid) scales which do not overlap in the usual manner of fish scales. The long snout is a beak; its jaws studded with small sharp teeth recall those of the gharial among crocodilians, the beak being twice as long as the rest of the head. The dorsal and anal fins are set far back on the body. The back is olive to silver, the underside white.

The shortnose gar, up to 2 ft long, lives mainly in the Great Lakes. The tropical gar of Mexico is said to reach 10 or even 12 ft, and the alligator gar which ranges from southern United States to Panama and Cuba is about the same size. Its snout is very like that of an alligator.

Indolent fishes

The gars live mainly in still waters, where they lie almost motionless among water plants, looking more like floating logs than fish. They move quietly and slowly to stalk passing prey, which is seized with a sudden sideways slash of the snout. Although apparently so lethargic gars can move rapidly when necessary. Their food is mainly other fishes but little animal food is refused. Frogs, salamanders and worms are readily accepted and the young gar feeds largely on water insects. They soon take to catching fish, however, and a young 2 in. gar is on record as taking 16 young minnows in quick succession. It is easy to imagine from this the predatory nature of the gar and why fishermen hate them, and gars also take

bait from their hooks. A gar can, with one snap of its jaws, seize a whole group of small fishes. With larger fish the prey must be gradually worked round in the mouth into a position from which it can be swallowed head first. All food takes 24 hours to digest, which is slow compared with most other freshwater fishes.

Eggs and babies stick to rocks

The males mature in 3—4 years, the females taking 6 years. Spawning is from March to May in shallow waters, each female being accompanied by 3 or 4 males. The average number of eggs laid per female is about 28 000 but may vary from 4 000 to 60 000 according to her size. The eggs are sticky and cling to rocks and water plants. In a few days they hatch and the baby fishes fix themselves to water plants by cement organs, adhesive discs at the end of the snout, and hang there until the yolk sac has been absorbed. After this they swim freely, feeding at first on mosquito larvae.

Rapid growth

In spite of its reputation for voracity, justified if by nothing else by its almost shark-like teeth, a gar has a low food consumption, feeds irregularly and has a slow rate of digestion. Yet it is one of the fastest growing of freshwater fishes. In its first year a young male gar grows on average just over $\frac{1}{10}$ in. a day to reach $19\frac{1}{2}$ in. by the end of the first season, the female reaching 22 in. in the same period. After that growth slows down to 1 in. a year but continues for 13—14 years in the females, which outlive the males. Because it moves about so little—even its feeding is leisurely—and because it has a high metabolic efficiency (that is, its body makes the fullest use of all its food), the energy supplied by the food goes into growing in size instead of being dissipated by moving about quickly and continuously.

Arrowheads and ploughs

In all probability it is because its scales are so closely set, forming such a rigid covering, that a gar must lead an inactive life. This

△ *The dart-shaped body of short-nosed gar helps it merge with surrounding water plants.*

tough scaly armour of the gar has, however, proved very useful and been used by different peoples in different ways. The original inhabitants of the Caribbean islands are said to have used the skin, with its diamond-shaped, closely fitting scales, for breastplates. Some of the North American Indians separated the scales and used them for arrowheads. The early pioneers in what is now the United States found gar skin hard enough to cover the blades of their wooden ploughs.

class	**Osteichthyes**
order	**Amiiformes**
family	**Lepisosteidae**
genus & species	***Lepisosteus osseus*** longnose gar ***L. platystomus*** shortnose gar ***L. spatula*** alligator gar ***L. tristoechus*** tropical gar

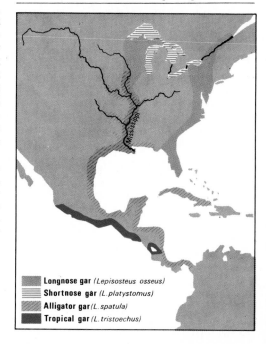

■ **Longnose gar** *(Lepisosteus osseus)*
▤ **Shortnose gar** *(L.platystomus)*
▨ **Alligator gar** *(L.spatula)*
■ **Tropical gar** *(L.tristoechus)*

Garden snail

All too familiar to most gardeners, the garden snail is the second largest land snail in Britain. Its shell is up to 1½ in. across, with 4½–5 whorls. Its tabby appearance is due to 5 dark brown spiral bands on a fawn, yellowish or buff background, the bands being broken by streaks of the ground colour making it look mottled. The shell is calcium carbonate (chalk) covered by a glaze of protein material which tends to wear off with age. The snail itself is dark grey. The head has two pairs of tentacles, the larger of which has eyes at the tips and can be pulled inside out by a muscle running up the inside. The smaller pair has other sense organs. When the snail withdraws, the opening into its shell is filled by a collar of soft tissue finely speckled with

Rock-boring snails

Needing calcium for their shells, snails tend to flourish where soils and rocks are rich in it, and they are less fond of clay soils. Where calcium is scarce, the shell may be very thin, as in some populations in the Channel Isles. On the other hand, some areas are notable for the holes bored in limestone by these snails. These are about 1 in. across and may extend 3 or 4 in. upwards into the rock, worn by generations of snails. The garden snail is absent from northern Europe but occurs in the Netherlands, France, Spain, Portugal and around the Mediterranean and the Black Sea. It has also been introduced, or has found its way, to North and South America, Australia, southern Africa, Cuba, Mauritius and St Helena. In Britain it is widespread, except in the north of Scotland, and is most abundant in southern England, especially near the sea, and is found in gardens, hedges and quarries, under cliffs and banks and in old walls, particularly if ivy-covered.

outwards. Evaporation and the production of slime can lead to excessive loss of water but these are greatly reduced when the snail withdraws into its shell, as it does during dry periods. Its rate of living also slows down and months or years can be endured without re-awakening. There are records of snails remaining inactive for as long as 4 years and the Rev W Bingley wrote in 1805 of snails re-awakening after they had been more than 15 years in somebody's collection.

Under normal conditions this sleep may be ended by the return of wet weather, with a dramatic reappearance of active snails. Any deficiency in body water is then made up by absorption through the skin. Consequently, the amount of water in a snail's body is forever fluctuating, and the volume and concentration of the blood varies more particularly.

Home after a meal

Inside the mouth is a hard, curved plate, 2–3 mm across, called the jaw, and below

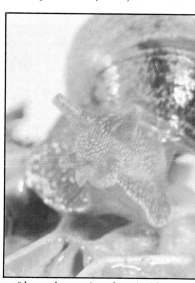

Emerging from its shell, a snail spreads its two pairs of horns by turning them inside out, and raises its head to survey the scene before setting off.

Series by Jane Burton: Photo Res.

yellowish grey, and this has a hole, called the pneumostome, passing through it that periodically opens and closes. This lies a little to the animal's right side and leads into the 'lung', a cavity just beneath the shell used in breathing and also, by decreasing in volume, allowing the snail into its shell.

The garden snail **Helix aspersa** (aspersa for 'besprinkled') is often known as the common snail and 'garden snail' is commonly applied to **Cepaea hortensis**, a close relative of the banded snail (p 130). Confusion is avoided if one uses the proper scientific name.

Freak shells are sometimes found in which the whorls twist in the reverse direction or are separated, making a corkscrew or cornucopia. Sometimes the colouring may be a more or less uniform yellow. Artificial monstrosities were once made for amusement. A snail would be removed carefully and placed in a shell of similar size but of another species. Eventually the snail would anchor itself in the shell and lay down new shell whorls of a different pattern and colour.

Multi-purpose slimes

A snail moves by waves of muscular activity passing forwards along the sole of the foot. Generally 7 at a time can be seen as it moves over a sheet of glass. It gives out slime from just behind the head to make its slime track. This is not a continuous smear, but a series of patches where the foot has touched the ground. Slime of other kinds is given out from other parts of the body, including a bright yellow slime discharged when the snail is irritated. Slime, secreted by the collar, dries to form one or a series of membranes, sealing the opening of the shell when the snail is withdrawn, or it may be used to seal the opening against a flat surface.

Snails spend much of their lives drawn inside the shell during dry spells and in winter. Preparation for hibernation may begin as early as September, the snails congregating among the roots of shrubs or in old walls or burying themselves several inches in the earth, the mouth of the shell then being sealed. Young snails may spend a shorter time hibernating or may awaken temporarily on mild days in winter, but adults seldom stir until the following April.

The moist surface of a snail, unlike our own skin, allows water to pass inwards or

this is the file-like radula or tongue with 15 000 file-like horny teeth arranged in rows (see abalone p 6).

Garden snails, generally less of a pest in gardens than slugs, eat the leaves of many plants including lettuce, hops, primrose, nasturtium, alder and, more remarkably, nettle and holly. They are fond of fruit and they may eat dead slugs and earthworms. Spindle and yew are said to be poisonous to them, and one may sometimes find large numbers of empty shells under yew trees. Snails will also eat paper. They have a well-developed homing instinct and regularly return from their foraging expeditions to the same roosting place, which is often communal. Gardeners who try to get rid of snails by throwing them over a fence should know they will return, even climbing the fence to do so.

Uneven life history

Each snail has both male and female organs, being hermaphrodite. Mating, which may last half a day, takes place throughout spring and summer. Two snails, after mutual fondling, plunge their 'love darts' into each other. They are small chalky darts ⅓ in. long (see banded snail, p 130), slightly curved and with four longitudinal blades, ejected

from special muscular sacs. Then follows an exchange of sperm contained in long packets called spermatophores. The eggs, 40–100 or so, are laid soon after in holes in the soil and covered over. They are slightly oval, $\frac{1}{6}$ in. long, with tough, whitish coverings. They hatch in 2–4 weeks.

Although eggs are laid soon after pairing, the sperm can survive for a long while after being exchanged so eggs can be laid months later without further mating. In another species this interval has been known to extend as long as 4 years.

The young snails hatch with a glossy, unbanded shell of about 1½ whorls and grow to a third or half of the final size by the time they are ready to hibernate. Growth, like their lives so influenced by the weather, is not even. It involves the periodic rapid addition of shell around the aperture, sometimes as much as 1 in. in 2 weeks. The outer protein layer is produced first. Individuals have been known to live 5–10 years, but 2 years is more usual.

A neglected delicacy

Enemies are rats, moles, hedgehogs, field voles, rabbits, ducks, geese, domestic fowls, thrushes, blackbirds, glowworms, certain beetles and flies—and man. In Britain winkles (sea snails) and oysters are eaten with relish, and sometimes the Roman or edible snail. But although land snails of various kinds are eaten on the European Continent, few people in Britain can be persuaded to eat the garden snail. This was not always so, and in the 19th century 'wall fish', as garden snails were called, were on sale in markets at Bath, Bristol, Swindon, Covent Garden in London, and probably elsewhere. The glassmen of Newcastle enjoyed a feast of them once a year until at least 1880. An excellent imitation cream could be made from milk plus the slime.

Above and top: Garden snails mating. Although snails are hermaphrodite, they reproduce by exchanging the products of their gonads after stabbing each other with their 'love darts'.

Shells found in Wick Barrow, Stogursey, suggest that garden snails were eaten in the early Bronze Age, about 1 800 BC, and they seem to have been used in Roman-British times in the west of England. The Romans cultivated snails in 'cochlearia', the first of which were set up about 50 BC by Fulvius Hirpinus at Tarquinium. This was recorded by Pliny the Elder who also recommended snails (but not *aspersa*) for coughs and stomach aches (to be taken in odd numbers!). Snails and slugs have been used to treat a variety of ailments, notably pulmonary tuberculosis, coughs and colds. In Yorkshire, at one time, they provided a greenish salve for corns, and in the 1880s, plasters, sold at a penny each in London,

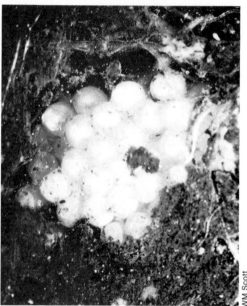

Snails lay clusters of whitish eggs in the soil soon after mating. These take 2–4 weeks to hatch, and the baby snails emerge complete with a glossy, unbanded shell.

were made from papers over which garden snails had crawled.

Two additional uses for the garden snail were recorded by Martin Lister in 1678. He noted that the fluid obtained by pricking snails was used in bleaching wax for artistic purposes and also for making a firm cement when mixed with the white of egg.

phylum	**Mollusca**
class	**Gastropoda**
order	**Pulmonata**
family	**Helicidae**
genus & species	***Helix aspersa***

Garter snake

Garter snakes are the commonest and most familiar snakes of the United States and Canada. They also occur in Mexico. They are found farther north than any other reptile in the Western Hemisphere, the common garter snake as far north as 67 degrees latitude, in the Yukon. Garter snakes are non-venomous, slender, marked with longitudinal stripes, commonly 2 ft, sometimes 3 ft long, the record being 4½ ft. The common garter snake may be black, brown or olive with three yellowish, orange or red stripes. The stripes may be vivid or dull. The belly is usually yellow or greenish. All-black individuals may occur. One species, known as the ribbon snake, has three golden-yellow stripes, and its scales are more markedly keeled than in other garter snakes. It lives in southeastern Canada and the United States east of the Mississippi, especially in marshy areas, and takes readily to water. Another subspecies, the western ribbon snake **Thamnophis sauritus proximus***, lives west of the Mississippi.*

From sea level to the Rockies

Garter snakes live in a variety of habitats from sea level to high up in the Rockies. The mountain garter snake is the only reptile in the Rocky Mountain National Park. The Mexican garter snake is found up to 13 000 ft. They are, however, often restricted to the neighbourhood of streams and lakes in the western half of the United States but are found almost everywhere in the humid eastern half. The plains garter snake is found even in the suburbs of towns such as New York and Chicago, where they hibernate in cracks in the ground near the bases of buildings.

They are the last reptiles to go into winter quarters and the first to come out, as early as March, from a hibernaculum which may be as deep as 3 ft underground. A saying of one tribe of North American Indians is that the first clap of thunder brings them out of hibernation.

It is said there is one or another subspecies of garter snake in every state, and in places the species overlap. Where they do there is no competition. The different species tend to occupy slightly different habitats, one preferring damper ground than the other, for example, and usually they show slightly different food preferences. They also tend to breed at different times.

Early food is worms

Young garter snakes feed almost entirely on earthworms in their first year. After that, although worms are the chief item in their diet, they also eat frogs, toads and salamanders, sometimes fish and occasionally birds' eggs. Large garter snakes may eat mice.

Very large litters

Mating takes place near the winter quarters, soon after the snakes come out in late winter. The male has tiny barbels on his chin which

Des Bartlett: Photo Res

he passes along the female's back as he prepares to mate with her. Once mating is over the snakes disperse to their summer ranges. The young are born alive in summer in litters of usually 50–60 but the number may vary from 12 to 78. The newly-born garter snake is 6 in. long. It grows a foot a year for the first 2–3 years, is mature at 2 years old, is ready to mate in its third spring and may live 12 years. There is, however, a very heavy death-rate during the first few months, due mainly to predators and deaths from starvation.

Killed in error

Their enemies are snake-eating snakes, hawks, owls, skunks and domestic cats. All-black individuals, or those with indistinct stripes, are apt to be killed by people in mistake for poisonous snakes. They are also killed in large numbers on the roads.

Garter snakes take readily to water; this wandering garter has hunted down a small speckled dace and is dragging it onto a stretch of floating algae before tucking in.

A garter snake's defence is to give out an obnoxious fluid from a pore on either side of the vent. It may bite but this has little effect on the human skin.

Some snakes lay eggs; others, such as garter snakes, bear their young alive. The first is called ovipary, the second is ovovivipary and in this the eggs remain inside the mother until they hatch. In both the eggs contain yolk for feeding the developing embryo but in ovoviviparous snakes oxygen for breathing and moisture must be supplied by the maternal tissues, so the shells must be very thin, virtually no more than a transparent membrane in most cases. In garter snakes, as well as European adders, sea snakes and the Australian

copperheads, a sort of placenta is formed to carry nourishment from mother to developing young. It is a very simple affair, nothing like as efficient as the placenta of mammals, but it is enough to supplement the yolk supply already in the egg.

The main advantages of ovovivipary are that there is no chance of the eggs drying up and the temperature remains fairly constant. The mother can choose basking areas with suitable temperatures. This is important in latitudes where summers are short and where even summer temperatures are not high. Add to this the advantages of having even a simple placenta and it is easy to see why garter snakes can live so far north. The disadvantages of ovovivipary are that the mother is encumbered, less agile and therefore handicapped in hunting and in dodging enemies. In most species this is minimized by the broods

△ *Colourful version of the common garter, with three stripes of vivid yellow.*

carried being small in numbers. It is the more remarkable, therefore, that garter snakes should commonly have 50–60, even 78 young in a brood.

class	**Reptilia**
order	**Squamata**
suborder	**Serpentes**
family	**Colubridae**
genus & species	***Thamnophis sirtalis*** common garter snake ***T. elegans*** mountain garter snake ***T. elegans vagrans*** wandering garter snake ***T. radix*** plains garter snake ***T. sauritus*** ribbon snake, others

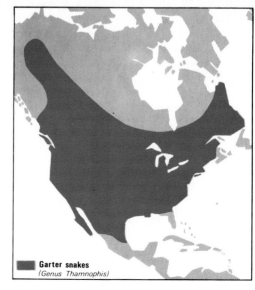

Garter snakes
(Genus *Thamnophis*)

Gaur

The gaur is the largest species of wild cattle, usually standing 5½–6 ft, but one male shot in Burma stood 7 ft high with a girth of 8½ ft. The average weight of males is just under 1 ton with females somewhat smaller. Both sexes are black, with legs whitish from the knees and hocks down. Young gaurs are brownish-orange until they reach maturity. The horns are semicircular, curving sideways and corrugated at the base. They grow to 25 in. Male gaurs are immensely muscular and usually have a dewlap.

Closely related to the gaur are the banteng and the kouprey. Both are smaller than the gaur. Gaurs are still common in many places and banteng are not rare, but the kouprey is scarce. The male bantengs are black in the southern parts of their range and tawny in the north. Females are khaki or tawny. The legs and rump are white. The kouprey is the same size as the banteng. Both sexes are grey, with white patches on shoulders and rump as well as the legs.

The gaur lives in India, Burma, Vietnam and Malaya, where it is called the seladang. Recently it has been found in Yunnan, in southern China. The banteng inhabits Burma and Vietnam, is not found in Malaya or Sumatra, but is found again in Java and Borneo. The kouprey is restricted to northern Cambodia and southern Laos.

Cows lead the herds

These huge wild cattle live in mountain forests in small herds that are basically associations of cows with their calves. In January and February a herd of gaur usually consists of 5 or 6 animals of which 1 or 2 will be bulls. Then, in April or May, bulls join the herds for the rut, swelling the numbers to 9 or 10, although individual bulls may move from herd to herd. In May or June, they leave to form small herds of bulls only, or to live singly.

Each herd has a home range in which it is usually to be found. The home range is not exclusive, and several herds may cover one area, wandering 2–5 miles in a day. Sometimes the small herds join together so 50 or more gaur may be seen feeding in one valley. While they are feeding, one member of the herd, usually a cow, may stand, with head raised, on a mound or anthill, presumably acting as a sentinel, giving a loud whistling snort if danger threatens. A cow will also lead the herd while it is on the move.

Both gaur and banteng have been domesticated. The domestic gaur, called the gayal or mithan, is sometimes said to be a separate species, formed by the crossing of wild gaur and common cattle. The gayal has shorter horns and a wider forehead than the gaur. It is kept only by the Nagas

▷ *Heavyweights in the wild: Indian gaur cattle in a forest clearing.*

and Mishmis of Assam who use it as a status symbol and for sacrifices, rather than for meat or milk. Banteng are domesticated on the islands of Java and Bali where they are the common domestic stock.

Fond of salt licks

Gaurs feed mainly on grass or occasionally bamboo shoots, but also eat leaves and nuts. They feed in the open, usually at night, returning to the forest to chew the cud during the day. Like many jungle animals, gaurs are very fond of visiting salt licks. These are specially provided by man as a lure when gaurs are needed for domestication.

Wild bull rings

During the rut the bulls move from herd to herd, each mating with many cows, and because the herd is continually changing the hierarchy of bulls is continually changing. The dominant bulls are the largest and they display at each other by standing broadside with head lowered, 10–20 ft from their rival. Then one begins to circle while the other stands still, except to remain broadside-on. This display may last 10–15 minutes, or even as much as an hour, until one bull is intimidated and moves away.

There is no strict breeding season but the peak of the rut is in March and April when the bulls have joined the cows. Gesta-tion takes 9 months, so most calves are born in December or January. The cows leave the herd to give birth, returning after about 4 days.

Mass attack

Tigers may kill gaur calves, but are no match for an adult. A bull gaur advances with head lowered and sweeping up and down, threatening to impale any potential enemy on its horns. Sometimes the whole herd will advance *en masse*, presenting a formidable array of horns.

The last great beast

In 1937, the director of Vincennes Zoo was travelling through Cambodia, when he came across the head of an odd-looking ox hanging as a trophy in the house of a vet, Monsieur Sauvel. Thus the kouprey was first made known to western science and became the last large mammal to be found. It had probably been overlooked because it is rare and lives in country that is hardly penetrated by westerners. When it was first seen it was probably mistaken for banteng or for domestic cattle that had gone wild. Even now little is known about it. It has been suggested that koupreys are cross-breeds between banteng and gaur, Indian buffalo or zebu, the Oriental domestic cattle. Another suggestion is that they are the

△ *A family of banteng, probably a smaller domesticated variety of the gaur.*

descendants of the domestic stock of the ancient Khmer empire. Both its form and its behaviour, however, suggest that the kouprey is a true species. The shape of the horns differs from those of other cattle in Asia, being cylindrical in section, recurved in males and lyre-shaped in females. Old male kouprey fray their horns near the tips, apparently by rubbing them on tree-trunks or anthills. Fraying has not been recorded in other wild cattle, except the European bison.

It is very likely that the kouprey forms a link between the gaur and banteng on the one hand and domestic cattle and the aurochs, the now-extinct wild ancestor of European cattle, on the other (see p 398). As such it is of interest to scientists, but the population, estimated at only 1 000 in 1940, is probably nearly extinct because of the recent wars in its homeland.

class	**Mammalia**
order	**Artiodactyla**
family	**Bovidae**
genus & species	***Bos gaurus*** *gaur* ***B. banteng*** *banteng* ***B. sauveli*** *kouprey*

Gazelle

Gazelles are slender antelopes, dainty and graceful in movement. The males have sweeping, lyre-shaped horns but the females have short spikes or no horns at all. There are 10 species of true gazelle, genus **Gazella,** in Asia and northern and eastern Africa. The best known are, the smallest of all, the Dorcas gazelle, of Algeria to Egypt and the Sudan, only 21 in. at the shoulder, and Grant's and Thomson's gazelles of East Africa. There used to be vast herds of the last two before they were slaughtered by hunters or driven from their homes by the spread of agriculture. All are fawn-coloured with a white rump and belly, and a dark band along the flanks. They have a white streak on either side of the face from eye to muzzle and usually a dark streak below this. Grant's gazelle, together with Soemmerring's and the red-necked gazelles, are the largest, 33–37 in. at the shoulder with a white wedge-shaped patch on the rump.

Three other species are also known as gazelles. These are the Tibetan, Prze-walski's and the Mongolian gazelle, all of the genus **Procapra.** They live on the grassy plains of Siberia, Mongolia, China and Tibet. They lack the glands on face and 'knees' that are features of the true gazelles.

Common or rare
Gazelles usually live in dry country, although some live on fertile plains. Most species are widespread and exist in large numbers. Speke's gazelle, with an inflatable swelling on its nose, is found only in the deserts of Somalia; and Loder's gazelle, a very pale species with narrow, spreading hooves, is restricted to the Ergs, the dune areas of the Sahara. The red gazelle is known from only four specimens, all bought at souks, or markets, in Algeria.

The goitred gazelle, named for the small cartilaginous swelling in the throats of the males, is also a desert animal, living from Arabia to Mongolia. Like many other desert animals it migrates in search of food. In Soviet Asia, around Lake Balkash, the herds come down from the mountains to escape from winter snows and in Kazakh-stan they migrate south some 300 miles across the steppes in winter. In the summer they return to feed on fresh vegetation growing under the snow. During the summer a herd may range over a few square miles but in winter it may have to move over 100 square miles in search of food.

△ A couple of Thomson's gazelle, enjoying a quiet scratch on the high veld.

Water from absorbent shrubs
Gazelles eat grass when it is available, but in dry country they browse low-growing bushes and succulents. Many of them can go without drinking for long periods. Some Grant's gazelle were watched during a drought in East Africa when they ate mainly a certain dry shrub. Experiments showed that at night, when the relative humidity of the atmosphere was higher, this shrub absorbed water from the air, and so by eating at night the gazelles were able to get all the water they needed.

Territorial bucks
The goitred gazelle has a fixed breeding season. In September the bucks join the herds of does and begin to separate them into groups of 2–5, each protected by one buck. At the end of the rut in December the doe herds reassemble. Other species in more tropical areas have no fixed breeding season. In East Africa the strongest bucks of Thomson's gazelle establish territories of 20–60 ft diameter in open country which they defend against other bucks. When the herd, mainly of does, passes through the territory, the buck mounts several does. Any bucks travelling with the does are tolerated, but the rest form a separate herd

on the edges of the open country. In the dry season, the bucks leave their territories and join the main herd migrating to fresh pastures. When they return the territories have to be set up again, and it may not be the same animals that are successful in doing so.

When first born the young crouch hidden until they are strong enough to run. In a few days they can run fast enough to keep up with their mothers.

Wary but unafraid

In East Africa Thomson's gazelles are preyed upon by all four large predators: lions, cheetahs, leopards and cape hunting dogs, as well as hyaenas. Eagles also take the young. In Asia, wolves and tigers prey on gazelles. It is the bucks of the all male herds that suffer most. They live on the fringes of the bush where their enemies can lie in wait.

Although built for running, gazelles do not use their speed to the full. They will run for 200–300 yd, then stop and look back at their enemies, or else they will run about, jinking, rather than trying to put as much space between themselves and their enemies as possible. By contrast, they approach waterholes very carefully. The main herd halts some 200 yd from the water, then a few young bucks will rush up to the water's edge, quickly look round, then dash back to the herd. This is repeated two or three times, before the herd, convinced that there is no danger, comes down to drink.

Domesticated dorcas

Gazelles could be one of the greatest sources of animal protein in the dry parts of Africa and Asia, even though their numbers have been reduced by overhunting. In Kazakhastan, in Asia, for example, where they have been hard hit, there are 100 000 gazelles still alive. The domestication of gazelles along the lines being carried out with eland (p 701) would be no new undertaking. The dorcas gazelle was apparently domesticated by the Ancient Egyptians and the Romans. About 7 000 BC gazelle meat formed an important item in the diet of the people of Jericho, and in Egypt writings in a tomb dated 2 500 BC indicate that the occupant had owned 1 135 head of gazelle. Later gazelles were kept by the Romans. Paintings in Pompeii show them in butchers' shops and they were also used for drawing children's chariots. Their skins were used for leather, their horns for knife handles and their ankle bones for dice.

Gazelle portraits
Gazelle species differ only slightly, and one distinguishing feature is seen in the males — the difference between their sweeping lyre-shaped horns. The females usually have stumpy spikes or no horns at all.
1. Grant's gazelle.   2. Mongolian gazelle.
3. Thomson's gazelle.   4. Goitred gazelle.
5. Dorcas gazelle.
Left: Siesta time — a male Grant's gazelle lies lazily in the afternoon heat near a female, while a herd of zebra grazes peacefully close by.

class	**Mammalia**
order	**Artiodactyla**
family	**Bovidae**
genera & species	*Gazella cuvieri* Thomson's gazelle *G. dorcas* dorcas gazelle *G. granti* Grant's gazelle *G. subgutturosa* goitred gazelle *Procapra gutturosa* Mongolian gazelle

Gecko

Geckos form a family of lizards noted for the large number of species, the structure of their feet, their voices, the differences in the shape of their tails, and for the ease with which some of them will live in houses. The smallest is $1\frac{1}{3}$ in. long; the largest—the tokay—may be 14 in. long.

Geckos are found in all warm countries: 41 species in Africa, 50 in Madagascar, about 50 in Australia, the same in the West Indies, with others in southern and southeast Asia, Indonesia, the Pacific islands and New Zealand, and South America. There are geckos in the desert regions of Mexico and southern California. Several have been introduced into Florida from the Caribbean islands. Spain and Dalmatia, in southern Europe, have the same wall gecko as North Africa.

A liking for houses

The majority of geckos live in trees, some live among rocks, others live on the sandy ground of deserts. Tree geckos find in human habitations conditions similar to, or better than, those of their natural habitat: natural crevices in which to rest or take refuge and plenty of insects, especially at night when insects are attracted to lights. Because geckos can cling to walls or hang upside-down from ceilings they can take full

△ *Pinhole sight: pupils shrunk to four tiny holes, to keep out excessive glare of the sun.*

advantage of these common insect resting places, and so many of them are now known as house geckos.

Hooked to the ceiling

Most geckos can cling to smooth surfaces. Their toes may be broad or expanded at the tips with flaps of skin (lamellae) arranged transversely or fanwise. The undersides of the toes look like suction pads but apparently no suction is involved, nor are the undersides sticky. They have numerous microscopic hooks that catch in the slightest irregularities, even those in the surface of glass, and so a gecko can cling to all but the most highly polished surfaces. The hooks are directed backwards and downwards and to disengage them the toe must be lifted upwards from the tip. As a result, a gecko running up a tree or a wall or along a ceiling must curl and uncurl its toes at each step with a speed faster than the eye can follow. Some of the hooks are so small the high power of a microscope is needed to see them, yet a single toe armed with numbers of these incredibly small hooks can support several times the weight of a gecko's body. In addition to the hooks, most species have the usual claw at the tip of the toe which also can be used in clinging. One species has microscopic hooks on the tip of the tail and these help in clinging.

Tails for all tastes

The tail is long and tapering, rounded or slightly flattened and fringed with scales, according to the species, or it may be flattened and leaf-like. A South American gecko has a swollen turnip-shaped tail. It has been named *Thecadactylus rapicaudus* (*rapi* for turnip, *caudus* for tail). The flying gecko of southeast Asia has a leaf-like tail, a wide flap of skin along each flank, a narrow flap along each side of the head and flaps along the hind margins of the limbs. Should the gecko fall it spreads its limbs, the flaps spread and the reptile parachutes safely down.

Geckos can throw off their tails, like the more familiar lizards, and grow new ones. In some species 40% have re-grown tails. Sometimes the tail is incompletely thrown and hangs by a strip of skin. As a new tail grows the old one heals and a 2-tailed gecko results. Even 3-tailed geckos have been seen. Temperature is important in growing a new tail. It has been found that when the wall gecko of southern Europe and North Africa grows a new tail with the air temperature at 28°C/82°F it is short and covered with large overlapping scales. With the temperature around 35°C/95°F the new tail is long and is covered with small scales.

Permanent pair of spectacles

One difference between snakes and lizards is that the former have no eyelids. In most geckos the eyelids are permanently joined and there is a transparent window in the lower lid. The few geckos that are active by day have rounded pupils to the eyes. The rest are active by night and have vertical slit-pupils like cats. In some species the sides of the pupils are lobed or notched in four places, and when the pupils contract they leave four apertures, the size of pinholes each one of which will focus the image onto the retina.

Surprisingly small clutches

All geckos except for a few species in New Zealand, which bear live young, lay eggs

*Top: Close pursuit. As firm as the flies it is hunting, a diurnal gecko **Phelsuma vinsoni** pauses on a vertical tree-trunk, unaware of the apparent impossibility of its position.*
Right: Living crampons. Geckos get a grip from tiny hooks in the flaps of skin on their feet.
Far right: After partial loss, regrowth and healing, the result is a three-tailed gecko.

Anthony Banister: NHPA

SC Bisserot: Photo Res

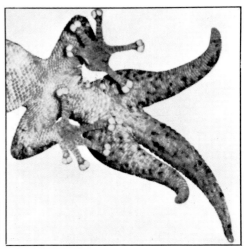

John Visser

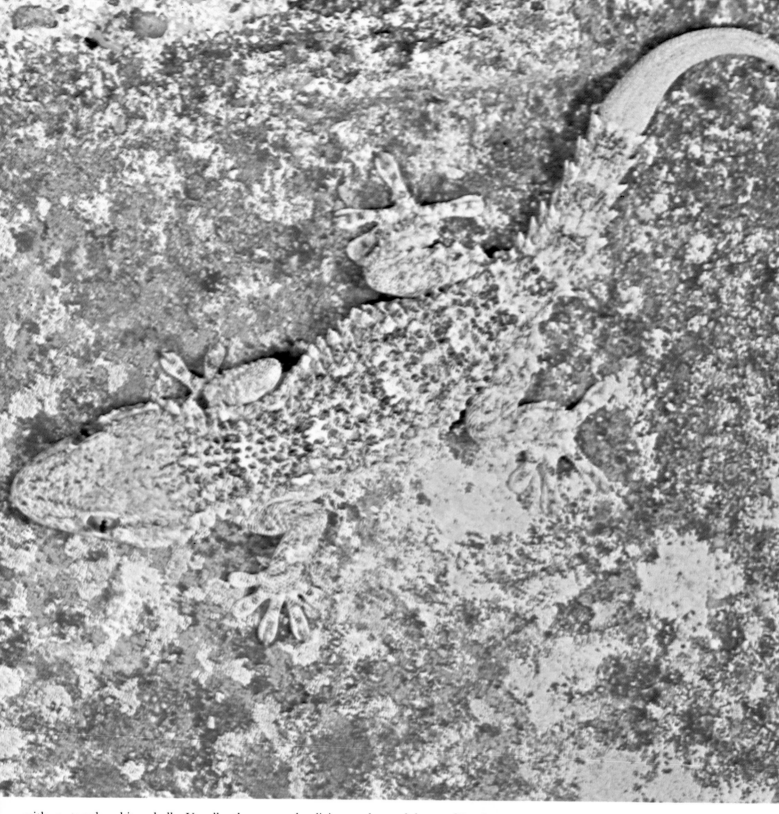

with a tough white shell. Usually there are two in a clutch, sometimes only one. The eggs are laid under bark or under stones and take several months to hatch.

The ghostly gecko

Geckos eat only insects. They are harmless and wholly beneficial to man, yet among the people of Africa, South America, Malaysia and the aboriginals of Australia there are widespread beliefs that their bite makes them dangerous to handle. Possibly such beliefs spring from some of the more remarkable species, like the gecko that stalks insects as a cat does a mouse, even lashing its tail from side to side just before the final pounce. Then there are the web-footed

geckos living on the sand dunes of Southwest Africa. They not only use the webbed feet to run over loose sand but also to burrow. They scrape the sand away with the forefoot of one side and shovel it back with the hind-foot of the same side while balancing on the feet of the other side. Then they change over. They walk with the body raised high and the tail held up and arched.

One web-footed gecko has a delicate beauty. It is pinkish-brown with a lemon yellow stripe along its flank. Its eye has brilliant yellow lids, the iris is black, patterned with gold and coppery tints, while the edges of the vertical pupil are chalky white. Its skin is so transparent its spine and some of its internal organs can be seen clearly. GK Brain, writing in *African Wild*

*Not good enough: regrown tail of **Tarantola manritanica** shows that, despite camouflage, only desperate measures saved its life.*

Life, claims its two ear openings are almost in direct connection, so by looking into one earhole the light coming in through the other can be seen.

class	**Reptilia**
order	**Squamata**
suborder	**Sauria**
family	**Gekkonidae**
genus & species	*Gekko gecko others*

Genet

The genet looks like a cross between a tabby cat and a mongoose. With the civets and mongooses, genets make up the family Viverridae that lies between the weasel family (Mustelidae) and the cat family (Felidae). Three genets are well known and numerous; three are rare and little known.

The feline or small spotted genet is cat-like but more slender, elegant in build and graceful in movement. Up to 40 in. total length, of which nearly half is tail, its fur is soft and spotted with brown to black on a light ground colour. The head tapers to a pointed muzzle; the ears are large and the whiskers long. The tail is ringed with dark and light bands, and there is a crest of long black hairs along the back which is raised in moments of excitement. The legs are short, the paws are small and the toes have retractile claws.

The feline genet ranges over most of Africa apart from desert and semi-desert, and is also found in Spain and southern France, but the blotched or tigrine genet is more numerous throughout Africa. It is similar to the feline genet in form and habits but it has larger spots on a more yellowish ground and no crest along the back. The rusty-spotted genet is like the blotched genet except for its more reddish spots and it is found south of Tanzania. Some scientists believe it to be a colour variety of the blotched genet. The Abyssinian genet of the highlands of Ethiopia is small, has ash-coloured fur with longitudinal black stripes and is very rarely seen. The Victorian genet is like the feline genet but has richer markings. It lives in the Ituri Forest in the Congo and is known almost entirely from skins brought back by pygmy hunters of the Ituri. The first skin sent to London by Sir Harry Johnston in 1911 was obtained in the region of Lake Victoria, but the animal does not live there.

The water genet is known from only three skins. It is the size of a domestic cat, has a rich chestnut fur with white markings on the face and a black bushy tail. It was unknown, except to the local people, until 1919.

Ghostly markings have a purpose

A notable feature of genets is their white face markings. They bring to mind the white facial markings on badgers and foxes, two other nocturnal animals, and the markings of the genet may provide a clue to the use of these. When a genet is seen on a dark night, these white marks on the face stand out in the same way as the luminous paint on a clock face. To only a slightly lesser extent the pale whitish parts of the pattern

▷ *The genet: quick as a cat, curious as a mongoose, it even looks like a cross between them.*

on its body and tail also stand out in the dark. The best comparison is with the way the lights of a ship stand out on a dark night, so although the rest of it is obscured by blackness we still know it is a ship. So we can imagine a genet can recognise another genet in the dark by the ghostly white pattern of its body and tail, or, when seen head-on, by the white markings on the face.

Sure-footed night climber
The feline genet lives alone (at most in pairs) in bush country, sleeping by day among the branches and hunting by night. It can move swiftly over the ground, with the body held low and tail straight out behind, in an almost snake-like movement. It is most at home in bushes and trees, a skilful sure-footed climber, stalking its prey like a cat and seizing it with a swift sharp pounce. Normally it is silent but when alarmed or about to attack it purrs loudly with the sound of a kettle boiling, raising the crest on its back and fluffing the hair of its tail to form a 'bottle-brush'—typical mongoose behaviour when danger is imminent.

Genets are typical carnivores and their canine teeth, though small, are needle-sharp. They feed on any small animal food, especially small rodents, birds and insects, particularly night-flying moths and beetles. A small amount of grass is eaten fairly regularly.

Hidden secrets of breeding
Little is known of the breeding. In the northern parts of its range the genet appears to have 2—3 in a litter, born in spring after a gestation of 10—11 weeks. The nest is in a hollow in a tree or among rocks. In South Africa, at least, there is a second litter in autumn.

Animal night-craft

We, who move about by day or carry a lamp at night, may wonder how an animal that hunts at night among branches can find its way so surely when moving at speed. Perhaps the behaviour of a tame genet tells us this. When first put into a strange room, with branches for it to climb over, the genet will make a circuit of the room, going over

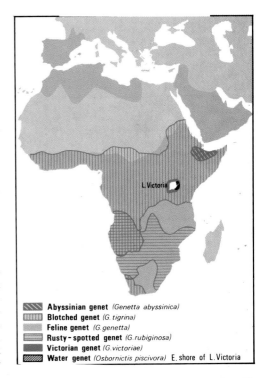

Abyssinian genet (Genetta abyssinica)
Blotched genet (G. tigrina)
Feline genet (G. genetta)
Rusty-spotted genet (G. rubiginosa)
Victorian genet (G. victoriae)
Water genet (Osbornictis piscivora) E. shore of L. Victoria

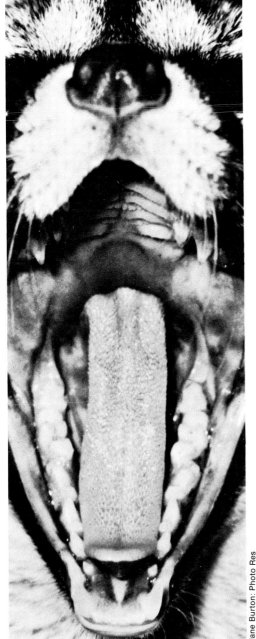

Jane Burton: Photo Res

Jane Burton: Photo Res

Far left: After a stealthy stalk and quick pounce, a feline genet settles down to a meal.
Left: Prey's-eye view: a genet yawn shows typical carnivore teeth, relatively small, perhaps, but needle-sharp.
Above: Inquisitive, if a little wary, a pair of genet kittens explore the world around them.

the floor and over every branch and other solid object. It goes very slowly, putting each foot down in turn and not putting its weight on that foot until it is sure of its foothold. At the same time it is investigating everything around, with its nose, probably also with its eyes; and since its ears are quivering all the time it is probably bringing the sense of hearing to bear as well. Having thoroughly investigated the whole of its surroundings in this tediously slow and painstaking way, it repeats the circuit, this time going slightly faster. At the completion of this second circuit it makes a third, this time rapidly. From then on it can race around in total darkness and never put a foot wrong. So far as we can see it

memorizes the whole of its surroundings mainly by touch and smell, perhaps by sight and hearing to a lesser extent.

One genet, put into a fresh cage furnished with branches, slipped at one spot in its first circuit so that it swung under the branch and had to do a 'handspring' to regain its position on the branch. It lived many years in this same cage and always, whenever it came to this same spot on the branch, it swung under it and did a handspring, just as it had on the first occasion.

class	**Mammalia**
order	**Carnivora**
family	**Viverridae**
genera & species	*Genetta abyssinica* Abyssinian genet
	G. genetta feline genet
	G. rubiginosa rusty-spotted genet
	G. tigrina blotched genet
	G. victoriae Victorian genet
	Osbornictis piscivora water genet

Gerbil

Gerbils, or sand rats, live in desert or semi-desert parts of Africa and Asia. There are many species going by different names—usually describing their characters—such as naked-soled gerbils, fat-tailed mice, and fat sand rats. Two genera are known as jirds, while another whose habits have not yet been recorded is called the ammodille. Gerbils are rat-like and belong to the same family as the common rat, but in some features of appearance and habits they resemble the jerboas or desert rats. The fur is fawn on the upper parts, the hairs often tipped with black making it darker. The under-parts are white. In most species the tail is long and slender often with a small tuft of hairs at the tip, but the fat-tailed gerbil has a very short plump tail. The hindlegs are long, and with the long tail give the gerbils a kangaroo-like appearance.

Most gerbils are found in Africa, especially around the Sahara, but the large naked-soled gerbils live as far south as South Africa, spreading over most of the continent except the equatorial forests. These gerbils, also known as Indian gerbils, are also found in Asia from Turkey and Arabia to India and Ceylon. Others are found in Asia; great gerbils and Przewalski's gerbils are limited to the central Asian deserts of Mongolia, Turkestan and Iran.

Desert hopper

Although they are sometimes found in bush or scrub country, the typical home of gerbils is in the dry, sparsely covered regions around deserts. They have many of the features found in desert animals: the bullae or earbones are large, indicating sensitive hearing and water is conserved so some gerbils can live almost indefinitely without drinking. They live in burrows and are usually nocturnal, so avoiding the worst of the sun's heat. Some species have hairy soles on their hindfeet which probably insulate them from the hot sand and many travel by leaping when in a hurry. This is a common feature of desert rodents, such as the jerboa or the kangaroo rat of North American deserts, and is thought to be an economical method of moving about in search of the scant supplies of food in dry regions. The Indian gerbil has been given the name of antelope rat for it progresses in bounds of 15—16 ft.

The habits of gerbils are not well known as most are nocturnal, but many are now kept in laboratories as experimental animals and they are becoming popular as pets. They are expert burrowers and need to be kept in a cage with plenty of earth or sand. Some species make only a simple short burrow. The entrance may be blocked with loose earth, presumably to keep out either enemies or the heat. Other gerbils make complicated systems of burrows with several entrances, and chambers where they make their nests or store food. Often several gerbils make their tunnels close to each other, forming distinct colonies. Observations of great gerbils in winter showed that they never strayed far from their burrows. Footprints in the snow were never found more than 60 ft from a burrow's entrance and most trails never went this far. These gerbils became less active when temperatures fell and the snow became deeper. By midwinter only a few entrances remained open.

Food stored in burrows

Gerbils live mainly on the herbs that flourish in desert country during winter and spring. Leaves, seeds, flowers and roots of many different kinds of plants are eaten, and are often stored in the burrow for future use. The great gerbil stores winter supplies either in the burrow or just outside where they can easily be dug out of the snow: Over 100 lb of food has been found in one burrow. A few gerbils are also carnivorous. The short-eared gerbils sometimes feed on locusts and grasshoppers which they take back to the burrows and eat at the entrance, scattering the discarded wings and bodies. The Indian gerbil occasionally eats the young of its own kind and takes eggs and chicks from nests of birds.

Foot-stamping drummers

Some gerbils have breeding seasons restricted to a few months in the year, while others breed all the year round. The breeding habits of most species are unknown. Both sexes of the great gerbil mark their territories by rubbing their bellies on rocks, which transfers a musky secretion from glands on their bellies. A common habit of gerbils is to stamp their hindfeet, presumably to advertise themselves. It is possible to hear the slow, muffled thud coming from the burrows. The males will also fight, sitting back like kangaroos on their hindfeet while they bite and kick.

There may be several litters a year of 1—8 babies. The birth takes place after about 3 weeks gestation and the young stay below ground for about another 3 weeks. Then

◁ Apprehension: A gerbil swings onto its hindlegs to look round before bounding away.
▷ Mid-leap: **Gerbillus pyramidum** jumping.

they come to the entrance of the burrow and, after much hesitation, make short trips above ground. They gradually gain confidence and eventually start searching for their own food.

Agile enemies

Gerbils are eaten by all kinds of flesh-eating animals including snakes, foxes and shrikes. Their safety lies in being able to dash into a burrow or in jinking. Gerbils are very agile, being able to change direction at each bound, although the bat-eared fox (p 163) is skilful at out-jumping them. A fat sand rat will often stop at the entrance of its burrow and sit back on its hindlegs to peer at the source of disturbance before disappearing below ground. It would seem better to bolt straight in, and the Indian gerbil has short burrows, distinct from its main burrow, where it can hide when in danger. This gerbil is also said to be able to elude dogs by jumping on their backs and the naked-soled gerbils of Nigeria escape by suddenly leaping to one side and hiding motionless in the cover of grass.

Plague carrier

Gerbil activities sometimes clash with man's interests. They are occasionally a pest to crops or desert reclamation schemes. In Iraq the jird steals grain and stores it in temporary burrows in the fields. Later it removes its booty to permanent stores under stones, where it may be stolen by hamsters. Much more serious pests are the gerbils of South Africa. They are carriers of bubonic plague and unceasing efforts are made to control their numbers.

It is the general rule for small desert animals to come out from their holes at night (see fennec, p 747) but several species of gerbil are diurnal. The fat sand rat can be seen out feeding even during the heat of the afternoon. The intense sunlight in the desert can damage an animal's tissues because some of the radiation is able to penetrate very deep into the body. Nocturnal activity removes this risk. Some observations by a Russian zoologist suggest that the diurnal gerbils are protected from the harmful effects of the sun. The midday jird has very dense fur, with nearly twice as many hairs per square inch as a coypu, which is noted for its thick fur. It also has a thick skin. This is unusual as thick-furred animals usually have thin skins and vice versa. The great gerbil, another diurnal species, has layers of pigment in the skin that prevent the harmful rays from penetrating, whereas the nocturnal gerbils that were studied had no such protection.

class	**Mammalia**
order	**Rodentia**
family	**Cricetidae**
genera & species	**Gerbillus gerbillus** *pygmy gerbil* **Meriones meridianus** *midday jird* **Psammomys obesus** *fat sand rat* **Rhombomys opimus** *great gerbil* **Tatera indica** *Indian gerbil* *others*

Rough but effective: a female gerbil drags her babies to safety after being disturbed. They are helpless until about 3 weeks old.

Gerenuk

Also known as Waller's gazelle or giraffe-necked gazelle, the gerenuk was not set on scientific record until 1878. It is often said that the gerenuk was known to the Ancient Egyptians and was figured in their tombs. In fact only one Egyptian antiquity has been discovered bearing a representation of a long-necked, long-legged antelope and this is more likely to have been the dibatag (see p 631).

The gerenuk stands up to 41 in. at the shoulder, the length of head, neck and body totals 4½ ft, the tail is 9 in. long and the weight up to 115 lb. The male carries short, thick, lyre-shaped horns up to 17 in. long. The coat is fox red on the back, lighter on the flanks and white below.

Sir Walter Brooke first described the gerenuk from specimens sent to him by a missionary, the Rev Horace Waller, a friend of David Livingstone. Waller had received them from Sir John Kirk, British Consul in Zanzibar, the specimens having come originally from the coast of Somalia. Brooke gave them the name **Gazella walleri**. *An Austrian scientist, Dr Kohl, studied their anatomy and concluded they were not gazelles. One feature he noted was that the skull extended unusually far back behind the horns and that this part was almost solid bone. So he changed the name to* **Lithocranius** *(stony skull)* **walleri**, *but misspelt it* **Litocranius**.

The horizontal position . . .

Gerenuks are excessively shy and readily move away trotting with the head held horizontally forward, so they easily pass under low branches in the thorn bush. A gerenuk when disturbed moves away about 200 yd then stops and raises its head from behind a bush to survey the intruder.

Gerenuks live singly, in pairs or in small herds of 3—10 in the drier parts of southern Ethiopia, Somalia and northern Kenya.

. . . and the vertical

Gerenuks browse foliage, especially acacia, with their long, hairy mobile lips and long tongue. Characteristically a gerenuk will stand on its hindlegs to reach leaves 6 or 7 ft up. They may place the front hooves on the trunks to do this. Where water is available they will drink, but in the drier parts of their range they seem to go long periods without drinking. In the Frankfurt Zoo it has been noticed that gerenuks will drink each other's urine, which may be a means of water conservation in the wild.

Wife-kicking

Although Kohl decided the gerenuk was not a gazelle it has one trick which is seen in Thomson's and Grant's gazelles of East Africa. Before mating the buck throws a front leg forward in the direction of the doe, but instead of inserting it between her hindlegs, as the two gazelles do, he aims it

▷ *Female gerenuk and young.*

Okapia

at her forelegs or flanks. Then he nibbles her muzzle and rubs his head against her, particularly the part of his face just in front of the eye, which is marked with a dark patch. This is the opening of a scent gland, the preorbital gland. In other antelopes it has been found that when the buck's scent is rubbed onto the head and the neck of the doe it brings her more quickly into breeding condition.

There is relatively little information on breeding. Females in zoos had bred for the first time at 19–22 months and, in the wild, the young are born in time to browse the tender new shoots that appear with the rains.

There is no precise information about enemies, but presumably these include any carnivores in their range large enough to take either the kids or the adults. The Somalis refuse to eat the flesh of the gerenuk believing it is a relative of the camel and that if gerenuks are killed, sickness will afflict their camels.

Fauns and satyrs

The most striking thing about the gerenuk is that it can, and habitually does, stand erect on its hindlegs with the neck, back and hindlegs in a straight line. This, however, is not so astonishing as those freak quadrupeds which always walk on two legs. They show how readily an animal can pass from the quadrupedal to the bipedal posture. The most famous of these is known as Slijper's goat.

Professor EJ Slijper wrote in a Dutch scientific journal in 1942 about a he-goat born without forelegs. It lived for a year, and even then only died of an accident. It moved about by jumps on its hindlegs in a semi-upright posture, its body making an angle of 45 degrees with the ground, the hoofs of the hindlegs placed much farther forward than usual to bring them under the centre of gravity.

Buried in various scientific journals in Britain, France, Germany and the USSR are similar accounts of dogs, horses, sheep, goats, cats and other domestic animals born without forelegs or only stumps and compelled to walk erect or nearly so. One dog lived for 12 years despite the handicap.

There is a further interest in this. If this can happen to domesticated animals it could also happen to wild animals. They might not survive so long, especially those like dogs or cats which must hunt for a living. But a herbivore, like a goat, might well survive, and one wonders whether stories of fauns and satyrs may not have sprung from the sight of a bipedal goat. Even the great god Pan may have been nothing more than a Slijper's goat living in classical times.

Full stretch: noses buried in foliage about 7 ft from the ground, a gerenuk couple browse in satyr-like poses.

class	**Mammalia**
order	**Artiodactyla**
family	**Bovidae**
genus & species	*Litocranius walleri*

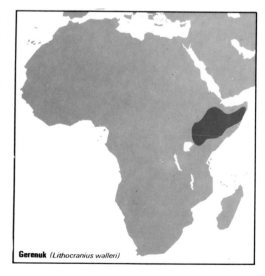

Gerenuk *(Lithocranius walleri)*

866

Gharial

The gharial is a long, slender-snouted crocodile living in the rivers Indus, Ganges and Brahmaputra and in a few other rivers of this same region. The alternative name of gavial, although Latinized to give its scientific name, was originally due to a misspelling.

The Indian gharial can grow to 20 ft in length. The eyes are set well up on the head and the nostrils are at the tip of the long slender snout. The jaws are armed with small sharp teeth of nearly uniform size. The upper surface of the neck and the back have an armour of bony plates. The legs are longer proportionately than in most other crocodiles and the toes, especially those of the hindfeet, are webbed.

A crocodile very similar to the gharial lives in the rivers and marshes of Malaya, Borneo and Sumatra. Its snout is long but proportionately shorter than that of the gharial, and the two are similar in habits. It is, however, known as the false gharial and is one of the crocodile family (see p 575) or **Crocodylidae,** *while the gharials have a family of their own, the* **Gavialidae.**

Inoffensive crocodiles
Gharials keep to the water more than other crocodiles. They tend to lie just under the surface with only the eyes and nostrils exposed. When anyone approaches, the eyes sink slowly out of sight, leaving only the nostrils breaking surface. With the closer approach of an intruder the tip of the snout is then submerged. Both gharial and false gharial are little danger to people although there are rare records of fatal encounters. The gharial is sacred to the Hindus, and although its stomach is sometimes found to contain articles of personal adornment, such as bracelets, these have come almost certainly from human corpses committed to the sacred River Ganges.

Handy snout for feeding
The food of the gharial and false gharial is almost entirely small fishes, seized with a sideways snap of the jaws. The slenderness of the snout allows quick movement sideways; it is easier to wave a stick from side to side in water than a plank.

Two-tier incubator
The male gharial has a hollow hump on the tip of the snout with the nostrils at the centre of it. Otherwise there is little outward difference between the sexes. In the breeding season the female lays about 40 eggs in sand on a river bank, each $3\frac{1}{2}$ in. by $2\frac{3}{4}$ in.

△ *Gharial siesta, slumped on a warm bank to make the most of the midday sun.*

These are in 2 layers, probably laid on separate days, and each layer is covered with a fairly deep covering of sand. The newly-hatched young, 14 in. long, have absurdly long snouts and they are coloured greyish-brown with five irregular dark oblique bands on the body and nine on the tail. The adults are mainly dark olive.

Same head, same feeding

Crocodiles in general and their immediately recognisable ancestors have a very long history going back over 200 million years. The crocodiles proper, living today, which must include also the caimans and alligators, do not differ much from their earliest ancestors, except that some of the extinct crocodiles are larger than the largest living today. There was, however, a separate group of crocodilians whose fossils also date from those very early times, known as the Mesosuchia. They also had 'frying-pan' heads like the gharials, but they lived in the sea and they died out 120 million years ago. The gharials came into existence much later, less than 70 million years ago, and one of them was 54 ft long, the largest crocodilian we know of, living or extinct.

The Mesosuchia and the gharials are,

apart from being members of the order Crocodilia, not related. But they both had the long slender snout and both had many small sharp teeth. They both had the same feeding habits, seizing fast-moving slippery prey with a sideways slash of the head. We know gharials do this because people have watched the living animals feeding. We know false gharials do also, for the same reason, and we can deduce the Mesosuchia did this from the finer details of their bones. So we have three kinds of crocodilians with the same shape of head, feeding in the same way but all three unrelated. We know the gharials snatch fish; we can deduce the Mesosuchia snatched squid.

Many animals have pebbles in their stomachs. Living crocodiles are one example. Extinct crocodiles are another, and we know this because when their skeletons are dug out of the ground groups of pebbles are found lying where the stomach would have been.

How do we know the Mesosuchia ate squid? Because the stomach stones found where their stomachs would have been are stained with the ink contained in the bodies of squids.

class	**Reptilia**
order	**Crocodilia**
family	**Gavialidae**
genus & species	*Gavialis gangeticus*

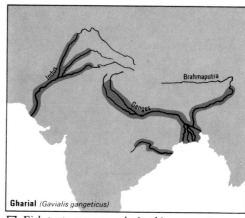

Gharial *(Gavialis gangeticus)*

▽ *Fish trap: once caught in this array of vicious teeth by a sideways slash of the gharial's head, few fish, slimy or not, can escape.*

Ghost frog

The ghost frog of South Africa gets its name from the white skin of its underside, which is so thin that the digestive organs are visible through it. Its back is green, marked with a reddish network. Compared with other frogs, its body is small relative to the head and unusually long legs, and there is almost a suggestion of a neck. The head is flattish with the eyes more prominent than is usual in frogs, and the toes of all four feet end in discs. When an animal species is placed first in one family, then in another, it usually means that its relationship with other animals is not clear. Some scientists put the ghost frogs in a family of their own, the Heleophrynidae, others put them in the Leptodactylidae, but all leading authorities now agree on the latter. The animals normally end up in a genus of their own. This is true of the ghost frogs, of which there are three species. One species **Heleophryne rosei** *lives on Table Mountain, another* **H. purcelli** *is found in Cape Province, and the third* **H. natalensis** *is in the Transvaal and Natal. The frogs are elusive in another way: they are very hard to find, but the real reason for their name is that you can almost see through them.*

John Visser

The ghost frog gets its name from the white skin of its underside. It is very difficult to track down and as a result is rarely seen. This may be partially explained by the fact that it is nocturnal— as shown by its diamond-shaped pupils formed during daylight to keep out bright light.

Equipped for climbing

Ghost frogs have toes shaped like those of tree frogs, although they climb little. Instead, they tend to spend the day crouching in holes in the ground, under stones or in caves, and they also spend much of their time in water. At night they come out and clamber over large rocks or into trees. Another unusual feature is that the skin of the undersides of the forelimbs and the tops of the fingers has groups of small hooks, and similar hooks form a double row on either side along the lower jaw with scattered hooks on the upper jaw and the snout. It has been suggested that these help the frog to cling to the surfaces of slippery rocks. This description applies to the best known of the ghost frogs, *Heleophryne rosei*. Another species also has spines on the skin, and this one climbs into bushes.

Mainly insect-eaters

Frogs shed their skins periodically and in most species the frog eats the cast skin, which is sloughed more or less in one piece. Ghost frogs shed their skins in pieces and make no attempt to eat them. It should be emphasized, however, that in this as in everything else concerned with their biology we have only a small amount of information. Ghost frogs are difficult to track down and are rarely seen. Possibly part of the explanation is seen in their eyes, diamond-shaped with the long axis of the diamond vertical—an unusual eye, showing nocturnal habits.

Ghost frogs probably eat insects, and one species *H. purcelli* has been seen capturing flies by leaping up at them.

Holding on to food

By dissecting the dead female ghost frog it is known that she lays about 30 large eggs. Where she does this is not known, and the guess is that she lays them in a hole in a river bank just above water level. More is known about the tadpoles which are somewhat flattened, especially in the head. Seen from above they are wedge-shaped except for the tail. Around the mouth is a large sucker by which the tadpole can cling to submerged rocks and browse the small algae on their surfaces.

Mountain chicken—frogs of the West Indies

Those not versed in field natural history may wonder why, once a species is known to exist, somebody does not set to work to learn all about it. To illustrate the difficulties we cannot do better than tell the story of the mountain chicken of the West Indies. This is a frog *Leptodactylus fallax* which belongs to the same family as the ghost frogs if we accept the majority view. It is nearly 6 in. long, weighs up to 2 lb and lives on the islands of Dominica, Montserrat and Martinique. The frog lives in the steep-sided valleys which are heavily forested and difficult of access. During the day, so far as anyone can tell, it rests in burrows in the ground or in cavities among boulders. The females have never been seen and nothing is known of the way they breed. They do not live near streams, so possibly they make foam nests in the trees like related species living in South America are known to do. The males come out at night and call

with a musical, bird-like 'song', but the reason why they are called mountain chicken is that the flesh of their legs cooked with egg and bread crumbs is delicious, like the best chicken. The frog has been almost eliminated from Martinique, partly because introduced mongooses have preyed on them and partly because they are much prized for the table.

An English zoologist visiting Dominica tried to find the females in the hope of studying the life history of the species. He found some of the males, but even this entailed climbing the steep slopes at night in rain, negotiating tangles of tree roots, creepers and boulders, finding his way by electric torch and guided by the somewhat ventriloquial musical calls of the males, which go on singing all night. Even to find a few males was a small reward for all the effort and discomfort he expended. The males themselves do not help because they tend to sit near the mouth of a burrow or cavity among the boulders into which they can readily retreat.

After all, if you can only find males your knowledge of a species must be very incomplete. And if you eat those males it cannot be long before a population of spinster frogs is created—and that means the end of the species.

class	**Amphibia**
order	**Salientia**
family	**Leptodactylidae**
genus	*Heleophryne natalensis* *H. purcelli* *H. rosei*

Ghost moth

Swinging to and fro, as if on an invisible thread, with the white uppersides of its wings flashing on and off, this moth is aptly called 'ghost'. It is one of the five species of **Hepialus** *found in Britain and is remarkable for the great difference in appearance between the male and female. Males have the uppersides of all four wings shining white. Females have the hindwings dusky and the forewings yellow with a pattern of reddish markings, and they are generally larger than the males. Ghost moths are $\frac{3}{4}$ in. long with a wingspan of just under 2 in. They are found throughout the British Isles and all over central Europe and western Asia. The larva is a large, whitish, rather grublike caterpillar, with a brown plate on the segment just behind the head. It lives underground.*

Spooky husbands

Ghost moths frequent open spaces where rough grass and weeds are allowed to grow, and are on the wing in June and July. The males execute a kind of aerial dance, swinging to and fro just over the herbage as if suspended on invisible threads. As they fly they vanish and reappear as the dark underside and white upperside of the wings are alternately exposed. The dance is performed for about half an hour after sunset and again shortly before dawn; at other times the moths hardly fly at all. It is a courtship display and serves to attract the females, which fly about the countryside and are guided visually to their palely glimmering partners, their search being assisted by a scent, given off by the males, that has been likened to that of a carrot. This is one of the few cases known among insects where the females fly in search of the males. More usually female insects remain static in courtship and the males are attracted to them, in most cases by the emission from the female of a specific scent.

Non-hopping moths

The eggs are laid at random among grass in June and early July and the larva feeds underground on the roots of various plants until May of the next year, when it pupates in the burrow that it has made. The adults have vestigial mouthparts and do not feed. There is no association with the hop, as the specific name *humuli* suggests.

Shetland ghost moths

In the Shetlands a peculiar race of the ghost moth is found, in which the males differ in their colours from the ghost moths of both the British and the European mainlands. It is regarded as a subspecies and has been named *H. humuli thulensis*. The hindwings of the males are dusky and the forewings dull white with a brown or ochreous pattern similar to that of the female.

The shining white coloration of the typical male ghost moth is not characteristic of

GE Hyde

△ *Male ghost moth. In June and July the males execute a kind of aerial courtship dance. This serves to attract the females who fly in search of these glimmering partners.*

▽ *The female is slightly larger than the male usually being $\frac{3}{4}$ in. long with a wingspan of just under 2 in. After mating she lays eggs at random among grasses and herbs.*

GE Hyde

△ *In the courtship dance the male swings to and fro just above the herbage as if suspended on invisible threads. The dance is performed for about half an hour after sunset and again shortly before dawn. At other times they hardly fly at all. The dance attracts the females, helped by a carroty scent given off by the males.*

▽ *Ghost moth larva—a large, whitish, rather grub-like caterpillar—it lives beneath the ground feeding on the roots of plants such as burdock, dandelion and dead-nettle.*

swift moths in general. Presumably it is maintained by natural selection, on the principle that the most conspicuous of the twilight dancers will be more readily found by females and so are most likely to leave progeny. In the almost Arctic latitude of the Shetlands, however, where there is no darkness at midsummer and the sun disappears at midnight for only half an hour, the males must perform their dance in broad daylight. They do not need the porcelain-white wing colour of their relatives farther south to make them visible to the questing females. The selection pressure being relaxed, it is supposed that the males have reverted to an appearance more characteristic of the Hepialid moths in general, probably more like that of their ancestors.

This is, however, an academic point and there is another, more practical explanation. In the Shetlands ghost moths are heavily preyed upon by gulls, which by flying above the moths will see white individuals more readily than darker ones against the background of heather, rock or peat. In these circumstances the pure white coloration is a definite disadvantage. Here the tables are turned. The white males are more likely to make a meal for a gull than a mate for a moth, and therefore are less likely to leave progeny.

class	**Insecta**
order	**Lepidoptera**
family	**Hepialidae**
genus & species	***Hepialus humuli***

Giant forest hog

This forest hog, the largest wild pig in the world, very nearly became extinct before the western world ever knew about it. It was unknown to Europeans until 1904 when a skull and pieces of skin were given to Colonel Richard Meinertzhagen by the local hunters of the Kakamega Forest in western Kenya. Since then it has been found on Mount Kenya, in the Aberdare Mountains and in the mountain forests of Uganda and westwards through the Congo to Liberia.

A large boar may be 5 ft long with a 13 in. tail, 3 ft high at the shoulder and weigh up to 600 lb. The body is thickset, the head broad and stout, the clay-coloured skin covered with long black bristles. The snout is heavy, with large upper tusks growing out at right angles. The skin in front of the eye is naked, and behind each eye is a pair of warts. These are much the same as the warts on the face of the more ugly warthog but their position and shape is different—and nobody knows what they are for. On the naked skin in front of the eye is a slit, the entrance to a facial scent gland which no other pig has. Another unusual feature is that on the top of the head is a deep depression 'large enough to take a tangerine orange', as one French zoologist put it.

Pig with clean habits

Forest hogs, shy and retiring, move about in groups or 'sounders' of 4–20 in dense undergrowth of rain forests, where they have their runs and bedding-down places. They also frequent swampy places to wallow. They seldom use a burrow and even less do they construct one, but they dig holes at the bases of trees to use as latrines. Their usual habit is to keep well out of sight but old boars brought to bay by dogs or wounded can be dangerous. They have also been known to attack humans in defence of the sounder.

Little more is known about them except that they feed mainly on lush grass and shrubs, and unlike most species of wild pig do not root in the ground for food. They come out of the dense undergrowth in the early morning to feed, and again in the late afternoon and evening. The litters may contain 2–6 young, born after a gestation of 125 days.

Tracking it down

The story of why so little is known about these giant hogs is one of the most romantic in the annals of large mammals. Several of the early explorers in Central Africa, including Sir Henry Stanley as well as Sir Harry Johnston, who discovered the okapi, had heard stories about it from the Africans but none had been able to see it. Then, in 1903, Colonel (then Lieutenant) Richard Meinertzhagen, a professional soldier, since famous as a naturalist and author of books on birds, heard about it when he was in Kenya. He determined to find it but bad luck dogged him. First he heard one had

A sounder of giant forest hogs on a night feeding expedition. A sounder is made up of 4–20 hogs. The largest wild pig in the world, a large boar may be 5 ft long and over 600 lb in weight.

been killed by African hunters but by the time he had reached the spot the carcase had been carved up and all he could get were two pieces of the skin. A little while later he heard of another having been killed. This time he got some of the skin and also the skull. These few relics, and especially the skull, were enough to show the animal belonged to an unnamed species, so Meinertzhagen sent them to London where they were shown to the Fellows of the Zoological Society. An account of them was published in that Society's Proceedings for 1904.

The pig that nearly died out

In following years several more skulls as well as drawings of the animal were sent to the Natural History Museum in London. Occasionally white hunters in Central Africa had a sight of it, and people who visited Tree Tops, the famous look-out in Kenya, were sometimes able to see it. All the same, the giant forest hog is one of the rarer animals. So far as it has been possible to piece the story together it seems that it used to be much more numerous. Then, in 1891, the disease known as rinderpest swept across Africa and the giant forest hog suffered so badly that it is now rare.

Colonel R Meinertzhagen who tracked the hog.

Fact and fable

Many of the stories told to the early explorers by the Africans were highly coloured as to the hog's ferocity. This was the natural reaction to being attacked unawares. For example, the women going into the forest to gather firewood were sometimes ambushed. Although some of the estimates of its size given by the Africans proved accurate, others were often badly exaggerated. This also is the reaction of people everywhere to mystery animals. Nevertheless, there could in this instance be some justification, for, as as result of Dr LSB Leakey's discoveries in Kenya in the last 20 years, we now know there used to be giant animals in that part of Africa, including hogs the size of a rhinoceros or hippopotamus.

class	**Mammalia**
order	**Artiodactyla**
family	**Suidae**
genus & species	***Hylochoerus meinertzhageni***

The distribution of the hog is localised.

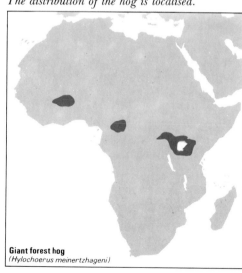

Giant forest hog
(Hylochoerus meinertzhageni)

Giant rat

Some rats are little bigger than mice, but others are nearly 3 ft long and have deservedly been called giant rats. A few not quite as long as this have been called giant rats, but one that deserves the title is the African giant pouched rat, also called the Gambian pouched rat. It is found from Gambia in the west to the Sudan and Kenya in the east and southwards to the Transvaal. It is nearly 3 ft long of which just over half is tail. Its fur may be sleek or harsh, grey to brown on the back, lighter on the flanks and whitish on the under-parts, with the feet and legs noticeably white or pink. Some are mottled, almost spotted. The head is long and narrow and the ears large. The tail is naked.

The Gambian, pouched or African giant rat, numerous over so wide an area, has many local names, in the African languages as well as in English. In Sierra Leone it is the ground pig, in Ghana the bush rat. In northern Nigeria it is the bandicoot and in western Nigeria the rabbit.

Short-sighted giant

The African giant rat lives in the rain forests of west central Africa, in the bush, on farms, in grassland, under piles of logs, even on the summits of the huge bare rocks, known as insulbergs, standing in the savannah. It is solitary, living in a burrow that may have 2—6 entrances, and it is said these are often closed from the inside with leaves. Mainly active at night, it may some-times be seen by day sitting on its haunches, sniffing in all directions as if blind, despite its bright eyes, and it can be seen doing exactly the same at night. This suggests it is very short-sighted and doubtless depends mainly on its nose and, more especially, its large ears, which are constantly on the move. When running it holds its tail well up. It is wholly inoffensive and docile, and can be picked up by the tail and handled without fear of its biting. When not feeding it keeps up a constant bird-like chirping.

Built-in shopping bags

The food of the giant rat is any plant material, especially grain, fruits and nuts. It is called the pouched rat from its capacious cheek-pouches, which have earned it the additional name of hamster rat. It stuffs these pouches with food until its face is twice the normal size, then runs away and, working the food forwards with its paws, spits it out in a heap to store it.

Pink and white rats

The breeding season seems to vary from one part of its range to another. Usually 2—3 young are born at a time after a gestation of about 42 days. They are pink and white at first, the body and head about 4 in. long with a tail half as long again. Brown fur begins to show at about 3 weeks.

African 'small beef'

Little is known of natural enemies but they must include almost any local beast or bird of prey. Their greatest enemy is probably man, since the Africans regard their flesh as a delicacy and dig the giant rats out of their burrows. To them the flesh is 'small beef'.

Many island giants

By contrast with the giant pouched rat the five species of giant naked-tailed rat, or African big-toothed mouse *Uranomys*, only $8\frac{1}{2}$ in. long overall and covering much the same range, are all rare. They are hardly worthy of the name of giant. For really big rats we need to go farther west, to the islands of the Indo-Pacific. The New Guinea giant tree rat *Mallomys rothschildi* lives among rocks 4—8 thousand ft up and feeds on plants, especially fern shoots. It is 34 in. overall with thick woolly brown to grey fur, a scaly tail and long curved claws. Another New Guinea giant rat is *Hyomys goliath*, grey with light underparts and also nearly 3 ft total length. Little is known of the habits of either of these giants. A third species on New Guinea is the giant naked-tailed rat *Uromys caudimaculatus*, 28 in. long, of which half is tail, and there are species related to it on the islands of Aru and Kei, of the Bismarck Archipelago and the Solomons, as well as in Queensland, Australia. Again little is known about them. There is a giant tree rat *Papagomys armandvillei* on the island of Flores of which practically nothing is known and very few specimens have been obtained. On the island of Luzon, in the Philippines, are two species of cloud rat, both nearly 3 ft long, one of them with a bushy tail, and this one is trapped by the aboriginal inhabitants of the island and their pelts sold in the markets. Yet we are in almost complete ignorance of how they live. There are three species of giant water rat: one in New Guinea, one in New Britain and the third in Australia and Tasmania and also on a number of the islands to the north of Australia. A little more is known about

Giant rat or Gambian pouched rat youngster stuffs its food pouches with food. It will push in fruit, grain and nuts until its face is twice the normal size before going off to store it.

Jane Burton: Photo Res

Jane Burton: Photo Res

these, but still not very much. They are nocturnal, sleeping by day in a burrow in the bank, a hollow log or under a pile of vegetable litter, and they feed on water snails, mussels, fish, frogs and water birds. They have a long flattened head, eyes set high up on the head, small ears and seal-like fur and their feet are partially webbed. Starting in 1937 they were extensively trapped in Australia for their fur and now they have to be protected.

class	**Mammalia**
order	**Rodentia**
family	**Muridae**
genus & species	*Cricetomys gambianus* *others*

◁ *Baby giant rat.*
▽ *Cocoa bean investigation: this giant rat may be eaten by Africans who regard its flesh as a delicacy—to them it is 'small beef'.*

Jane Burton: Photo Res

Giant snail

A pest in many parts of the world,
Achatina fulica *is a large land-living
snail, native to East Africa. With its
pointed shell, 5 or even 8 in. long, it
weighs about ½ lb. This species deserves
the title of giant snail, although there are
other large terrestrial snails in many of the
warmer countries, because of its notoriety
and economic importance. The fact that
even larger snails live in the sea seems
somehow less remarkable.*

*In other respects, there is little of
note in the appearance of the giant snail
as compared with the snails of our gardens.*

Dusk feeder

The giant snail feeds mainly by night or
at dusk, usually returning after its forays
to a regular 'home'. However, it will also
come out by day if there is rain or if the sky
is overcast. For continued activity, dampness
and a temperature above about 24°C/75°F
are needed. On the other hand, during dry
or cold periods it remains inactive, often
deep in some hollow log or under a rock
and withdrawn into its shell, the aperture
closed off with a thin membrane. This state
of inactivity, or aestivation as it is called,
has been known to last for as long as a year
—a long enough time, but not to be compared with the 6 years recorded for an
individual of another species of snail. When
so much time can be spent in suspended
animation, records of longevity have little
meaning, but one specimen is recorded as
having lived 9 years in captivity.

A taste for whitewash

To a large extent the giant snail feeds on
rotten plant matter and dead animals but
it will also feed voraciously on the leaves,
fruit, bark and flowers of a great variety of
plants—including, unfortunately, crops
like beans, breadfruit, cabbage, cacao,
citrus trees, melons, yam plants and rubber.
Needing calcium to form its shell, it may
even climb walls of houses to ravage the
whitewash on them for its lime content.

Pea-sized eggs

These giant snails begin breeding when
about a year old and, like their smaller
relatives, are hermaphrodite. They lay eggs
the size of small peas, like miniature bird's
eggs with lemon-yellow shells. These they
deposit, 40−500 at a time, in or on the
soil, doing so every 2 or 3 months. The
young hatch in 1−10 days. A single snail
can apparently lay eggs without mating
after months of isolation, for evidently
sperm can be stored for this time before
being used. One result is that a single snail
can suffice to found a new colony if it was
fertilised before being transported.

Growth of a pest

In its East African home, the giant snail
is hardly a pest, but it has spread from
there to many of the warmer parts of the
world, becoming in most of them a considerable pest. Like the rabbit in Australia,
it is one of too many examples of animals
or plants, originally fairly innocuous,
that have become pests outside their native
lands. Everything about this snail, such as
its ability to eat almost any plant material
and its high rate of reproduction, combined
with its hardiness and a scarcity of natural
enemies, favour its chances of colonising
new areas, provided that the climate is
suitable. Just a few individuals need be
introduced—even one is enough.

The spread of the giant snail started in
about 1800 when some were taken to
Mauritius by the wife of the governor on
doctor's orders (medicinal properties have
been ascribed to these snails as to others).
There they multiplied and became a pest.
Some were taken to the island of Réunion
and to the Seychelles and, in 1847, some
were released in Calcutta. From then on the
snail has appeared in more and more countries—particularly in the Indo-Pacific area,
including Malaya, Indonesia, the Philippines, Thailand, Vietnam, and China.

*This West African giant snail has a pointed shell 5−8 in. long and weighs about ½ lb. Introduction
into many parts of the world mainly for its food value has resulted in it becoming a pest.*

Sometimes introductions have been acci-
dental, the snails being transported while
aestivating in bananas, in soil, or in motor
vehicles. Sometimes they have been deliberately introduced. In 1928, for instance,
they were introduced to Sarawak to be used
as poultry feed and in 1936 to the Hawaiian
islands by a lady wishing to keep two in her
garden as pets. The Japanese forces took
them as food for themselves into New
Guinea and elsewhere and, before the
Second World War, they were eaten by
Malays and by Chinese in various places.
Other related giant snails are important as
food in parts of West Africa. In Ghana
they are the greatest single source of animal
protein. The value of snails as food, however, even to those willing to eat them, is

more than offset by the damage they can
inflict on crops and gardens, for they can
occur in huge numbers, like apples under
an apple tree.

The nuisance does not end there, for in
places the ground may become slippery
with slime, excreta and dead snails, and
roads in Ceylon and Saipan have been turned into 'stinking nightmares' as more
and more were attracted to their crushed
fellows. Worse still, the slimy mess provides
breeding grounds for disease-bearing flies.
With others dying in drinking wells, de-
vouring with impunity the warfarin bait
and springing the traps put out for rats,
it is hardly surprising that much effort is
devoted to their control. Poisons have been
used as well as various predators—including
other carnivorous snails—but always there
is the danger in these methods of upsetting
the balance of nature in yet other ways,
such as the controlling predators attacking innocuous species, and so becoming
pests themselves. The best method of all,

if it can be used in time, is a rigorous system of control to prevent the spread of the
snail. It is encouraging that, in some areas,
after an initial heavy infestation, the population diminishes to a steady level at which
they are not such serious pests.

phylum	**Mollusca**
class	**Gastropoda**
order	**Stylommatophora**
family	**Achatinidae**
genus & species	***Achatina fulica*** *East Africa* ***A. achatina*** *West Africa*

Gibbon

The most agile of mammals and smallest of the five apes (including man) the gibbon is distinguished by its extremely long arms, which may be 1½ times the length of the legs. Most gibbons are about 3 ft high when standing upright, but the largest species, the siamang, reaches 4 ft. The fingers are long and the thumbs appear long because they are deeply cleft from the palms of the hands. The thumbs are also very mobile and gibbons are adept at manipulating objects. The nails are clawlike and the fangs, which in other apes are long in the males and short in females, are long in both male and female gibbons. As the males are only slightly larger than the females, the sexes tend to look alike except for their colour.

The six species of gibbon live in southeast Asia from Assam south to Java. The siamang lives in Malaya and Sumatra and the dwarf siamang lives on some small islands west of Sumatra. The species differ in colour. The siamangs are entirely black. The males of the concolor, hoolock and black-capped gibbons are black and the females fawn. Both sexes of these gibbons are whitish when born, turning black in their first year. At maturity the males remain black while the females turn fawn. The sixth species, the lar gibbon, the one most often seen in zoos, has several races. The white-handed and agile races of Malaya and Sumatra have light and dark colour phases, independent of sex. The silvery gibbon of Java and Borneo is uniformly grey or brown. The concolor gibbon differs in that the male has a crest of hair.

Superb acrobats

Gibbons live high in the trees, where they travel by swinging by their arms. They are popular in zoos for the way they will swing from one end of the cage to the other, grabbing bars with their hands and throwing themselves forwards without a check in their progression. Their agility is quite incredible, as they make apparently effortless leaps of 30 ft or more, and their reflexes match it. A gibbon was once seen to jump from a branch just as it broke, and so fail to get enough momentum to reach the next branch. Twisting in mid-air, the gibbon grabbed the stump of the broken branch, swung right around it and flew off to its destination. The gibbon's agility is mainly due to its long arms, which can move freely in all directions, its light body and the long fingers that are held in a hooked position with the thumbs out of the way. Gibbons are also agile on the ground. Apart from man, they are the only apes that

◁ *The swinging primate: the ability to swing hand over hand is the art of the gibbon. Its wrist, long arm and shoulder are adapted for this movement, known as brachiation.*

▷ *Almost human: a silvery gibbon stands erect.*

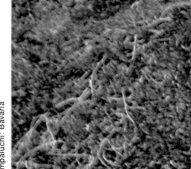

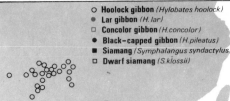

○ Hoolock gibbon *(Hylobates hoolock)*
● Lar gibbon *(H. lar)*
□ Concolor gibbon *(H.concolor)*
● Black-capped gibbon *(H.pileatus)*
■ Siamang *(Symphalangus syndactylus)*
□ Dwarf siamang *(S.klossii)*

not found

?

probably
throughout

probable extent of range

At home with the gibbons

A 6 day old gibbon clings instinctively to its mother (above). The mother will lavish intense care on her offspring until it is weaned. Portrait of a lar gibbon (above centre). The eyes are designed for binocular vision. They are forward directing giving overlapping sight which enables the gibbon to focus accurately on branches it is aiming for in its aerial acrobatic movements (above right).
Siamang family (right). The siamang is the largest of the six gibbon species with an arm-spread of as much as 5 ft. It has a throat sac which can be inflated to about the size of its head when a call is given. This call has been described as the combined bark of a dog and the hoot of a grouse. In the early morning all the members of a family give a short 'concert', hooting in unison for several minutes. This noise carries for considerable distances — often over two miles. The map marks (left) show the positions of recorded specimens. Apart from the siamang which is rather different from the others, the species of gibbon have separate ranges which overlap only slightly so there is no real competition.

habitually walk upright on their hindlegs. When walking on the ground or along a branch, they hold their arms out to help in balancing.

Other apes are becoming rare, but the gibbon is still quite numerous in the wild; soldiers returning from Vietnam often bring home pet gibbons. They are not the best of pets, the females in particular being liable to fits of bad temper, but the males usually become tame and affectionate.

Gibbons live in small groups, often a pair with up to four offspring. Each group owns a small territory varying from 40 to 300 acres. They sleep in the centre of the territory, huddled together on a branch, squatting on their ischial callosities, or sitting pads— hard patches of skin on their rumps. Gibbons probably mate for life and they are very aggressive to other gibbons. Each morning some, usually the females, begin calling, uttering the 'great-call' which is used as an advertisement. This attracts the groups towards each other and they often meet at the boundaries of their territories. The males leap about uttering the 'conflict-call', a series of hoots, and eventually one male may chase another, forcing him back into his own territory, then rapidly retreating. Very occasionally there is a fight and the two males scratch and bite each other. After an hour or so the conflicts die down and the groups wander back into their territories to feed.

Each species of gibbon has a very characteristic great-call, by which it can be recognised even if the gibbons are hidden in the tree canopy. The black-capped gibbon has the most musical call consisting of a rising crescendo of wistful-sounding whoops followed by a rapidly descending series. The hoolock gibbons produce a call that is imitated by the name. It is stimulated by another gibbon calling or by a sudden change in the weather such as a shower of rain or the appearance of the sun. The siamang has a special throat pouch. Filling it produces a deep resonant boom, followed by a harsh, honking exhalation, which can be heard over a wide area.

Snatching birds from the air

Gibbons eat mostly fruit, such as figs, grapes and mangoes. They also eat leaves, insects, eggs and occasionally birds, which they have been seen catching in mid-air as they leap from one branch to another. In the tropical forests a group of gibbons can usually find all the food it requires within its territory as the trees fruit all the year round. Occasionally, however, the trees along the boundary are disputed with the neighbours.

Breeding all the year round

Gibbons breed all the year round. A single baby is born after a 7-month gestation. At first it is helpless and is carried, clasped to the mother's breast. A few weeks later it begins to take an interest in its surroundings and is carried clinging around its mother's waist like a belt. When she is swinging through the trees she raises her legs to give the baby extra support and protection. After weaning, the baby joins in the social life of its family. Mature at 6 years old, gibbons live to about 25 years.

Smallest but the most successful ape, a gibbon hangs by a hand. The hands have long fingers and the thumbs appear long because they are deeply cleft from the palms of the hand.

Not so dim

Gibbons are often said to be the least intelligent of apes, but recent tests have shown that they may be as intelligent as chimpanzees. The reason for the gibbons' supposed lack of intelligence was that they were not so adept at problem-solving tests as the other apes. The tests are absurdly simple for a man. Food such as a banana is placed out of reach beyond the bars of the apes' cage. A piece of string is tied to the banana and led to the bars. The ape has no trouble pulling the string to get its banana but the situation is made more difficult by having two pieces of string. One, for instance, may run straight from banana to cage, but pulling it does not draw the banana nearer, while the other runs first away from the cage then back, and is the right one to pull to get the banana. The ape can solve the problem by trial-and-error, pulling strings at random until it gets the right one, or by insight, that is by working out the problem in its head.

Gibbons were apparently unable to solve these problems, but it seems that they were unfairly set. The strings ran along the ground and gibbons had difficulty in grasping them. If, however, the strings are raised, the gibbons, being adapted for hanging on to branches or vines, could take hold of them. This is a point of great importance in designing tests of an animal's intelligence. It has to be able to carry out the necessary movements. For example, it would be no good expecting a dog to pull a suspended string with its paws. Using the improved tests it was found that gibbons could solve the problems as well as other apes. First they would pull the wrong string, and give up and climb round the cage. Then, suddenly, they would return and without hesitation pull the right string. Apparently they had been thinking about the problem and worked it out.

class	**Mammalia**
order	**Primates**
family	**Pongidae**
genera & species	***Hylobates concolor*** *concolor gibbon*
	H. hoolock *hoolock gibbon*
	H. lar *lar gibbon*
	H. pileatus *black-capped gibbon*
	Symphalangus syndactylus *siamang*
	S. klossii *dwarf siamang*

Giganturid

*This name, which looks very queer to the non-zoologist, is deliberately used to introduce a very odd deep-sea fish, one that breaks all the rules. There are several species in one genus **Gigantura**, belonging to one family placed in a suborder on its own. The several species, which differ from each other in small details only, have been brought up from depths between 1 500 – 6 000 ft in both Atlantic and Indian Oceans. The name suggests giant fishes but they are usually between 2 – 5, rarely as much as 8, in. long. In fact, when we break up the name we find it is made up of a Latin word **giganteus** and a Greek word **uros** meaning tail. It refers not to the size of the fish but to*

made. The shape, number and disposition of the fins of a giganturid suggests that they do not swim rapidly. On the other hand, it is a mystery why it should be silvery or why it has no scales. And the long lower tail fin is hardly more easy to explain. We are on firmer ground about the way it feeds because the strong jaws and sharp teeth mark it as predatory. Moreover, because its teeth are depressible we could suppose it swallows large prey, the teeth being lowered to allow more room for large prey to be taken into the mouth. This line of argument is supported by the elastic stomach of a giganturid and by those brought to the surface that have recently swallowed a fish as large or larger than themselves. One giganturid, appropriately named *Gigantura vorax*, itself 3 in. long, had swallowed another fish 5½ in. long. Moreover, this fish was doubled up, suggesting that the giganturid had seized it by the middle

they can. A further theory is that the eyes, which have an accessory retina of short rods as well as the main retina, are specially adapted for picking up the luminescence from the light-organs of their prey.

Problems to be settled

The eyes of fishes are essentially like ours but there are differences, one of them being that the lens, instead of being oval, is spherical and bulges well through the pupil. Consequently, with the eyes set on the sides of the head a fish has a wide all-round vision, necessary because it has no neck and cannot turn its head to look for food or keep watch for enemies. It has, so to speak, the next best thing to having 'eyes in the back of its head'. Most fishes, also, are long-sighted despite a popular belief that they are short-sighted. In addition, many fishes can swivel their eyes forward

Gigantura — tubular-eyed fish with a body 2 – 5 in. long is found in the deep waters of both the Atlantic and Indian Oceans.

Malcolm McGregor

the extraordinarily long lower lobe of the tail fin. And if the name is misleading this is appropriate because almost everything else about the fish is misleading.

Catalogue of oddities

Giganturids have slender rounded bodies. They lack pelvic fins as well as a number of other anatomical parts, normally considered essential to the life of a fish, including several bones of the head. They also lack light-organs which are such a feature of deep-sea fishes. They have needle-sharp teeth that can be raised and lowered. The pectoral fins are tolerably large for the size of the body. Their bodies are scaleless and whereas other fishes living at these depths are black or dark brown, giganturids are a bright, metallic silvery colour, like fishes that live near the surface. Above all, these fishes have tubular eyes directed forwards, as if they were wearing binoculars. There are a few other fishes with tubular eyes but usually these are directed upwards.

Huge meals at long intervals

As with all deep-sea animals virtually nothing is known of the way they live except what can be deduced from the way they are

and had swallowed it bent into a V.

Then comes the question: how does a giganturid breathe while swallowing such large prey, which must take an appreciable time? One suggestion is that while doing this, and so prevented from taking in water through the mouth to pass across the gills, the pectoral fins are used to fan water into the gill-chamber for breathing.

Why do they wear binoculars?

So far as the food and feeding habits are concerned, all that has so far been deduced fits into the general pattern of what is already known for the carnivorous deep-sea fishes. That is, they are living in depths where food is not abundant so they must take whatever food presents itself even to swallowing prey larger than themselves. So they make up for the infrequency of their meals by taking huge meals when opportunity offers. What is now needed is to guess why the tubular eyes are required. One view is that they act like the telephoto lens of a camera so the giganturid can see prey a long way off, even in the murky gloom at great depths. Another is that they need this improved vision because they are poor swimmers and, presumably, must stalk prey that cannot see as far as

to give better vision forwards. This can be seen when we look at a fish in an aquarium as it faces us head-on as in the angelfish, picture on page 51. It can also be seen on the television screen when underwater close-up pictures of fishes are being shown. These considerations show how specialised are the eyes of giganturids, which can only look directly forwards. Perhaps one day we may know how they are compensated for this loss of all-round vision, with eyes in the front of the head only. They may have other senses for detecting the approach of food or enemies from behind. Perhaps the scaleless skin means it is more sensitive to vibrations in the water. And then, there is the long lower tail fin — the giant tail — to be accounted for, giving only one of the many problems to which answers will be eagerly awaited.

class	**Osteichthyes**
order	**Cetomimiformes**
family	**Giganturidae**
genus & species	*Gigantura vorax* others

If looks could kill: massive-headed, belly-dragging, obese and ugly, the Gila monster is among the more repulsive of reptiles and one of the only two poisonous lizards. Surprisingly, many people have kept it as a pet; enough, in fact, to make it rare. It is now protected by law.

Gila monster

Only two out of about 3 000 kinds of lizards are poisonous: the Gila monster (pronounced 'heela') and the beaded lizard. They look alike and live in deserts of the southwestern United States and adjacent parts of Mexico respectively. The first is named for the Gila basin in Arizona where it is plentiful, the second after the beaded nature of its scales.

The Gila monster is up to 23 in. long and weighs up to 3¼ lb. It is mainly pink and yellow with black shading. The beaded lizard, up to 32 in. long, is mainly black with pink and yellow patches. The Gila monster has 4—5 dark bands on the tail. The beaded lizard has 6—7 yellow bands. Both have a stout body, large blunt head, powerful lower jaw, small eyes, an unusually thick tail, short legs with 5 toes on each and remarkably strong claws.

Alternate gluttony and fasting

These lizards move about very slowly, although when captured they can move swiftly and struggle actively, hissing all the while. They spend long periods of time in their burrows in the sand, coming out at the rainy season and even then mainly at night. Being slow movers they must eat things that cannot run away. These are mainly eggs of birds and other reptiles, baby birds and baby mice and rats. They track them down partly by smell but more especially by taste, using the tongue to pick up scent particles on the sand from birds' nests or rodents' burrows. These are conveyed by the tongue to Jacobson's organ, a sort of taste-smell organ in the roof of the mouth. They eat insects and earthworms in captivity and from the behaviour of these captive animals it seems unlikely that venom is used to kill prey. Eggs are either seized, the head raised and the shell crushed so the contents flow into the mouth, or bitten in two and the tongue used to lap up the contents as the shell lies on the ground. The Gila monster drinks liquid food by lapping it up and holding its head back to let the liquid run down its tongue.

While active these lizards eat all they can find and store the surplus as fat in the body and especially in the tail. When well-fed their skeleton represents a small part of the total weight of the body and the lizards can then survive long periods of fasting. The fat tail will then shrink to ⅕ its former girth and the rest of the body will be little more than skin and bone. The lizard will quickly recover once it can find food. One that had survived three years drought, during which it took no food, was taken into captivity and in 6 months its tail had doubled in size and the body was as plump as usual.

Inefficient venom apparatus

The venom glands are in the lower jaw although teeth in both jaws are grooved. Each gland has several ducts that open into a groove between the lower lip and the gum, and the poison finds its way from this to the grooves in the teeth. Neither of the lizards can strike as a snake does but must hold with the teeth and hang on with a vice-like grip sometimes chewing to help conduct the venom. If bitten by a monster, the main problem is to free the tight-gripping jaws.

Nests in the sand

Mating takes place in July and eggs are laid a few weeks later. These are laid in a hole dug by the female with her front feet and covered with sand. There may be 3—15 in a clutch, each egg about 1½ by 2½ in. and oval, with a tough leathery shell. They hatch in about a month, the young lizards being 3½—4¾ in. long, and more vivid in colour than the parents.

Legally protected monster

Little is known of the natural enemies of the two poisonous lizards but by 1952 the Gila monster was becoming so rare it had to be protected by law to save it from extinction. It was being caught and sold in large numbers as a pet. Those who caught them were paid 25—50 cents an inch, and the lizards were then sold at 1—2 dollars an inch.

Lizard with a bad name

In striking contrast with the popularity of the Gila monster as a pet are many erroneous beliefs that have gathered around it in the past. One is that it cannot eliminate body wastes, which is why it is so poisonous. For the same reason its breath is evil-smelling. Another is that it can spit venom, whereas at most, when hissing, it may spray a little venom. The lizard has been credited also with leaping on its victims, largely the result perhaps of the way it will lash out from side to side when held in the hand. Its tongue has been said to be poisonous, the lizard itself impossible to kill and possessed of magical powers. Lastly, it has been said to be a cross between a lizard and a crocodile.

More than 400 years ago, a Spaniard, Francisco Hernández, wrote that the bite of the lizard though harmful was not fatal, that it threatened no harm except when provoked and that its appearance was more to be dreaded than its bite. Although his writings had been overlooked the first scientists to study it seem to have taken much the same view when they named it *Heloderma suspectum*, because they were not sure whether it was poisonous, only suspected of being so. They were more certain about the beaded lizard which they named *H. horridum*. Now we know that the poison is a neurotoxin which causes swelling, loss of consciousness, vomiting, palpitations, laboured breathing,

△ *Lizard connoisseur: using tongue and 'nose', a Gila monster tests its surroundings.*

dizziness, a swollen tongue and swollen glands. Not all these symptoms appear in one person, however. The swelling and the initial pain are due to the way the poison is injected. The lizard must hold on and chew with a sideways action of the teeth.

In 1956 Charles M Bogert and Rafael Martin del Campo published in America the results of their thoroughgoing investigation into the injuries suffered by human beings from the bite of the Gila monster. They found only 34 known cases of which 8 were said to have been fatal. Most of those who had died were either in poor health at the time or drunk. In several instances there were signs of repeated biting, as in the case of the man who carried the lizard inside his shirt, next to his skin. This may explain the drunks who fell victim. They teased the lizards in zoos and probably did not realise they were being repeatedly bitten.

▽ *Section through Gila monster's head, showing Jacobson's organ in the roof of the mouth. This is a specialised organ of smell, supplementing or replacing the nose. Scent particles are picked up and conveyed to it by the tongue.*

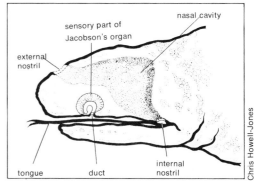

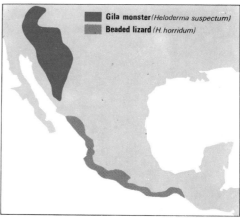

class	Reptilia
order	Squamata
suborder	Sauria
family	Helodermatidae
genus & species	*Heloderma horridum* beaded lizard *H. suspectum* Gila monster

883

The lofty ones

Dappled freaks of the African veld: a group of giraffes rear their extraordinary necks against the skyline of a pale sunset.

Giraffe

Tallest animal in the world, the giraffe is remarkable for its long legs and long neck. An old bull may be 18 ft to the top of his head. Females are smaller. The head tapers to mobile hairy lips, the tongue is extensile and the eyes are large. There are 2—5 horns, bony knobs covered with skin, including one pair on the forehead, a boss in front, and, in some races, a small pair farther back. The shoulders are high and the back slopes down to a long tufted tail. The coat is boldly spotted and irregularly blotched chestnut, dark brown or liver-coloured on a pale buff ground, giving the effect of a network of light-coloured lines. A number of species and races have been recognized in the past, differing mainly in details of colour and number of horns, but the current view is that all belong to one species. The number of races recognised, however, varies between 8 and 13 species depending on the authority.

The present-day range of the giraffe is the dry savannah and semi-desert of Africa south of the Sahara although it was formerly more widespread. Its range today is from Sudan and Somalia south to South Africa and westwards to northern Nigeria. In many parts of its former range it has been wiped out for its hide.

A leisurely anarchy

Giraffes live in herds with a fairly casual social structure. It seems that males live in groups in forested zones, the old males often solitary, and the females and young live apart from them in more open country. Males visit these herds mainly for mating.

Giraffes do not move about much, and tend to walk at a leisurely pace unless disturbed. When walking slowly the legs move in much the same way as those of a horse. That is, the right hindleg touches the ground just after the right foreleg leaves it, and a little later the left legs make the same movement. The body is therefore supported on three legs most of the time while walking. As the pace quickens to a gallop the giraffe's leg movements change to the legs on each side moving forward together, the two right hoofs hitting the ground together followed by the two left legs moving together.

The long neck not only allows a giraffe to browse high foliage, the eyes set on top of the high head form a sort of watch-tower to look out for enemies. In addition, the long neck and heavy head assist movement by acting as a counterpoise. When resting crouched, with legs folded under the body the neck may be held erect or, if sleeping, the giraffe lays its neck along its back. To rise, the forelegs are half-unfolded, the neck being swung back to take the weight off the forequarters. Then it is swung forwards to take the weight off the hindlegs, for them to be unfolded. By repeated movements of this kind the animal finally gets to its feet.

Adult giraffes apparently sleep little: not at all according to some authors, one-half hour in 24 according to others.

Necking parties

The habit of 'necking' has been something of a puzzle. Two giraffes stand side-by-side and belabour each other with their heads, swinging their long necks slowly and forcibly. Only rarely does any injury result, and the necking seems to be a ritualized fighting, to establish dominance, and confined exclusively, or nearly so, to the male herds.

Not so dumb

One long-standing puzzle concerns the voice. For a long time everyone accepted the idea that giraffes are mute—yet they have an unusually large voice-box. During the last 25 years it has been found that a young giraffe will bleat like the calf of domestic cattle, that the adult female makes a sound like 'wa-ray' and that adult bulls, and sometimes cows, will make a husky grunt or cough. Nevertheless, there are many zoo-keepers who have never heard a giraffe utter a call and there is still the puzzle why there should be such a large voice-box when so little use is made of it. Some zoologists have suggested the giraffe may use ultra-sonics.

Controlled blood pressure

In feeding, leaves are grasped with the long tongue and mobile lips. Trees and bushes tend to become hourglass-shaped from giraffes browsing all round at a particular level. Acacia is the main source of food but many others are browsed, giraffes showing definite preferences for some species of trees or bushes over others.

Giraffes drink regularly when water is available but can go long periods without drinking. They straddle the front legs widely to bring the head down to water, or else straddle them slightly and then bend them at the knees. Another long-standing puzzle concerns the blood pressure in the head, some zoologists maintaining a giraffe must lower and raise its head slowly to prevent a rush of blood to the head. In fact, the blood vessels have valves, reservoirs of blood in the head and alternative routes for the blood, and so there is no upset from changes in the level of the head, no matter how quickly the giraffe moves.

Casual mothers

Mating and calving appear to take place all the year, with peak periods which may vary from one region to another. The gestation period is 420—468 days, the single calf being able to walk within an hour of birth, when it is 6 ft to the top of the head and weighs 117 lb. Reports vary about the suckling which is said to continue for 9 months, but in one study the calves were browsing at the age of one week and were not seen suckling after that. The bond between mother and infant is, in any case, a loose one. Giraffe milk has a high fat content and the young grow fast. Captive giraffes often live for over 20 years.

Defensive hoofs

Giraffes have few enemies. A lion may take a young calf or several lions may combine to kill an adult. Even these events are rare because the long legs and heavy hoofs can be used to deadly effect, striking down at an attacker.

Symbol of friendliness

Rock engravings of giraffes have been found over the whole of Africa and some of the most imposing are at Fezzan in the middle of what is now the Sahara desert. The animal must have lingered on in North Africa until 500 B.C. Some of the engravings are life size, or even larger, and many depict the trap used to capture giraffes, while others show typical features of its behaviour, including the necking. The engravings also show ostriches, dibatag, and gerenuk. Giraffes were also figured on the slate palettes, used for grinding malachite and haematite for eye-shadows, in Ancient Egypt, similar to that believed to portray the dibatag. The last giraffe depicted in Egyptian antiquities is on the tomb of Rameses the Great, 1225 BC.

There are references to the animal in Greek and Roman writings and a few pictures survive from the Roman era, but from then until the 7th or 8th century AD the principal records are in Arabic literature. The description given by Zakariya al-Qaswini in his 13th-century *Marvels of Creation* reflects the accepted view, that 'the giraffe is produced by the camel mare, the male hyaena and the wild cow'. The giraffe was taken to India by the Arabs, and from there to China, the first arriving in 1414 in the Imperial Zoological Garden in Peking. To the Chinese it symbolized gentleness and peace and the Arabs adopted this symbolism, so a gift of a giraffe became a sign of peace and friendliness between rulers.

In medieval Europe, and until the end of the 18th century, knowledge of the giraffe was based on descriptions in Greek and Roman writings and on hearsay accounts. It was at best a legendary beast.

class	**Mammalia**
order	**Artiodactyla**
family	**Giraffidae**
genus & species	***Giraffa camelopardalis***

Wiped out for its hide in many parts of its range, the present day distribution of the giraffe is much reduced. A number of races are recognised within the single species.

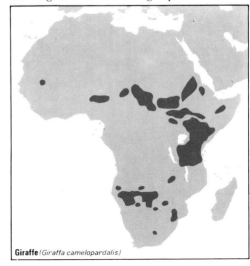

Giraffe *(Giraffa camelopardalis)*

One more . . .

Below: The happy couple. A pair of giraffes circle one another in courtship ceremony.
Right: Casual birth. With a minimum of fuss, a calf is born in London Zoo — all 6 ft and 110 lb of it. After wobbling to its feet straight away, the calf can walk within an hour — very necessary in the wild, with many predators only too ready to snatch an easy meal.
Below right: First food. Although opinions differ about the time a giraffe calf spends suckling, it is known that the milk is highly nourishing, and the baby grows at an extraordinary rate.

Despite these happy domestic scenes, the relationship between mothers and calves is quite casual — they merely live in the same herd once weaning is over.

RS Virdee

Giraffes at home

Far right: Using long tongue and mobile lips, a giraffe feeds on ground-growing plants.
Right: Top gear. A herd of females and young gallop away from a disturbance.
Below: Feathered grooms. A pair of oxpeckers feed on the parasites from the neck of a somewhat disgruntled giraffe.
Below right: The long way down. Giraffe at a waterhole during a drought in Nairobi Park. One might expect the blood to run into a giraffe's head in this awkward position, but a system of reservoirs and valves, inside the arteries, prevents this. A giraffe will drink regularly if there is water nearby, but in times of drought it can abstain for some time.
Below far right: Tough tongued eater. Ignoring thorns in its mouth, a giraffe makes the best of a sharp meal, while avoiding prickly branches with its flexible neck.

Okapia

N Myers: Bavaria

Phillipa Scott: Photo Res

*See-through skin and shining colours make glassfishes popular in aquaria. Left: Siamese glassfish **Chanda wolfii**. Above: **Chanda lala**.*

Glassfish

This is an obvious name for fishes that are transparent, with the skeleton and some internal organs clearly visible; yet although transparent they do not lack colour. A number of fishes are transparent or translucent but the name 'glassfish' is reserved for certain small fishes that are favourite aquarium fishes. In the same family, however, are large game or commercial fishes, including the snooks and the Nile perch. As we shall see, the glassfish and the Nile perch, although so different to look at, have one thing in common; they have both, at different times, ended in the ground.

The body is deep and strongly compressed from side-to-side. The dorsal fin is in two parts, that in front being supported by hard rays, the rear portion having one hard ray and up to 18 soft rays. The tailfin is either rounded or deeply forked.

The 8 or more species are found from East Africa through southern Asia to eastern Australia, the majority being in southeast Asia.

The 8 species of snooks live in the seas of tropical west and east Atlantic and the eastern Pacific. They readily enter rivers and may be 4½ ft long with a weight of 51 lb. The Nile perch, up to 7 ft long and more than 250 lb weight, is only one of several related African game species. It looks much more substantial than the glassfish and a special account of it will be given later.

Living gems for fertilizers

The Indian glassfish looks like a piece of crystal floating and reflecting colours in water. It is up to 3 in. long, greenish to yellowish but shining gold or iridescent bluish-green in reflected light. The flanks are marked with bars made up of tiny black dots, with a delicate violet stripe running from the gill-cover to the root of the tail. The fins are yellowish to rusty-red, the dorsal and anal fins with black rays and bordered with pale blue. Rays of paired fins are red or bluish.

It is the best known of the small glassfishes, and lives in fresh and brackish waters of India, Burma and Thailand. Its uneventful life is spent among water plants feeding on small aquatic animals such as insect larvae, crustaceans and worms. Its breeding habits are almost equally uneventful. In aquaria, according to Günther Sterba, spawning is triggered by morning sunshine raising the temperature, and a brief separation of the sexes, by putting them in separate tanks for a short time then reuniting them. The pair take up position side-by-side, quivering all the time. As the female lays the pair turn over to an upside-down position. The female lays her eggs among water plants to which they stick. She lays 4–6 at a time, repeating this until 200 or more have been laid. After this the parents take no further interest. The eggs hatch in 8–24 hours, depending on temperature, the baby fishes hanging from the water plants for 3–4 days after which they swim freely. Their food is small crustaceans, such as water fleas. The young glassfishes do not go in search of food but snap up any that drifts past them. It can be presumed that if food is scarce around the area at such times many young fishes will die of starvation. Nevertheless, large numbers survive for, as William T Innes remarks in his *Exotic Aquarium Fishes*, this little gem treasured by aquarists is caught in large numbers in India and Burma for use as a fertilizer.

Family likenesses

Two people when related even distantly often share what we call a family likeness. In height, girth, colour of hair and in almost every way the two may be wholly unlike yet there is something that marks them as belonging to a family. It may be something very small, for example, a peculiarity in the way they walk, the shape of the lower lip, and so on. It is the same in classifying animals, and the family we are considering here is a fine example. Included in it are glassfishes, small, transparent, delicate; as well as snooks that are large, sturdy and not transparent and the 7ft robust giant, the Nile perch. From a casual glance they look most unlike yet each has a similar outline, and each has at least one small feature we call a family likeness. In each the lateral line, the line of sense-organs running along the flanks of fishes, goes right to the end of the tailfin, which is most unusual.

class	**Osteichthyes**
order	**Perciformes**
family	**Centropomidae**
genera & species	***Chanda ranga*** *Indian glassfish* ***Centropomus unidecimalis*** *snook* *others*

Leonard Lee Rue

Glass snake

Glass 'snakes' are, in fact, legless lizards that look like snakes. The Scheltopusik or Pallas' glass snake of southeast Europe and southwest Asia is nearly 4 ft long and about 2 in. across the body. It was first discovered by the naturalist Pallas on wooded slopes bordering the Volga. Since then it has been found as far west as Hungary and it is widespread throughout the Balkan peninsula. Another living in northeast India and Burma is 15 in. long and the glass snake of southern China is 2 ft long. There is another glass snake in Morocco and 3 others in North America, up to 3 ft long, ranging from Lake Michigan southwards through the eastern and southern states and into Mexico. One American species ***O. ventralis*** *is brown, olive or black with green spots or stripes and greenish-white underneath.*

Two-thirds of their length is made up of tail, whereas in snakes the tail makes up only a small fraction of the total length. Pallas' glass snake is bronze, yellow or chestnut-brown, often with tiny pale spots, and very old individuals are coppery-red. The glass snake of southern China has an olive back and bright blue flanks. All glass snakes have a deep furrow running along each side of the body from the neck to the vent. There is no trace of the forelimbs and, in the European and North African species, there is a barely noticeable stump of a hindlimb at the rear end of the furrow.

Snake-like but not snakes

Glass snakes live in fields or copses, among heaps of stones or in bare rocky places. They avoid dense woods. They are not as agile as snakes but they can clamber over rocks easily. They do not climb trees, and they avoid water. Their habit is to hide under fallen leaves or burrow just beneath the surface where the soil is sandy and light. When they do come out they move over the ground like snakes but with a less graceful action. When chased they move with a rapid twisting of the body, stopping every 2–3 yd for a rest.

Glass snakes feed by day on insects, especially grasshoppers. They sometimes take mice, lizards, fledgling birds and the eggs of snakes and birds. Live prey is twisted rapidly round and round or beaten against the ground until stunned and then chewed with powerful jaws and swallowed whole. Glass snakes are said to eat snakes, including adders. When eating an egg they crack the shell with their jaws and ladle out the contents with their flat forked tongues. The American glass snake, also called glass lizard or joint snake, seems to spend more time burrowing than the European form. It has a similar diet but is said to eat earthworms as well as other underground animals.

The females lay their inch-long eggs under moss or dead leaves, 8–10 at a time. They take about a month to hatch, the female guarding them during that time in a half-hearted way. The newly-hatched glass snake is 5 in. long, ashen-grey with dark spots and bands along the back and dark vertical stripes on the sides of the head. They take several years to reach maturity and the glass snakes are said to live up to 60 years.

Two lines of defence

Little is known about the enemies of glass snakes. They would be likely to be taken by large birds of prey. They have, however, two lines of defence. Like other lizards they can shed their tails when attacked, and if held in the hand they twine round it in a most unpleasant manner, which would probably deter all but a large or a persistent predator.

Falling to bits

Glass snakes are named for their reputation of breaking into pieces when struck with a stick. The legend continues that the pieces

later reassemble and that the lizard is none the worse for its adventure. As in other lizards the tail is shed in moments of alarm, but in glass snakes it also breaks into several pieces. Because the tail is so long, the body of a glass snake that has just cast its tail looks very small, little bigger than one of the portions of the shed tail, so it looks as if the whole animal is in pieces.

class	**Reptilia**
order	**Squamata**
suborder	**Sauria**
family	**Anguidae**
genus & species	***Ophisaurus apodus*** *European glass snake* ***O. ventralis*** *N. American glass snake* *others*

△ *Brittle-tailed reptile: the 'glass' half of this animal's name is perhaps justified by the way its tail will fall off and break into several pieces in moments of alarm. 'Snake', however, does not apply; it is a legless lizard.*
▷ *Twisting sprinter—a European glass snake. Glass snakes do not move with the wriggling expertise of true snakes, especially when frightened; they use a twisting movement and have to stop for a rest every 2—3 yd.*

Gliding frog

There are a few species of frogs which are also referred to as 'the so-called flying frogs', or else they are called 'flying' frogs. The writer then goes on to say that of course they do not fly, they only glide. It is high time, therefore, that we stopped calling them flying frogs and followed the lead given, for example, by Doris B Cochran, of the United States National Museum, and called them gliding frogs, which is what they are.

The gliding frogs are members of a family of tree frogs, Rhacophoridae, which will be dealt with later. The most common are the Malayan and Wallace's gliding frogs which are 4 in. long in the head and body, shining green above, yellow on flanks and white underneath. They range from Malaya to Borneo. As with other tree frogs of this family the ends of the toes on all four feet have sucker discs at the tips, for clinging to trees. Gliding frogs differ in having the toes of all four feet longer than usual and fully webbed.

Jumping and gliding

Gliding frogs spend the day in trees and tall bushes holding on by the discs on their toes. In strong sunlight they are a greenish-blue, turning to green in the evening and finally to black, the change taking place more rapidly in the males than the females. They become active at night, leaping from branch to branch and taking gliding leaps from tree to tree. The leaps may be up to 6 ft but the glide may cover 40—50 ft to the base of the next tree. In a glide the toes are fully stretched and held rigid and the underside of the body is drawn up, giving a concave surface that increases the lift. The direction and length of a glide can be controlled to some extent.

Foam nests

Gliding frogs feed mainly on grasshoppers but take other insects as well, and when breeding they do not take to water but make foam nests among large leaves. While mating the male clings on the female's back, as is usual in frogs. As the eggs are laid quantities of albumen are given out with them and both female and male beat this into a frothy mass with a paddling action of the hindlegs. The outside of the mass hardens while the inside of it becomes more and more fluid. The eggs float in this until rain washes either the eggs, or the tadpoles, out of the nest, to fall into pools below. If no rain falls the outer crust eventually liquefies to release eggs or tadpoles.

Frogs' flying school

The first Europeans to learn about these frogs heard the story from Chinese labourers in southeast Asia who spoke of the frogs flying down from the trees. The story that there were frogs that flew was accepted at first. Then came disbelief and this was reinforced by a curious accident. Alfred Russel Wallace, the distinguished naturalist, who worked so much in the southeast Asian region, calculated that the area of the spread feet with their webs was sufficient to enable the frogs to glide. He made an error in his calculations and when this was detected the story of flying frogs became further discredited. Few zoologists had ever seen the gliding frog alive so it was difficult to check Wallace's statement or those of the Chinese in Malaya. In 1926, however, HB Cott carried out experiments with the Brazilian tree frog *Hyla venulosa* which showed that even tree frogs with less webbing than gliding frogs could fall from considerable heights and land safely on their feet. He dropped the frogs from a tower 140 ft high and the frogs landed on the ground 90 ft out from the base of the tower. They reached the ground at such a slow speed that they were quite unhurt. Almost any small tree-living animal will do the same and the reason is that they spread their legs and keep their body the right way up, as a cat does when it falls from a height, and this acts as a brake. By contrast, the ordinary common frog, although the webs on its feet are larger than those of a tree frog, simply tumbles head over heels when it falls and plummets straight down. It only needs that little extra webbing on the feet, which gliding frogs have, to keep them gliding.

class	**Amphibia**
order	**Salientia**
family	**Rhacophoridae**
genus & species	***Rhacophorus nigropalmatus*** *Wallace's gliding frog* ***R. reinwardtii*** *Malayan gliding frog*

▽ *Ready to go: a Siamese gliding frog* **Rhacophorus prominanus** *takes aim for the leap which will start its long glide towards the base of the next tree—perhaps 50 ft away.*

Lim Boo Liat

▽ *Airborne amphibian: Bornean gliding frog on the way down, each webbed foot a tiny parachute. Even the body is held concave to add to the gliding surface and so increase lift.*

D Davis

Glowworm

The glowworm is a beetle belonging to the family Lampyridae which also includes the fireflies (p 762). Centuries ago anything that was long and crawling was called a worm. The female glowworm lacks wings and it was this and her general appearance that was responsible for the name.

Male and female of the common English glowworm **Lampyris noctiluca** are yellowish grey-brown. The male has large eyes and two very tiny light-producing organs at the tip of the abdomen. He also has wings covered by the usual wing cases of beetles, and his length is about ½ in. The female, slightly longer than the male, differs little in shape from the larva and the last three segments of the body, on the underside, are yellowish and strongly luminescent.

A second species of glowworm **Phosphaenus hemipterus** has been found but rarely in parts of southern England. It is, however, widespread over continental Europe.

The lure of the lights

Adult glowworms are most active in June and July. Preferring slightly damp places, they may be found on hedgerow banks, hillsides and in rough meadows, especially where there is a plentiful supply of snails. By day they hide in cracks and crevices. After nightfall the female climbs onto a prominent piece of foliage and takes up a position head down so her luminous end is prominently displayed. Her method of light-production is the same as in the firefly (see p 752). Beneath the light-producing bands is a whitish, opaque layer which not only prevents absorption of the light into the body, but reflects it back, making full use of all the light. The winged male homes on the female's light for mating. The light may be visible to us over 100 yd or so under suitable conditions, but may be 'doused' as we approach and switched on again after an interval. By contrast, the larvae light up as a result of being disturbed, which suggests that in them the luminescence may serve as a defence, frightening away some enemies. The larvae's light also is slightly different from that of the adults, being more intensely green.

Short-lived adults

The pale yellow eggs are 1 mm diameter. Usually they are laid in ones and twos over a period of a couple of days on grass stems or moss, or in or on the soil. They hatch in a fortnight, the larvae being almost exact miniatures of the adult females except for the simpler structure of the legs and a series of paler spots at the front corners of each body segment. Growing by a series of moults, the larvae reach the adult stage in three years. The pupa of the male differs from that of the female, reflecting the different appearance of the adults. Emerging from the pupae after about 8 or 9 days, usually in April or May, the adults live for only a short while after mating and egg-laying. During mating neither sex glows.

John Markham

△ *Fickle flasher: having attracted three males to her powerful light, a female glowworm mates with one, ignored by her disappointed suitors.*

▽ *Incandescent cousin: female African beetle of the closely related family Phengodidae waiting in the grass for response to her light.*

Anthony Bannister: NHPA

Larvae feed, parents starve

Adult glowworms take no food, although it is often asserted that they do. The larvae feed on snails which they discover by following their slime trails. They drive their hollow, curved mandibles into the mollusc and inject a dark fluid, partly paralysing and partly digestive. This rapidly reduces the snail's tissues to a pre-digested soup-like liquid which the glowworm then sucks up. Newly-hatched glowworms are only $\frac{1}{5}$ in. long. They feed on the smaller snails. Sometimes the larvae feed communally, crowding round the lip of the shell and feeding side by side. After a meal the glowworm pushes out a white sponge-like device from its anus. With this it can clean away from its head and back any remains of slime resulting from its meal.

Lucky to survive

Glowworms fall victim to any insect-eating animal, despite the glowing lights on their bodies, but especially to toads and hedgehogs, both of which feed at night. Some are eaten by frogs and spiders, and there are mites which penetrate the soft joints between the body segments of the larvae and feed on their body fluids. The larvae are particularly vulnerable to mites when they have shed their skins at the periodic moults, making them fair game for these parasites.

On the decline

The twinkling lights of a modern city are an irresistible attraction to the eye of young and old alike. It is doubtful, however, whether any of the artificial illumination produced by man has the same aesthetic quality as that from a well-stocked colony of glowworms seen on a moonless night. It is not surprising that poets have made so much of this. Unfortunately, the chances of seeing it today, at least in Britain, are much smaller than in times past. Glowworms, useful and attractive insects, have died out from many areas where they were once common. The reasons for this are not easy to see, but it almost certainly springs from the pressure on land for housing, factories, intensive farming, combined with more efficient draining of the land. No doubt the use of insecticides is also partly to blame. What is quite certain is that it is not natural enemies that have brought about this fall in numbers, because toads and hedgehogs are all less numerous than they used to be.

Ironically, there may be another reason. Many insects are irresistibly attracted to artificial light, and in this the male glowworm is no exception, in spite of the fact that it has its own, highly individual 'bright light' to go to—that emitted by the female. Even the weak, flickering light of a candle-flame will attract a glowworm, as Gilbert White, father of field naturalists, records. In many areas, it seems, modern artificial lighting systems have become a serious threat to glowworm survival, in that the male glowworms are finding them far more alluring than the more modest glow produced by the females, which as a result may languish in vain and even die 'old maids'! Once attracted to the lights of large buildings the male insects may damage themselves in hitting or being burnt by them, and then fall to the ground stunned or dazzled, to be subsequently eaten by a variety of small animals; or the attraction may simply disrupt the delicate balance of nocturnal flight activity. Fortunately there are still many areas in England where such hazards are less pronounced, as is indicated by the fact that the greatest numbers of glowworms are found in areas which are comparatively less developed industrially.

phylum	**Arthropoda**
class	**Insecta**
order	**Coleoptera**
family	**Lampyridae**
genus & species	***Lampyris noctiluca***

Making the most of youth: doomed to starvation as an adult, a glowworm larva gorges itself on a tiny garden snail (12 × life size).

Gnu

Often known by their Afrikaans name, wildebeest, gnus are ugly cow-like antelopes, up to 4 ft at the shoulder, with short thick necks and large heads with a tuft of long hair on the muzzle, a throat fringe and a mane. The males weigh up to 460 lb, the females up to 360 lb. There are two species, the white-tailed gnu, or black wildebeest, and the brindled gnu, or blue wildebeest. The former, extinct

Following the young grass
The white-bearded race of the brindled gnu was studied in 1963 by Lee and Martha Talbot in West Masailand (centred on the Serengeti plains), where they counted 239 516 of them. The animals move about freely; in the wet season they are scattered over the plains, and in the dry season they move through the surrounding bush, along streams, seeking new grass produced by local showers. In the dry season the movements between these limited areas of new grass lead to massing, and huge numbers are to be seen in one place. It is not a true,

calves are well developed, and can follow their mothers within 4–5 minutes of birth. There is, however, a heavy loss through predation and through calves becoming separated from their mothers. Within a few weeks almost half the season's crop of calves are dead. When the surviving calves are 6–7 months old, a rinderpest epidemic further decimates them, and this lasts until 11–12 months after birth. This is known as 'yearling disease'. It arises at this time due to the loss of the initial colostral immunity, but does not bother adults. The colostral immunity is imparted by the

△ *Dawn patrol: Gnus trek in the cool of morning, seeking new grass before the intense midday heat forces them to rest in shade.*

in the wild but preserved on private land in South Africa, has a long-haired white tail and forward-curving horns. The latter, slightly larger, has an equally horselike black tail and laterally curved horns; instead of being blackish like the other, the brindled gnu is grey with brownish bands on neck, shoulders and the front part of each flank. The long tail is used to make fly-whisks, which are a symbol of rank in East and South Africa. The white-tailed gnu has always been restricted to South Africa. The brindled gnu occurs in both South and East Africa, and is still abundant.

regular migration, however, although the animals may move as much as 30 miles in a day. The gnu feed in the morning and evening, seeking shade in the heat of the day. They are sheep-like in that they tend to follow anything moving in a determined manner—other gnu, other animals, even Land Rovers. Several species of grass are eaten, but only the fresh young growth, when the sprouts are not more than 4 in. high. Where the grass is regularly burned, this helps the gnu.

Democratic love-making
The rut is in April and May. The peak of calving comes 9 months later, in January and February, when the plains are green. The

mother to the calf in the first flow of her milk. This milk is called the colostrum and contains proteins, which pass directly through the baby's stomach wall into the bloodstream. These proteins include some of the mother's antibodies, which temporarily protect the infant from disease. The severity of yearling disease depends on the density of population, but taking everything into account there is an average loss of 80% of the calves each year. The 20% left form 8% of the population. Since the numbers of gnu remain steady from year to year this means that 8% of adults are lost each year.

The calf stays with its mother until the next one is born, after which the cow prevents the elder calf from suckling. Bull

The wandering life

▽ *Panic on the plains: gathered to feed on the only available grass in the dry season, and suddenly frightened, a vast herd of gnus begins stampeding in a sea of bobbing tails.*
▽▽ *Peaceful co-existence: gnus and zebras bathe and drink together—when grazing gnus eat young grass, zebras eat old grass. Below right: Grassland nomads—searching over, a herd spreads across a plain to feed.*

A Root: Okapia

A Root: Okapia

The white-tailed gnu, with elegantly forward-curving horns, is extinct in the wild.

beest; since there are about 700 lions there the yearly kill per lion is about 16. In the Talbots' study, 91·1% of the predation was by lions, 3·3% by cheetah, 2·2% leopard, 2·2% hyaena, 1·1% wild dog. The toll due to hunting (poaching) and accidents is about twice as important as that due to predators other than the lion. Gnu do not defend themselves against lions, but against cheetahs and wild dogs they have been known to form a circle, like musk oxen.

Sharing out the food

The ecology of the hoofed animals on the Serengeti provides a striking lesson in natural land-use. The gnu feed only on young shoots, as we have seen. Zebra feed on the same grasses but at a later stage of growth. Topi feed on the same species but on old grass. Yet other species feed on different grasses growing in the same places. Thus the Serengeti can support a far greater quantity of wild hoofed animals than it could domestic cattle, and is potentially much more valuable as a source of protein.

The enormous wastage of calves in their first year gives great scope to natural selection and comes as a surprise to those accustomed to thinking of large hoofed animals as slow breeders and consequently slow in evolving. Several races of brindled gnu exist. This is because to support gnus a habitat must provide new grass all the year round. Such places are not common, so the gnus tend to be in areas isolated from each other. This gives rise to differences between the groups, just as animals on groups of islands develop into different species (see Darwin's finches p 616). On the Serengeti, they are second in abundance only to Thomson's gazelle, of which there are between 5 and 8 million there. And there are twice as many gnu as there are zebra. On plains, south of Nairobi, gnu were almost wiped out by hunting but they have recovered rapidly. There are now some 9 000 there.

class	**Mammalia**
order	**Artiodactyla**
family	**Bovidae**
genus & species	***Connochaetes gnou*** *white-tailed gnu* ***C. taurinus*** *brindled gnu*

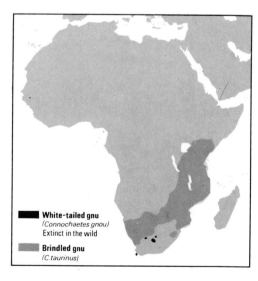

White-tailed gnu
(Connochaetes gnou)
Extinct in the wild

Brindled gnu
(C. taurinus)

yearlings now form separate herds, while the young cows remain in the cows' herd.

The rut takes place during the dry season. When the moving herds halt awhile where food is abundant, some of the males establish harems, which may contain as few as 2–3 females or as many as 150 females and young. Each male herds his harem tightly, running round and round it. Often as many as three bulls herd the same harem. They are not aggressive towards one another, and they have no hierarchy. A bull herding runs with a rocking gait, head held high. The females, the young and the non-active bulls keep the normal head-down position. The harem forms the centre of a territory established for the time being by one or several bulls. If a male approaches in rut position from the neighbouring herd, the bulls of the threatened herd go to meet him. The nearest one rushes forward, the rivals drop to their knees, butt and spar, get up, snort, look round, then retire or do it again. The breeding herds are stable for several days until the food is gone and the gnus must move on. Then the males retire to the margins of the migrating herd either singly or in small groups. Each time there is a pause in the mass movement, the males round up harems, and merge back into the mass when it begins to move again. Only a small proportion of bulls form harems each time, so different individuals are active at each stop. Non-active bulls can feed close to the breeding herds without being attacked. In fact, if they graze too close, they may be rounded up by other males like cows and calves! Some males establish a territory first, and then try to drive females into it. Some old males do not even migrate, but establish home ranges near water.

Gnus may live 20 years. Each year 83% of yearling cows breed; and 95% of the rest. At birth there are 170 males to 100 females; after a year the ratio is 117:100, and after 1½ the adult ratio of 108:100 is reached.

Lions most feared

Far and away the most important predator of the gnu is the lion. The 8% turnover of the population each year represents 18 000 animals, and these are almost entirely accounted for by lions. At least half of the lion's prey on the Serengeti consists of wilde-

Goats browsing in semi-desert. When presented with more lush conditions they will soon eat and spoil them until the land is like this.

Goat

Scientifically, it is not easy to sort sheep from goats. The distinguishing features are that the horns of sheep grow to the sides of the head, those of goats curve upwards and backwards and are worn by both sexes. Male goats have a strong smell and wear beards. In goats the forehead is convex, not concave as in sheep.

There are five species of wild goat, including the ibexes and the markhor. The wild goat Capra hircus from which the domesticated goat was derived, ranges from southeast Europe through Asia Minor to Persia and Pakistan. Domestication can be traced to 6—7 thousand years ago and it may have been earlier.

Goats are 4½ ft long in body and head, the tail is 6 in., they are 3 ft high at the shoulders and weigh up to 260 lb, the males being larger than the females. The horns of males are sweeping and scimitar shaped, up to

52 in. long, compressed sideways and ornamented along the inner front edge with large knobs. The horns of the females are shorter and more slender. The coat is typically reddish-brown in summer, greyish-brown in winter with black markings on the body and limbs.

Desert-making goats

Goats usually live in rugged, rocky or mountainous country, but sometimes on lowland plains. Where hunted they become extremely wary, and difficult to stalk, as their sure-footed skill as they progress from rock to rock is legendary. They generally move about in herds of 5—20, led by an old female. When living on mountains they may go up almost to the snow-line but in winter migrate down to lower levels, returning in spring to the fresh pastures. Goats do not sleep; they merely have periods of drowsiness.

Goats will eat straw, and have been seen to scratch their backs with straws held in the mouth. Like sheep, goats chew the cud,

but whereas sheep take mainly grass, goats browse chiefly on leaves and twigs as well. They will eat desert scrub and climb into trees to browse, and goats have been seen to jump onto the backs of donkeys to reach the lower boughs, and from there move to higher and higher boughs by jumps. They readily take bark, will eat paper and are notorious for eating linen cloth. In this they are helped by protistans living in the gut which pre-digest cellulose. Domestic goats will eat the foliage of yew, which may be fatal to horses and cattle, and suffer only a temporary diarrhoea. Released on oceanic islands, goats have reduced earthly paradises to barren soil with only low vegetation. In the Near and Middle East herds of goats have contributed to the formation of deserts.

Climbers from birth

A female goat over two years old is known as a nanny-goat, the male is a buck or billy-goat. Both are relatively recent names, the first having been used since 1788, the second since 1861. Mating is normally in autumn and the kids, born 147—180 days later, are able to run shortly after birth and soon

△ *A magnificent face in the crowd; even this buck with sweeping scimitar horns obeys the old nanny-goat who leads the herd.*

◁ *Adept climbers from birth—A goat has even been known to jump on a donkey's back to reach the boughs of an appetising tree.*

△▷ *Out on a limb; but the sure-footed agility displayed by these youngsters merely extends the area goats can devastate.*

▷ *Every kid needs its mum now and then, especially if he is the only one as a goat is likely to be.*

▽ *Domesticated 7 000 years ago, the goat has lived alongside man and provided him with milk and meat. But even a small herd left to run wild will multiply at an embarrassing rate and soon convert an island paradise into the barren hillside which is its natural habitat.*

become adept at climbing. There are one, sometimes two at a birth, exceptionally three or four. Sexual maturity is reached in about 12 months, when the male is known as a buckling, the female as a goatling. The life span is up to 18 years.

Indestructible spoilers

Goats have probably always been more useful for their milk than for their hair or flesh. Their flesh is somewhat rank and the hair short, but sometimes used for spinning, especially from longhaired breeds such as the Angora and the Kashmir. In the days of sail, ships took goats on board to provide fresh milk as well as meat. Ships' captains would put goats ashore on oceanic islands for the use of castaways, or to get rid of surplus. The marooned goats multiplied and, as on St Helena and other islands, denuded the flora. In 1773 Captain James Cook put goats ashore in New Zealand. These went wild and multiplied. Later goats were taken there for other purposes, to feed those building roads and railways, for use in miners' camps, and also to prevent introduced bramble, gorse and bracken running amok.

In fact, the goats barked trees, ate shrubs, brought many native plants to the verge of extinction and cleared the ground of mosses that not only held water but protected the topsoil from wind erosion. Their hoofs cut the turf so that it was washed away by rain, so adding to the erosion. The natural home of a goat is the barren hillside and wherever goats go they convert the landscape into their natural habitat.

The speed at which goats multiply is also an embarrassment. In 1698 an English ship put into the harbour of Bonavista. Two Negroes went aboard and offered the captain all the goats he cared to take away. There were only 12 people living on the island and not only were the goats eating everything but they were so tame nobody could go anywhere without a crowd of goats following.

Holinshed, in his *Chronicles of England*, 1577, wrote: 'Goats we have in plenty, and of sundry colours, in the west parts of England; especially in and towards Wales, and among the rocky hills, by whom the owners do reap no small advantage.' What the advantage was he did not say but it is believed that goats were deliberately allowed to go wild in these regions by the sheep farmers. In the Welsh mountains grass grows lush in inaccessible places. Sheep attracted up by the grass cannot get down and have to be retrieved. Wild goats, better climbers than the sheep, climb the high rocks and eat the grass (so removing temptation for the sheep) and have no difficulty in descending.

class	**Mammalia**
order	**Artiodactyla**
family	**Bovidae**
genus & species	*Capra hircus*

The humble goatfish, once worth its weight in silver at a Roman banquet, where it was brought alive to the table in a glass bowl.

Goatfish

The red mullet or surmullet is the member of the family Mullidae best known in Britain, but as most of the 42 species have been called goatfishes the name is used here. The true mullets belong to the family Mugilidae and are only distantly related. Goatfishes are long-bodied with two short dorsal fins, the one in front being spiny, the other soft. Their chief feature is a pair of long barbels under the chin, fancifully likened to a goat's beard. The barbels are flexible and can be swung forward or brought back to lie under the throat, where they are barely visible. The majority of goatfishes are under 10 in. long but a few species reach 2 ft.

Goatfishes live mainly in tropical waters but some are found in temperate seas. The red mullet is tropical and subtropical but ranges as far north as Norway. It is abundant in the Mediterranean. The spotted goatfish of the Bahamas and Atlantic seaboard of North America is mottled red. All goatfishes are red, orange or golden. The red mullet, for example, may be all red or it may be red on the back and sides with 3—5 longitudinal bright yellow stripes along the flanks. All goatfishes are noted for their rapid colour changes, not only while alive but also when dying.

Touch and taste in one

Typical goatfishes live inshore, in shallow waters and around coral reefs. Some are solitary, others live in shoals. They feed on worms, molluscs and crustaceans like shrimps. As they swim over the seabed they use their barbels as fingers, moving them actively to search the sand for food. As well as organs of touch the barbels are organs of taste, each bearing many taste-buds.

Spawning is in June and July, in the red mullet, and as in all goatfishes the eggs float at the surface. They are about $\frac{1}{80}$ in. diameter and hatch in 3—4 days. At first the baby fishes have a large yolk sac which projects well forward beyond the tip of the head.

Technicolor death

The colours of a goatfish, like those of the dolphin fish (p 652) are brightest at the moment of capture and fade when the fish is dead. In Roman times, when the red mullet was, as it is now, a valuable food-fish, it was brought alive to the banqueting table in a glass bowl. The guests were able to watch it swimming round and round and then enjoy the spectacular display of colour changes as it died. From tints of brightest scarlet the fish would flash to greenish red against streaks of ash-grey. Such was their popularity that red mullet were kept in special ponds and at least one wealthy Roman was reportedly more concerned with the welfare of his mullet than of his slaves. Each fish was worth its weight in silver, and was the equivalent of one slave in value.

Inevitably there arose a legend, but not about the colour. Michel de Montaigne, 16th-century French essayist, claimed that when the mullet was hooked a companion would swim across the line just above the hook, trying to cut it with the saw edge formed by the spiny dorsal fin.

class	**Osteichthyes**
order	**Perciformes**
family	**Mullidae**
genera & species	*Mullus surmuletus* red mullet *Parupeneus multifasciatus* common goatfish *Pseudupeneus maculatus* spotted goatfish, others

Fingers with taste buds: goatfish barbels.

John Tashjian at Steinhart Aquarium

Goat moth

The goat moth is so called on account of the strong and unpleasant smell of its larva, which burrows in the wood of trees. It is a large, stout insect with brown intricately mottled wings spanning 3 in. or more and is one of three British species belonging to the family Cossidae. These are regarded as primitive moths related to the family of small or minute moths called the Tortricidae. They are also called carpenter moths.

Don't take it home

The goat moth flies at night and is attracted to light. By day it sits on the trunks and branches of trees, where its colour and markings give it very effective camouflage. The larva burrows in the living wood, especially of willows and poplars. It is over 3 in. long when fully grown and stout in proportion, and its burrowing severely damages the timber of the tree in which it feeds. Affected trees exude a dark fluid from the openings of the burrows and this has a powerful smell, somewhat like that of a male goat. In spite of its unpleasant smell, other butterflies and moths are strongly attracted to the fluid, and an infested tree is worth keeping under observation by day and night.

The caterpillar is fully grown sometime in spring or summer, and often comes out of the tree in which it has lived and fed, to wander about seeking a place to pupate. This is the stage at which it is most often seen, the huge chestnut- and flesh-coloured larva being very conspicuous. If such a larva is taken home and put in a tin with some pieces of decayed wood it will spin a cocoon and pupate. It is useless to confine a goat moth larva in a wooden box as it will eat its way out in a very short time, and probably not all members of the household will be happy to encounter it in its subsequent wanderings.

The other two British moths of the family Cossidae are the leopard moth, whose larva also feeds in trees, and the reed leopard. The latter is rather rare, confined to fens and marshes, and its larva lives in the stems of reeds. The larva of the leopard moth lives in the trunks and branches of various trees, including fruit trees, where it may do some damage. It has been introduced into the United States, no doubt in timber imported from Europe, and is a considerable pest in trees in city parks. Both these moths are also found in Japan, and the reed leopard is found in China.

In the tropics and subtropics, especially those of Australia, some very large relatives of the goat moth are found. One *Xyleutes boisduvali* has a wing span of up to 10 in. and a body that has been described as resembling a small banana in shape and size.

Three-year larva

The eggs are laid on the bark of a tree and the larvae on hatching burrow under the bark and feed there for a year or so, eating their way into the solid wood as they grow larger. In the wild state they take up to three years to complete their growth.

Young goat moth larva. (6 × actual size)

Recipe for quick growth

The proboscis of the adult moth is vestigial and it must be supposed that the insect does not feed at all. Rather curiously, however, there are records of it visiting the bait of treacle painted on to tree trunks by moth collectors.

The larva eats wood throughout its long life and must consume great quantities of it. It is a matter of interest that if young goat moth larvae are fed on beetroot they complete their growth and come to full size in only a year.

Goat moths in history

The caterpillar of the goat moth has always attracted attention. In the 1750s a French entomologist, P Lyonnet, made a most detailed study of this larva and published a book about it. Among the facts he established were that, from the time of hatching from the egg to full growth, it increases its weight 72 000 times. Also in the course of dissecting it he discovered 4 061 muscles in its body. A second book, describing the pupa and the moth, was published after the author's death.

The Roman writer Pliny, who lived in the first century AD, wrote a monumental Natural History in 37 volumes, and one

Poplar riddled by grown larvae.

of the items he describes is a sort of large 'worm' that lived in the wood of oak trees and was highly esteemed as a luxury by gourmets of the time. The goat moth larva does sometimes live in oaks, and it has generally been assumed that this is what Pliny's edible wood-boring worms were, though there is no detailed description of them to serve as proof of this. If the ancient Romans did really eat these huge smelly caterpillars they must have had remarkably robust appetites.

phylum	**Arthropoda**
class	**Insecta**
order	**Lepidoptera**
family	**Cossidae**
genus & species	***Cossus cossus***

Adult goat moth. The larvae of this drab insect increase their weight 72 000 times to become fat and 3 in. long. Their voracious appetite damages poplars and willows, but their greed was repaid in kind many years ago; despite their goat-like smell, the Romans considered these repulsive larvae a delicacy, if the writer Pliny is to be believed.

Goby

Gobies are the Lilliputians of the fish world, most gobies being under 3 in. long and many not much more than 1 in. long. The giant goby **Gobius cobitis** *of the Mediterranean and western Europe does not exceed 9 in. and is usually 4 – 5 in. Most of them have little commercial value and so tend to be overlooked. Some of the largest among the nearly 500 species in the family are the mudskippers, which will be covered under that name. Other large gobies are the guavina* **Gobiomorus dormitor** *of Central America, 2 ft long, and the several species of* **Bunaka** *of the Indo-Australian region, of nearly the same size, which are valuable food-fishes. The smallest is the Luzon goby* **Pandaka pygmaea** *of the streams and lakes of the Philippines, barely ½ in. long, the smallest vertebrate.*

Mainly marine, but with many species entering brackish estuaries, gobies are colourful fishes with flattened heads, large eyes and short snouts. The eyes are high up on the head, often almost touching each other. There are two dorsal fins and the margins of the pelvic fins are joined to form a sucker.

Holing up for safety

As they are small it is natural that gobies should live in places where safe retreats are near at hand. Usually each fish has its own retreat from which it sallies forth to feed and to which it returns. The habitat is variable. Many gobies are bottom living, especially on rocky shores, some being left behind as the tide ebbs and sheltering under stones in rock pools. Others live in burrows in sand or mud, or shelter among branching corals. Some gobies have been elusive, regarded as rare for years, and then turning up unexpectedly in large numbers in a bay or a fiord. Since biologists began skin-diving, so-called rare species have been found to be common. The Catalina or blue-banded goby, for example, was first found in 1890. Few specimens were seen then or later until 1938 when an early skin-diving biologist found it was common, living in crevices in the rocks. New species have been discovered which could not have been otherwise brought to light because they live among rocky reefs, spending much of their time in crevices, where nets cannot reach them. A few gobies live among seaweeds in shallow inshore waters, and fewer still live in shoals in open water. Wherever they live their food is small invertebrates, especially the small crustaceans, and they also eat any small items of dead flesh that come to rest on the seabed.

Model fathers

By contrast with their retiring nature at other times the male gobies are aggressive towards each other during the breeding season. This is a matter of fighting over territories, in this case an area of rock, coral or other surface where the female will lay her eggs. After pairing, the male goby

Jane Burton: Photo Res

acts as guardian to the female while she is laying her eggs. Each egg is oval or pear-shaped, about $\frac{1}{16}$ in. long, and usually has a short stalk, the clump of eggs being fastened to a solid surface as they are laid. The 'nest' may be on rock or coral or in an empty shell. Having laid her clutch of about 100 eggs the female departs, leaving the male to guard it for anything up to a fortnight. He aerates the eggs by fanning them with his fins. The newly-hatched gobies are well developed and soon grow to look like their parents. Douglas Wilson has watched the sand goby *Pomatoschistus minutus* guarding eggs in an empty mollusc shell. If a shrimp or baby flatfish comes near he drives it off. When the shell with its eggs is removed for a few moments he swims back and forth over the spot in what seems a frenzied manner, and when the shell is put back he fusses over it like any conscientious mother to restore it to its original position, carrying tiny stones away with his mouth until the shell and the eggs are in order again.

Fried fish fry
Gobies are eaten by the usual predatory fishes, as well as diving seabirds such as divers, but little more is known of their enemies. Gobies are sometimes accidentally included in whitebait but apart from the few larger species taken for food in the Far East the only important fishery is in the northern Philippines. There a freshwater goby spawns in the sea and its $\frac{1}{2}$in. fry return in huge shoals to the mouths of the rivers. From September to March these are netted in the streams and rivers and sold under the name *ipon*, which is fried in oil or made into a paste called *bagoong*.

Unlikely partnerships
Gobies of the genus *Parioglossus* depart from the usual habit of keeping near their hiding places and 'hover' in mid-water in shoals of thousands. When disturbed they dive into the nearest coral heads. Related species of *Vireosa* do much the same except that they dive into the gaping shells of oysters and giant clams. Their entry alarms the molluscs which close their shells, so giving the gobies added security.

The habit of sheltering in cracks, crevices and burrows has led to several instances of commensalism (living together). The arrow goby *Clevelandia ios* of California shares

Leopard-spotted goby **Thorogobius ephippiatus** in its shelter (fan worm **Bispira volutacornis** in foreground).

DP Wilson

holes in mud-flats with a pea crab and a burrowing worm. The goby will carry large pieces of food, too big for it to swallow, for the crab to tear apart, then wait and pick up the crumbs. The blind goby *Typhlogobius californiensis*, also of California, lives in holes dug by the ghost shrimp. Should the shrimp die its goby companion is doomed unless it can find an unattached shrimp to live with. Several species of *Smilogobius* around the coasts of the Indo-Pacific region team up with snapping shrimps which dig and maintain the burrow, constantly shovelling away the loose sand, while the goby maintains a watch near its mouth. At the slightest alarm the goby dives into the burrow and the shrimp follows. The fish is the first to leave when things have settled down, and the shrimp then comes out to resume digging. It is a perfect partnership except that the goby is apt to feed on the shrimp's babies. A less damaging relationship is found between the neon goby *Elacatinus oceanops* and several species of larger fishes; it cleans parasites from them.

Looking before leaping
When dealing with genets (p 859) the suggestion was made that nocturnal animals carry in their memory a knowledge of their surroundings. Something of the same sort has been worked out for a goby *Bathygobius soporator*. This lives in pools when the tide is out and can find its way down the beach to the sea, if need be, by jumping from one pool to another. It is unable to see the next pool at the moment it takes off yet can leap with precision and not get stranded on dry land in between. This was carefully studied and the remarkable conclusion was reached that as the fish swims above the seabed at high tide it learns the topography of it so thoroughly that when the tide is out it knows the layout of the pools from high up the beach to the water's edge.

class	**Osteichthyes**
order	**Perciformes**
family	**Gobiidae**

◁ *Rock goby showing sucker of pelvic fins.*

▽ *Rock goby* **Gobius paganellus** *is a model father who cherishes the eggs until they hatch.*

Heather Angel

Godwit

Godwits are large waders related to snipe and sandpipers. Some are much rarer than formerly because of the destruction of their habitat. They have long legs and long, slender bills, straight in some species, slightly upturned in others. Of the two European species, the black-tailed godwit has a straight bill. It can be distinguished in flight by a broad white wing-bar and a white tail with a black band. The other European species, the bar-tailed godwit, has no wing bar and its tail is white with

The black-tailed godwit lives in Europe and Asia and migrates to Africa, south-east Asia and Australia. The bar-tailed godwit is a more northern species but migrates south in winter, occasionally reaching South Africa, Australia and New Zealand. Both these birds breed occasion-ally in Britain. The Hudsonian godwit lives in North America and migrates to South America, sometimes going as far south as the Falkland Islands. The marbled godwit is the most sedentary, breeding in North and Central America, but not migrating any farther south.

agriculture and building, so the numbers of black-tailed godwits have declined. In Britain their numbers fell drastically until the mid-19th century when they became extinct, but they now breed again in small numbers. In Central Europe there has also been a decrease but the bird has spread northwards to Finland in recent years and in the first half of this century its numbers increased in Holland, where it nested in the grass fields of reclaimed polders. The bar-tailed godwit is a coastal species, and in its isolated northern home it seems to be suffering less from man's activities.

Outside the breeding season godwits live in flocks, sometimes twittering to each other

G Rüppell

Arthur Christiansen

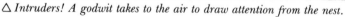

△ *Intruders! A godwit takes to the air to draw attention from the nest.*

△ *A pause for preening while fishing in the shallows.*

close black bars. Its bill is slightly upturned. On the ground, distinction is difficult. In summer both have chestnut plumage on head and breast, although the female bar-tailed godwit is much duller than the male. The winter plumage of both species is more like that of a curlew. In North America, the marbled godwit also has a curlew-like plumage and is the same size as a curlew. Its bill is slightly upturned. The Hudsonian godwit looks very dark from a distance. The under-parts are brown and the upperparts almost black.*

Reduced ranges

Godwits are becoming rare in many parts of their ranges. The marbled godwit has declined as its breeding haunts on the plains and prairies have been cultivated. In 1832, Audubon found flocks of many thousands in Florida, but AC Bent, writing in 1927, said that the species was then rare in Florida. The huge flocks migrating down from New England had been reduced to a few stragglers. The Hudsonian godwit is now very rare.

The black-tailed godwit nests in wetlands; bogs, moors and water meadows, or on dunes, and winters in marshes and estuaries. As wet country is progressively drained for

on the ground or calling in flight, but the winter flocks are not as noisy as the groups of godwits on the breeding grounds, where there is a babble of different calls. Flocks of bar-tailed godwits can often be seen gam-bolling in the air, especially at the end of the breeding season. Each bird dives and soars, twisting about, wheeling and turn-ing, in contrast with the neat, military manoeuvres usually executed by flocks of waders.

Chasing the waves

Inland, godwits feed on insects and their larvae and worms which they dig out of the soil with their bills or seek among vegetation or mud in shallow water. From water, small fish, tadpoles and water snails are taken, from land, grasshoppers and dragonflies. Along the shore, godwits search for food at the tideline. As a wave recedes, the flock rushes down the beach behind it, snapping up small crustaceans, marine worms and molluscs that have been exposed by the wave's action. Then, as the next wave rolls in, the flock retreats, opening their wings and sprinting pell-mell if the wave is too quick for them. If there is time they probe for lugworms buried deep in the sand, and sometimes they will bury head and neck as well as bill, in order to grapple them.

fly about calling and the male also displays on the ground, strutting around the female with tail spread. The black-tailed godwit, however, indulges in fewer aerobatics than the bar-tailed.

Godwits do not nest in colonies but their nests are usually grouped together. The nest is in a hollow made by pressing down grass and is liberally lined with dead grass and bents. Both parents incubate 5 bluish-grey eggs but the male appears to take the greatest share of incubation. The eggs hatch in 24 days and the chicks leave the nest shortly after their down has dried. They are cared for by both parents until they can fend for themselves.

and, at least formerly, they were present in large numbers for the taking. Shooting them was ludicrously easy because a flock will continually circle back over a fallen companion. Audubon found that the temptation to shoot more than were needed for specimens and food was often very great.

Occasionally a godwit is found to be as foolhardy as a dotterel (p 662). Bent once found a godwit's nest and decided to go back $\frac{1}{2}$ mile to collect his camera. (One did not carry the cumbersome cameras of 1906 around without good reason.) He got within 15 ft and set up the camera on its tripod and exposed a plate. Then he moved up to 10 ft and repeated the manoeuvre. Emboldened,

Pamela Harrison

△ *If one of the flock falls, the rest will circle overhead, presenting an irresistible target for hunters. No wonder it is becoming a rare bird.*

Aerobatic mating display

In the breeding season the male godwit performs a spectacular display flight. He flies up steeply on rapidly beating wings uttering a 3-syllable call. At a height of about 200 ft the wingbeats slow down and the call changes to the musical call that has led to the Dutch name of *grutto* for the godwit. During this phase of the display flight, the godwit rolls from side to side with his tail spread. He may continue like this for a mile before closing his wings and tail and nose-diving at speed. About 50 ft clear of the ground he spreads his wings and sideslips about, finally landing with wings held vertically. At other times male and female

Feigning injury

Like many seabirds, godwits fly out as an intruder approaches, circling and calling. It is then very difficult to find the eggs or young and the parents make it more difficult by feigning injury, luring a would-be predator away from the defenceless brood. The adults fall prey to hawks unless they can outmanoeuvre them and dive to cover or into the water.

Foolishly tame

Apart from their nesting grounds being destroyed, godwits have suffered from hunting. They are large enough to make a good meal

he crept up to 5 ft then to 3 ft, and, hardly daring to breathe and moving slowly, climbed under the cloth. In the end he decided to photograph the eggs and found that his caution had been wasted: he had to lift the godwit off its nest.

class	**Aves**
order	**Charadriiformes**
family	**Scolopacidae**
genus & species	***Limosa fedoa*** *marbled godwit*
	L. haemastica *Hudsonian godwit*
	L. lapponica *bar-tailed godwit*
	L. limosa *black-tailed godwit*

A potential stowaway; weighing in at ⅙ oz. the diminutive goldcrest has learnt to take advantage of its size. It has even been seen stealing a ride on the back of a migrating owl.

Goldcrest

*Once known as the gold-crested wren, this is the smallest British bird, but is not related to the wren, which is often thought to be the smallest native bird in Britain. The goldcrest, however, weighs only ⅙ oz, half the weight of a wren; by comparison, a house sparrow weighs 1 oz. Other names for the goldcrest are golden-crested regulus and golden-crowned kinglet. The name kinglet is applied to the other four members of the same genus, **Regulus**, all of which have brilliantly coloured patches on their heads. They belong to the warbler family. Of the two in the New World, the American golden-crowned kinglet probably belongs to the same species as the European goldcrest.*

The different names of the goldcrest refer to the bright golden-yellow patch, edged with black, in the centre of the crown. This can be seen only at close quarters, otherwise a goldcrest is a most inconspicuous bird, dull green with whitish underparts. In form it is much like a tit with a rounded body and short, pointed bill. The goldcrest breeds from the British Isles to Japan. It is found over most of Europe except the north of Scandinavia, most of Spain, Italy and southeastern Europe. In recent years the goldcrest has increased in many places because of the spread of conifer plantations.

Small birds similar to the goldcrest can be seen occasionally in the winter in Britain. These are firecrests that live in Europe, North Africa and many parts

of North America. They can be distinguished from goldcrests by black stripes on the head. Close inspection shows that the crown is more orange than that of the goldcrest.

Found in evergreens

Goldcrests are fairly tame and can be watched from close quarters flitting about rapidly from tree to tree. Outside the breeding season they live in small groups, sometimes mixing with tits and creepers. The first thing that attracts one's attention to them is their thin, shrill calls of 'zee-zee-zee', which are so high-pitched that they can only just be heard. Then they can be seen flying from trees or through foliage in a straight line with a titlike flight. They are usually found in evergreens, especially outside the breeding season. Goldcrests can be readily recognised by their habit of hovering hummingbird-like in front of foliage. They will hang steadily for 2–3 seconds while searching for food before moving on.

Some goldcrests migrate in the autumn. In the British Isles there is a general southerly movement and goldcrests of the continental race, slightly paler than British goldcrests, appear on the eastern coasts of Britain and spread inland. Before the next breeding season the movement is reversed.

Insect eaters

The continual flitting from tree to tree is in search of food. Goldcrests are insect-eaters and pick small insects, including beetles, aphids and flies, together with their eggs and larvae, from bark and foliage, often hovering, or hanging upside down like tits in the process. In the winter when insects are scarce, goldcrests will eat small seeds and buds.

Life on a swing

Breeding begins in April or May and two broods are raised by the end of the summer. The goldcrest's song is as thin and feeble as its call. This is characteristic of all kinglets except the ruby-crowned kinglet. Perhaps compensating for the weakness of the song, the males display their colourful crowns at rivals and prospective mates. The crown can be spread sideways and vibrated to make it conspicuous.

The nest is usually built in the foliage of an evergreen but has been found in ivy-covered trunks or, extremely rarely, in holes in trees. The usual nest is a cup of moss with a little grass, bound together by spiders' webs and lined with feathers. It is 3 in. across and 3 in. deep, and one can but admire the skill of the goldcrest, only 3½ in. long itself, that collects such a large amount of material and manages to form it into a nest that is slung like a hammock from the twigs and needles. It seems such a precarious position for a nest, as it is thrown to and fro by the slightest wind. The foliage, however, protects it, and squirrels are probably the only enemies that can climb out to it.

Goldcrests lay 7–10 eggs, sometimes as many as 13, each about ½ in. long—an awe-inspiring productivity. The eggs are incubated by the female alone, for about 16 days. Both parents feed the young, which fledge in about 3 weeks. Goldcrest populations are severely hit by hard winters, but with each pair producing a possible score or more offspring in one season, their numbers soon recover.

Hitch-hiker

Throughout Europe there are legends of the antagonism between the eagle and the wren, often about their vying to be king of the birds. The most familiar story is that of the competition to see which bird could fly highest. Surprisingly the diminutive wren won, but it was by means of a trick. It hid among the eagle's feathers and when the latter had flown as high as it could the wren emerged and flew a little bit higher, so becoming king of the birds. It has been suggested that the bird concerned was really the goldcrest, whose golden circle of feathers has led to its being given a name such as kinglet in several languages. In his book *The folklore of birds*, the Rev EA Armstrong dismisses this, pointing out that in many other languages the wren's name implies kingship, and that it would be surprising that the legend would have been transferred from one bird to another without any traces in the folklore of Europe. His view is that traditionally it is the Jenny wren that is the king of birds. But there is just one piece of evidence: a migrating short-eared owl was once found carrying a goldcrest on its back.

class	**Aves**		
order	**Passeriformes**		
family	**Muscicapidae**		
genus & species	***Regulus regulus*** goldcrest ***R. ignicapillus*** *firecrest* ***R. calendula*** *ruby-crowned kinglet* *others*		

Golden eagle

Often dubbed the 'King of Birds', only kings could use golden eagles for hawking in medieval Europe. Both flight and stance are majestic; golden eagles measure up to 36 in. long, females being larger than males. The plumage is dark, chocolate brown, tinged with yellow on the head. Young birds have white tails, with a broad, dark band across the base, and white on the undersides of the wings. In flight the wings appear broad with the primaries separated and curving upwards. From a distance, when size is difficult to judge, it is quite easy to confuse golden eagles and buzzards.

Golden eagles are found right across the northern hemisphere. In North America they range from Alaska to Mexico, mainly on the western side of the continent, but they range across Canada, between Hudson's Bay and the Great Lakes, to Nova Scotia. In the eastern hemisphere golden eagles range from northern Britain, Norway and Spain to Kamchatka and Japan. They are found over most of Asia north of the Himalayas, but in Europe they are found in Scandinavia, Scotland, northern Ireland and in parts of the south, including Spain, Greece and the Balkans, Italy and the central mountain ranges of Europe. In Africa they are confined to Tunisia, Algeria and Morocco.

Lord of vast territories

The home of the golden eagle is in open mountainous country, occasionally in forests or plains, but in these latter places it is usually replaced by the imperial eagle. In Scotland the golden eagle used to be found along the coast but it is now a Highland bird confined to inland mountain cliffs and crags overlooking deer forests or grouse moors. Each pair has a vast home range, up to 16 sq. miles, where they live all the year round. They do not necessarily hunt over all this range, and, in the Highlands at least, it appears that there is a surplus of food within the range of each pair. So the range size, and consequently the number of eagle pairs in an area is not determined by the food supply. In a 10-year study of some golden eagles in Scotland it was found that if the main source of food for a pair failed, as after myxomatosis, the eagles survived without difficulty.

The range is not defended so vigorously as is the territory of a garden songbird such as a robin or blackbird. Occasional squabbles break out but the limits of a range are usually demonstrated by a spectacular display flight following the usual hawk pattern. All through the year golden eagles can be seen, either singly or in pairs, flying upwards in a spiral then diving on half-closed wings, or flying up and down as if on a switchback. Other eagles especially juveniles are allowed into the home range and they may wander some distance. Golden eagles in Ireland have been found with the remains of the Scottish mountain hare by their eyries.

Carl Zwikl: Bavaria

△ *Talons and beak at the ready, the lord of the open mountain ranges prepares to pounce. This majestic bird is so confident of its power that it has been known to attack, and damage, an aeroplane.* ▽ *An outcrop on a craggy rock above vast hunting grounds is an appropriate setting for an eyrie.*

JH Sears

Arthur Brook

King of the crags

Majestic yet swift in flight, lord over vast territories, and faithful to his mate until death, the golden eagle is truly a monarch of the bird kingdom.

◁ *Power in action; the female, larger than the male, can have a wingspan of 8 ft. The nest of heather will be used by the couple year after year until one of them dies, when the survivor will search for a new mate.*

▽ *A watchful parent supervises the educational play of its offspring. The beak, strengthened by playing with twigs, will soon be tearing at carcases.*

Eric Hosking

Other places may be communal hunting grounds. The abundance of food within the range and the tolerance towards trespassers helps in winter when food may be abundant in one place but scarce elsewhere.

Sheep-slaughter myth

The food of golden eagles varies throughout its range. It consists mainly of small animals, predominantly mammals, together with birds, snakes, and rarely fish. A large amount of carrion is also eaten. In a survey made in the Highlands, mountain hares, rabbits, grouse and ptarmigan made up the bulk of the golden eagles' diet. They also ate foxes, stoats, pigeons, pipits, and voles

in small numbers. In America snakes and even tortoises are taken. On rare occasions lambs or deer calves were killed but these were usually eaten as carrion.

Golden eagles hunt by flying low over the ground or by perching on a favoured tree or rock, then swooping down at an incredible speed to seize their prey and kill it. They have been seen beating hares from cover and have been known to employ subtle stratagems. In the Hebrides a pair of golden eagles were seen to co-operate in capturing a lamb. One distracted the ewe's attention while the other approached to seize the lamb. They have also been seen trying to drive deer over cliffs.

Small well-tended family

In the breeding season the male and female indulge in the same display flights as are used for advertising their home range. The male also chases the female swooping or circling over her, while she may roll on to her back. They mate for life, but if one eagle is killed its mate finds a new partner at the next breeding season, and if both die the range does not stay vacant for long.

The same nest is used from year to year. In Scotland it is usually on a cliff edge, but may be on a tree or on the ground. In North America trees are used more often. The nest is built of sticks taken from trees, or in open country of sprigs of heather. Bracken and ferns are also used. Both birds bring material and pieces are added throughout the breeding season. Two eggs, white flecked with brown or grey, are laid and incubated by the female for about 40 days. The male only occasionally feeds his mate while she is incubating, but he brings most of the food needed by the chicks. At first the chicks, clad in down, are almost helpless and the parents have to feed them. Later they become stronger and crawl about the nest playing with sticks and learn to tear carcasses and feed themselves. They leave the nest after about 10 weeks and may not immediately fly but remain perched on a ledge waiting for their parents.

were found in mutton fat. Since then breeding success has returned almost to normal.

Dangerous to whom?

There are very few authentic cases of golden eagles attacking humans. Very rarely small children are attacked, but stories of children being found unhurt in eyries are all untrue because eagles habitually kill their prey before bearing it away. Golden eagles are tolerant of intruders at their nests, especially as compared with many much smaller birds such as drongos (p 670). In 1968, however, a helicopter flying over Uzbekistan was attacked by two golden eagles which dive-

bombed, then chased it. This is not an isolated instance. Once, golden eagles were controlled in Texas by shooting them from a plane. It was necessary to fly very close to the eagles. Sometimes the tables were turned and one eagle dived at a plane and flew right into it, tearing large holes in the aircraft.

class	**Aves**
order	**Falconiformes**
family	**Accipitridae**
genus & species	***Aquila chrysaetos***

A Himalayan golden eagle. This 20lb specimen was once used by Khirghity tribesmen to hunt wolves that threatened their flocks.

Keystone

Pesticides spell danger

Golden eagles are often killed because of the harm, real or imagined, that they do to livestock, but it is only in the last few years that they have really faced extinction. In the Scottish Highlands the percentage of pairs successfully rearing young fell from 72% up to 1960 to 29% in the next three years. This is an almost unbelievable drop and is almost certainly due to poisoning by DDT and the more toxic dieldrin. Most of this is from sheep carcasses, and is absorbed when the sheep are dipped to control insect pests. The poisons render the eagles infertile. In 1966, the use of dieldrin in sheep dips was banned because large amounts

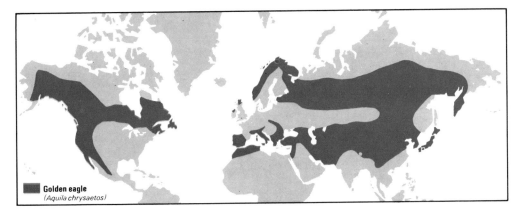

Golden eagle
(Aquila chrysaetos)

Nature's steam shovel with no reverse gears. The golden mole is prodigiously strong and can move a weight over a hundred times its own; but it cannot reverse against the set of its fur. It has to keep following its nose in the dark underground domains.

Golden mole

Golden moles look and behave like true moles but are more nearly related to shrews. It has even been suggested that they are not insectivores but should be placed in a separate order, an idea not favoured by most zoologists. The smallest is 3 in. long, the largest just over 9 in. They have the rounded, cylindrical body of a true mole, with very short legs and the claws on the front feet enlarged and used in digging. They are blind, the eyes being small and covered with hairy skin. The ears are small and hidden in the fur. The muzzle ends in a leathery pad and the nostrils are hidden under a fold of skin. The skin is tough and loose and the fur is thick with a dense, woolly underfur, and it has a metallic sheen which may be yellow, red, green, bronze or violet. There are 20 species of golden moles in Africa south of the Sahara, mainly in southern Africa.

Head used as a bulldozer

Golden moles are usually found where the soil is light and sandy, on plains or in forests, and they are especially common on cultivated ground. They burrow by thrusting their noses downwards into the soil and then bringing the head up. As the soil crumbles it is pushed backwards under the body with the short forelegs, which turn inwards, not outwards as in true moles. Each fore foot has four toes. One has a large curved claw, on the third of its four toes, and there is a slightly smaller one on the second toe. The remaining two are tiny and useless in digging. The hindfeet are used to push the soil farther back. The tunnels are usually just under the surface, the mole pushing its snout through the surface from time to time, wrinkling its snout as if sniffing, then submerging to continue its tunnelling. As a rule the tunnels are used only once. In very loose soil the roof caves in

behind the mole, leaving a furrow. Sometimes a golden mole will drive a shaft several feet down into the earth, possibly for making a nesting chamber.

Turns about by somersaulting

Unlike a true mole's fur, the golden mole's has a set. This means it cannot move against the lie of the fur so to turn around within its burrow a golden mole lowers its head slightly to one side, turns it, and with a quick flip brings the hind quarters over the head. It seems that golden moles are inconvenienced by dry soil in which they shake themselves vigorously. Their fur cannot be wetted and it is never groomed. If the fur gets muddy the mole merely continues burrowing until the mud is rubbed off. Generally, golden moles dig in a leisurely fashion compared with true moles and do not show the same restlessness.

We are told that some species are active by day and others active by night. This may mean that, as in the common European mole, the 24 hours are divided into 3-hourly or 4-hourly alternating periods of feeding and sleep. On the other hand, some may be nocturnal and some diurnal. Some species feed on insects, especially crickets, grasshoppers, locusts and cockroaches, earthworms and snails. Insects are crushed with a few snaps of the cheek teeth, then swallowed quickly. Snails are opened up with the incisors and crushed with the molars.

Earthworms are held in the forefeet and swallowed head-first in one continuous action, without being chewed. Certain legless lizards which burrow in the soil are also eaten.

Golden mole twins

Usually two young are born at a time in a grass-lined cavity in the ground. The Cape golden mole seems to breed in the rainy season, April to July, and the babies are suckled for two or three months, until they cut their first teeth, by which time they are almost mature. There is no information

about enemies, but it is known that one species, DeWinton's golden mole, shams dead when touched—after giving a sharp squeak.

Shivering while asleep

As long as it is awake a golden mole keeps on the move, and it is this exercise which keeps its body temperature normal. If it stays still too long, or if it is unwell, its temperature quickly falls. This suggests that waterlogged soil is probably a natural hazard. One golden mole that died in captivity was found to have contracted pneumonia through being kept in too damp soil. Clearly, sleep would be a hazard for a golden mole without some safeguard, so while it sleeps its muscles keep twitching, to supply at least some of the heat its body would generate when awake and moving about.

Strong-man mole

The South African zoologist, James A Bateman, who has studied golden moles, tells of their strength. A mole *Amblysomus hottentotus* was captured and placed in a glass bowl of the kind used for goldfish. It was filled with soil and over the top was placed a sheet of iron weighted down with a piece of railway metal. At one time the mole escaped by pushing this load of metal with its snout. The metal weighed 21 lb, the mole weighed 2 oz. This helps us to understand how a golden mole can almost literally bore its way through the earth with its nose.

class	**Mammalia**
order	**Insectivora**
family	**Chrysochloridae**
genera & species	***Amblysomus hottentotus*** *African golden mole* ***Cryptochloris wintoni*** *DeWinton's golden mole others.*

Goldfinch

The goldfinch is a very handsome bird, 5¼ in. long, named for the golden-yellow bar on each wing. Its back is a tawny brown, its underparts paler. The head is boldly marked with red, white and black. The wings are black with a gold bar and white tips to the flight feathers. The forked tail is black with white tips. The beak is short and conical: a seed-eater's beak.

*The young goldfinch lacks the red, white and black of the adult's head. Instead it has lines of spots or streaks on head, back and breast and, except for the golden bar on the wing, looks very like several other closely related finches. One of these is the siskin **Carduelis spinus**, which is about the same size and belongs to the same genus but has more yellow in its plumage. It spends the summer in pine-woods and the winter among the alders along the riverside. Another is the twite **Carduelis flavirostris**, a finch of Scandinavia and northern Britain. The serin **Serinus dermus** is very like the siskin in appearance and habits. It is a European bird that occasionally visits Britain, which also has the lines of dark streaks. In an evolutionary sense all three are less 'grown up' than the gold-finch and show their immaturity in the streaked plumage of the adult.*

The goldfinch ranges across Europe into western and southwestern Asia, also North Africa.

A charm of goldfinches

The goldfinch is a showy bird that appears to come from nowhere at certain seasons, especially late summer, when it feeds on the seed heads of herbaceous plants. Except in the breeding season, it goes about in small flocks and attracts attention by its musical twittering and its bold and conspicuous colours seen at close range. When not feeding it perches high up in trees, on the outer twigs, and seen then in silhouette so that its coloured head is obscured, it passes for any one of a half-a-dozen small finches. At night the flocks roost in trees and in winter use oak and beech, especially those in hedges, that are late in shedding their dead leaves. As with other small finches the flight is bounding or undulating.

A flock is usually spoken of as a charm of goldfinches. Originally this was spelled 'chirm', and meant a chorus of sounds and was applied to the chatter of any birds. In recent years it has become restricted to goldfinches. It was this musical twittering that made goldfinches, as well as the related linnets, popular as cage birds.

Diet of seeds

Goldfinches seldom feed on the ground although they may take insects, especially in summer. Their feeding is traditionally associated with the seeding thistle heads but they will visit the seeding heads of other

An agility at performing tricks with string made the goldfinch a popular cage bird in the past.

André Fatras

members of the daisy family Compositae. They also take seeds of pine and birch and may visit alders to feed from their catkins, in company with siskins, serins and red-polls. One goldfinch was seen to climb a dandelion stem until it bent over, then nip it, the stem folding at the weakened point. Then she held the top of the stem, as well as the part she was standing on, in her feet and ate the seeds. She did this repeatedly.

Away from the comparative safety of the nest, a young goldfinch faces the world.

F Blackburn: NHPA

Resourceful goldfinch hen

The breeding season begins early in May. The male flashes his golden wing bars at the female, as part of his courtship display, while swaying from side to side. The nest of interwoven roots, bents, wool, moss and lichens, lined with thistledown and wool, is built by the hen, usually well out on a branch but sometimes in a hedge. There have been a number of instances of goldfinches untying the strings of labels used on fruit bushes and weaving the strings into the nests. The 5–6 eggs are bluish white with red spots and streaks, each nearly ¾ in. by ½ in. The hen alone incubates for 12–13 days, fed by the cock, but both parents feed the chicks by regurgitation for another 12–13 days. There are sometimes 3 broods a year.

Hauling in the lines

The note included above under breeding behaviour, about goldfinches untying the strings of labels, may appear remarkable, but this is not beyond their known abilities. We are used to stories of tits pulling up strings of nuts to a perch in order to eat but for centuries, according to Dr WH Thorpe, the eminent authority on animal behaviour, goldfinches have been kept in special cages so people could watch what they do. In the 16th century the gold-finch was called the draw-water or its equivalent in several European languages. These captive goldfinches were in cages so designed that to survive they had to do precisely this. On one side was a little cart containing seed and this was held by a string. The goldfinch had to pull the string with its beak, hold the loop with one foot, then pull in another loop with the beak, hold that, and so on until it could take the seeds. Another string held a thimble of water. To drink, the bird had to draw this up in the same way.

Canaries and other captive birds have been seen to do similar things, and the performances are not confined to cage birds. In 1957, it was reported from Norway and Sweden that hooded crows were stealing fish and bait from fishermen's lines set through holes in the ice. A crow would take the line in its beak and walk backwards away from the hole. Then it would walk forward again, carefully treading on the line to stop it slipping back. It would repeat this until the fish or the bait was drawn to the edge of the ice, when it would seize it.

class	Aves
order	Passeriformes
family	Fringillidae
genus & species	*Carduelis carduelis*

A 'celestial' goldfish: his eyes are turned for ever towards the heavens.

▷ *An aquarium: a fish society in miniature.*

Goldfish

Goldfish are, in fact, a domesticated form of a wild carp native to China. The wild ancestral form is a very ordinary fish, sometimes used as food, green and brown in colour but occasionally throwing up red or red-gold individuals. These were collected and cultivated by the Chinese as far back as 960 AD and by the period 1173–1240 goldfish were being kept as pets in earthenware bowls and ornamental ponds. They were introduced into Japan in 1500 but reached Europe nearly two centuries later. There is reason to believe that the first reached England in 1692 on a ship that left Macao in 1691. From then on, goldfish reached France in 1750, the Netherlands in 1753 or 1754, Germany in 1780 and in Russia there were goldfish in bowls in Prince Potemkin's Winter Garden in 1791. Goldfish did not reach the United States apparently until 1859.

The relationships of the goldfish have been variously stated by experts. That its ancestor is the crucian carp which is also known as the Prussian carp when it is lean, is one variation. The opinion now seems to be that the goldfish **Carassius auratus** is Asiatic, and that the Prussian carp **C. auratus gibelio**, which is greyish-yellow to silver-grey, is a European subspecies. The crucian carp of Europe is a separate species **C. carassius**.

Usually regarded as a small fish, the goldfish can weigh up to 10 lb, although those bred as ornamentals are usually only a few inches long. There are two types of fancy goldfish, the scaled and the 'scaleless', the latter having scales that are transparent and hard to see. At first the scaled varieties are uncoloured, that is smoky or like tarnished silver, then black begins to show and later changes to red or white. The scaleless varieties do not have the metallic sheen of the others but show more delicate colours, such as lavender and blue. They are white at first, sprinkled with dark specks, and quickly gain their permanent colours. The shubunkin is a familiar example of the 'scaleless' type, blue tinged with red and mottled with yellow, red and dark brown, or in some combination of these colours.

Golden mudlarks

The life of the wild goldfish is no more eventful than that of the domesticated varieties. The natural food includes animal and plant, the first including water fleas, freshwater shrimps *Gammarus*, gnat larvae and worms (especially *Tubifex*). Among the water fleas are *Cyclops* and *Daphnia* (see p 611), the latter so familiarly known to aquarists as a food for aquarium fishes that the name is anglicized, usually to daphney. The plant food includes duckweed and, in the aquarium the small green algae that tend to coat the wall of the aquarium. This is augmented by mouthfuls of mud, the fish chewing this over by churning movements of the jaws. The inedible matter is spat out and the fragments of dead plant and animal matter swallowed. By what extraordinary means the two are sorted is not fully understood.

Pearly king

Male and female become recognizable at the breeding season because the female is then swollen with eggs while the male develops tubercles known as pearl organs on the gill covers and pectoral fins. These are difficult to see without viewing the fish from a certain angle. The female lays 500–1 000 eggs, each $\frac{1}{16}$ in. diameter, between May and August, which are fertilised after they have been laid, the male following the female around all the time she is spawning. The eggs stick to the water plants. They hatch in 8–9 days when the temperature is 16–18°C/60–65°F, in 5–7 days at 21–24°C/70–75°F. The larvae, $\frac{1}{5}$ in. long and tadpole-like in shape, hang on to the water plants for the next 48 hours, by which time the yolk sac is emptied, the fins have grown and the baby goldfish are able to feed on infusorians (microscopic protistans). When 18 days old they will be 1 in. long and will feed on water fleas, especially 'daphney'. In the aquarium they are usually given packaged foods, especially ants' 'eggs'.

Danger of infancy

Pet goldfish can be long-lived, up to 25 years having been recorded, but life for the wild form is more precarious. The enemies are predatory fishes, fish-eating birds such

A beautiful freak of nature bred by man, a veiltail would never survive outside the artificial world of the aquarium.

as herons and kingfishers, as well as aquatic mammals. The losses from these may represent perhaps 5 – 10% of the adult population. The real wastage takes place in the early stages of life, especially among the baby fishes, where the death-rate is 70 – 80% during the first 6 months to a year. The enemies then are many both for the wild stock and for goldfish in ornamental ponds.

Wherever in this encyclopedia the enemies of freshwater fishes are considered they must include much the same as those now to be listed for the baby goldfish. What follows here can, therefore, serve as a standard for the general run of freshwater fishes, with the advantage that those who keep goldfish in ornamental ponds can know who their enemies are. The freshwater hydra, leeches, pond skaters or water striders, water scorpions and water boatmen or backswimmers, as well as a variety of beetles are the main enemies, together with dragonfly larvae. On top of these there are bacterial and fungal diseases. The enemies that do the most damage are probably the various beetles, the whirligig, the great diving and the great silver beetles. The larvae and the adults of the first two attack

baby fishes, and so do the larvae of the third. The larva of the great diving beetle *Dytiscus* has been called the water tiger, the larva of the great silver beetle *Hydrophilus* is called the spearmouth by American aquarists. Both names are justified.

Beautiful freaks

The more fancy breeds of goldfish are freaks, no matter how attractive some of them may look. To recite their names is enough to make this point: veiltail, eggfish, telescope, calico, celestial, lionhead, tumbler, comet or meteor and pearl scale. There are also the water bubble eye, blue fish, brown fish, brocade, pompon and fantail and many others. Some breeds are monstrosities rather than freaks. The veiltail with long curtain-like tailfins, doubled in number, is a reasonable freak. The eggfish has a rounded body and has lost its dorsal fin. The telescope has large bulging eyes which may, rarely, be tubular. The lionhead has not only lost its dorsal fin and grown a rounded body but its swollen head is covered with rounded bumps and looks more like a raspberry.

Students of fishes have sometimes noted

that certain freaks arise more or less frequently in nature. Under domestication natural mutants or freaks, or monstrosities that appear are selected and bred to produce new strains. In goldfish the most frequent are the doubling of the tail fin or of the anal fin, the loss of the dorsal fin, and eyeballs that are outside the sockets. Where goldfish have gone wild, however, as they have in southern France, Portugal, Mauritius and the United States, the descendants of the more normal goldfish quickly revert to the wild form, in colour and in shape. Under these conditions the more freakish varieties are at a disadvantage and soon are eliminated – which is what happens to the freaks in any wild species.

class	**Osteichthyes**
order	**Cypriniformes**
family	**Cyprinidae**
genus & species	*Carassius auratus*

918

Hard going even for Good King Wenceslas; goral survive by digging for acorns, eating branches.

Male, with mate and family below.

All three are part of a Prague zoo study.

Goral

Like its relatives the serow, chamois and Rocky Mountain goat, the goral is a goat-antelope well adapted to a life on mountains. The male goral stands up to $2\frac{1}{2}$ ft at the shoulder – slightly larger than the female – and weighs 50 – 70 lb. The legs are long and stout, adapted for climbing and jumping, the coat usually long and shaggy with a short woolly undercoat and long coarse guard hairs, and the 6in. horns curve backwards. There are three species. The grey goral's coat is shaggy, grey to grey-brown, often grizzled with black, and there is a white throat patch. The brown goral has a short brown coat with white patches on throat and chest. The red goral has a long shaggy coat, bright fox-red with no throat or chest patches. It is smaller than the other two and has shorter ears. The grey goral ranges from northern Burma and Kashmir through the mountain systems of western and northern China to Korea and the Sikhote Alin region of eastern Siberia. The brown goral is known from a single specimen from the dry country of the upper Brahmaputra, in southeastern Tibet. The red goral lives in the mountains of northern Burma and Assam.

Inaccessible habitats

Goral occupy a variety of habitats in different parts of their range. In Szechwan the grey goral lives at altitudes of 5 000 – 8 500 ft in the steep, arid, often almost vertical gorges of the big rivers (Yangtse, Yalung, Mekong). The vegetation consists of short stubbly grass and thornbushes such as junipers, barberry and rose. Farther up, at 10 000 – 13 500 ft, it lives in the moist valleys of small mountain torrents, very craggy but still with thick vegetation, from thick bush to forest. In the northern part of its range, in the Sikhote Alin, it lives on the precipitous coastal cliffs, going down to sea level; the vegetation here consists of stunted oaks, stone-pines, and shrubby forms of maple and dwarf juniper, while at the top are oak forests. Inland in the same region the goral lives at altitudes of up to 3 500 ft on rubble-covered slopes interlaced with small wooded grasslands and deciduous forests.

Goral are found in small, isolated pockets, and it is difficult to see how inbreeding, with the deterioration that follows it, is avoided, since these animals do not move about much. The red goral is found at higher altitudes than the grey. It seldom comes much below 8 000 ft and ranges in summer above the tree-line, which is around 12 000 ft.

Eating whatever is to hand

In summer, goral live by grazing, but in autumn they go into more forested regions and eat mainly leaves, also acorns, which they dig out of the snow with their snouts. In February and March, when the snowfall is greatest, they eat mainly branches. In winter the animals are constantly up to their bellies in snow, and have to jump to move about. The ewes and juveniles live in groups of 2 – 12, but the adult males are solitary for most of the year. Goral are active mainly in the morning and evening. After the morning feed they go down into the valley to drink, then lie out in the sun on a ledge, motionless, with the feet tucked under and the head stretched out in front.

Philip Wayre: NHPA

Grey goral. These rare goat-antelope are being bred in a state wildlife park in the western Himalayas.

the high mountains nearby. In 1913 in the Mishmi Hills, just over the border in Assam, some of these red goral were shot. In March or April, 1922, HL Cooper was shooting in the Mishmi Hills and shot a takin at a salt lick. Grazing on a steep slope above the salt lick were some bright red goral, and the Mishmi tribesmen with him killed four or five of them for meat. In 1931, the Earl of Cranbrook shot a red goral in the Adung valley, on the extreme upper Irrawaddy in northern Burma, and presented it to the British Museum.

These facts did not come together to form a coherent picture until 1960, when Mr Cooper sent a rug from his home in Guernsey to the British Museum for identification. This was made from the skins of three of the animals shot in 1922. RW Hayman, at that time in the Mammal Section, recognised them as belonging to the same species as the Earl of Cranbrook's, and at once all the pieces of the jigsaw fell into place. Mr Hayman published a description of the species.

In a later paper, he described the skull of one of Mr Cooper's goral, sent over by the Bombay Natural History Society, and established that there were differences in the skulls too. At the same time, he re-examined the type specimen of the brown goral, described by Pocock as long ago as 1914 and named after Lt-Col Bailey, and was able to show that this, too, was a separate species and not just a race of the common species, as had been previously thought. Unfortunately, no second specimen of the brown goral is known. In January, 1964, a female red goral was captured near Lashio, in the northern Shan States of Burma, and sent to the Rangoon zoo where it still lives. It is a very agile animal; on one occasion it jumped the 6ft barrier of its enclosure from a standstill! It sleeps on the top of its hut, $5\frac{1}{2}$ ft above the ground.

class	**Mammalia**
order	**Artiodactyla**
family	**Bovidae**
genus	***Nemorhaedus baileyi*** brown goral
& species	***N. cranbrooki*** red goral
	N. goral grey goral

A mystery for zoologists: grey goral live in inaccessible places in isolated herds, yet there is no evidence of deterioration caused by inbreeding.

■ **Brown goral** *(Nemorhaedus goral baileyi)*
■ **Red goral** *(N.cranbrooki)*
▨ **Grey goral** *(N.goral)*

Dependent calves

The rams join the groups of ewes in the middle or end of September and go back to their solitary life after mating in the first half of November. The calves are born in early May in Szechwan, but not until June in the Sikhote Alin. They lie hidden among rocks while the ewes graze nearby. Usually there is only one at a birth; twins are rare, triplets rarer. They are suckled until late autumn, but stay with their mothers until the following spring. Goral may live as much as 15 years.

Enemies

In the really steep habitats, the only serious predators are eagles, which take the calves. In the higher, less steep country of the interior of Szechwan, leopards feed on them.

Goral offer poor trophies to the hunter but present a challenge to the sportsman because of the difficulties of their habitat. They are commonly hunted for sport, often with dogs, against which they defend themselves courageously with their horns. They make a hissing sound when frightened.

Species from a rug

Until 1961, only one species of goral was known, although evidence for the other two was already available. In 1863, Edward Blyth reported that the goral of Assam is 'bright rufous'. In 1912 Lt-Col FM Bailey saw people at Sanga Chu Dzong in SE Tibet wearing red fur coats. On being questioned they revealed that the fur came from a type of goral which was plentiful in

Gorilla

The gorilla is the largest of the man-like apes. The males average 5 ft 8 in. high and may exceed 6 ft, and the females are about a foot less. An adult male may weigh 400 – 450 lb but in a zoo he tends to get fat and may weigh 100 lb more. Unlike the chimpanzee whose skin normally turns black only at maturity, the gorilla's skin is jet black from a few days after birth. The hair is grey-black or brown-black in western gorillas, jet black in the eastern race. The adult male in both develops a silvery white back and this makes a strong contrast with the jet black of the eastern gorilla. He also has a large sagittal crest (a bony crest on the top of the skull) to which the jaw muscles packed with connective tissue are attached. This gives a helmet-like effect to the head. The nostrils are broad and the ear is small, in contrast with that of the closely related chimpanzee. The chest is broad and the neck short and muscular. The hands and feet are broad and strong, the great toe being less widely separated from the other toes than in the rest of the apes. A gorilla walks normally on all fours, with knuckles to the ground, in a semi-erect posture because the arms are longer than the legs. Adult gorillas seldom climb trees.

There are three very well-marked races. The western gorilla lives in lowland rain forest, from sea level to about 6 000 ft, in the Congo (Brazzaville), Gabon, Equatorial Guinea, Cameroun, extreme southwest of Central African Republic, and in the extreme southeast of Nigeria. The eastern lowland gorilla is found in a similar habitat in the eastern Congo (Kinshasa), ascending the mountains in the Central African Lakes region to about 8 000 ft. There are no gorillas in the vast lowland forest area between the ranges of these two races, and it is somewhat of a mystery why this should be. Finally, the mountain gorilla is found between 9 000 and 12 000 ft in the Virunga Volcánoes and Mt Kahuzi. All eastern gorillas are blacker than western, with larger jaws and bigger teeth; mountain gorillas are distinguished, in addition, by their comparatively short arms, long silky hair, and strikingly manlike feet.

Peaceful co-existence

Gorillas live in troops of a single adult male and several females with their young. Other males wander alone, sometimes travelling along with a troop for a while. There is thus a much tighter social organisation than with chimpanzees, with much smaller troops and only one adult male to each. The home ranges of the troops overlap extensively; there is no defended territory. A meeting between two troops may result in their mingling temporarily, or the two more or less ignoring one another. No fighting has

Popperfoto

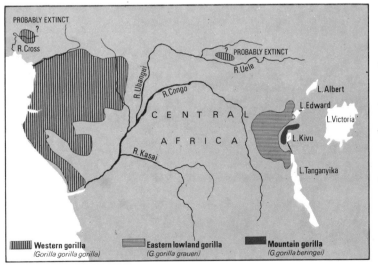

△ A relaxed snack: having torn away the tough outer covering of a plant stem, a young gorilla tucks into the juicy centre. Gorillas eat only plants, taking most of their water as well as food from them.
◁ The three gorilla races come from three distinct areas in Central Africa. Mountain gorillas have shorter arms, longer hair, and almost human feet. Eastern races are darker than western, with big jaws and teeth.

been recorded, although some gorillas have been seen with wounds, especially bruises and cuts about the eyes, which suggest they do occasionally come to blows. A troop tends not to wander over more than 10—15 sq miles. Their wandering is irregular.

Aversion to water

In the lowlands, gorillas feed on fruit and leaves, and raid banana plantations. They strip the stem from the banana tree and eat the marrow. In the mountains they eat much more tough, fibrous vegetation, such as bark, stems and roots. They get their moisture from their food, rarely drinking in the wild. When they do they soak the fur on the back of the hand and suck the water from it. They are afraid to cross even small streams, which limits their wanderings and makes it possible for them to be kept in by moats in zoos. They have not been known to eat eggs, insects or other animal protein. In lowland forests the density of gorillas is about 1 per sq mile; but in the open *Hagenia* forests at high altitudes in the Virunga Volcanoes, with dense ground cover and abundant fodder, the density of gorilla populations reaches 6 per sq mile.

Precocious babies

There is no special birth season and it is not necessarily the troop male who mates with the females in the troop. Often a wandering male who has joined the troop for a while mates with a female in it. Gestation is about 255 days—a little shorter than in the human. The young weigh about 4—5 lb at birth, which is less than a human baby, but the baby gorillas develop twice as fast: their eyes focus in the first or second

week, they crawl in 9 weeks, and can walk a few steps bipedally at 35—40 weeks. The infants play among themselves and with the adult male of the troop, who tolerates a great deal of nonsense from them. As they mature they become less playful. Females stay in the troop but the males leave it before they have developed the silver back of full maturity, to become wanderers. It is not known how a male becomes troop leader. The female is sexually mature at 6 or 7 years, the male a year or two later, but he does not reach full size until he is 12 or 14. Gorillas have been known to live 37 years.

No enemies but man

Leopards may take young gorillas and have even been known to kill adults, but this must be uncommon since gorillas show no particular uneasiness when leopards are around. There seem to be no other enemies except man, who kills them when they raid plantations and some tribes eat gorilla meat.

The gentle giant

The gorilla is not the savage, untameable ogre of popular imagination. He is normally a gentle peaceful creature. When disturbed gorillas of both sexes and all ages after about a year, beat their chests. This is a kind of tension-releaser, but in the male it is part of a full display of roaring, rising on hindlegs, beating the chest, a quick sideways run and, finally, tossing vegetation into the air. This is all very terrifying to a human being, and may precede a bluff charge, but an actual attack is rare. The male may, however, give chase if the in-

truder runs away, biting and scratching. Among gorilla-hunting tribes it is considered a disgrace to be wounded by a gorilla, for the man must have been running away! Unprovoked attacks are not known to have occurred.

Young gorillas have been kept as pets, but they are difficult to keep as they are subject to the same tantrums and fits of exhilaration as human children, and being much stronger they are more destructive. Moreover, they need constant companionship and affection and if the favourite person is not at hand the young gorilla will sulk, refuse food, become ill, even die. In zoos, keepers go in and play with young gorillas and every effort is made to obtain a companion to avoid the misery of loneliness and to prevent the animal becoming 'humanised'.

Gorillas are at least as intelligent as chimpanzees, less volatile in temperament and more patient and methodical. This stands them in good stead in the performance of intelligence tests, but they tend not to do well in tests involving manipulation. This makes sense, as they do not make use of natural objects as 'tools' in the wild as chimpanzees do.

class	**Mammalia**
order	**Primates**
family	**Pongidae**
genus & species	***Gorilla gorilla gorilla*** *western gorilla* **G. gorilla graueri** *eastern lowland gorilla* **G. gorilla beringei** *mountain gorilla*

◁◁ *Guy, a gorilla from the Cameroons, has been a star attraction at London Zoo since 1947.*
◁ *Tranquillisers ape-style; a disturbed gorilla beats his chest to relieve tension.*
△ *The Great Dictator; a troop of gorillas consists of several females and young dominated by an adult male.*
▽ *Normally afraid of the water, this lowland gorilla keeps cool at the Chester zoo.*
▷ *Freak of nature: a baby albino gorilla, Snowflake, survives at the zoo in Barcelona.*

Goshawk

A magnificent supremely manoeuvrable bird of prey, the goshawk is closely related to the sparrow-hawk. It has the same outline of long tail and rounded wings when seen in silhouette. When the bird is soaring, the primaries are splayed like fingers and the tail is fanned. The head and body length is nearly 2 ft, more than a sparrow-hawk and not much less than a golden eagle. The female is the larger, but otherwise the sexes are identical. The plumage resembles that of a female sparrow-hawk. The back is dark brown and the underparts white with close dark bars. Juveniles are light brown underneath with dark streaks rather than bars.

Goshawks are found on both sides of the Atlantic Ocean. In North America they range from Alaska to Newfoundland and extend into the northwest USA. They are found over most of Europe except the British Isles and across Asia to Japan and Kamchatka, south to a line running roughly along the latitude of the English Channel. There is an isolated population in the mountains of eastern Tibet, probably the relic of a population that lived in those latitudes when northern Asia was covered by glaciers in the Ice Age.

Related hawks in other parts of the world, also known as goshawks, include the black goshawk of Africa, the crested goshawk of southeast Asia and the white goshawk of Australia. The chanting goshawks of Africa feed mainly on lizards and insects which they chase on the ground.

Split-second manoeuvring

Like sparrow-hawks, goshawks are woodland birds preferring the edges of woods and forests with clearings. Their broad wings and long tails which can be spread to present a large area to the airstream are extremely well suited for split-second manoeuvres as they flit between the trees and pounce on their unsuspecting prey. Sometimes, when they are not too much persecuted, they extend to cultivated country near human habitations where there are only small coppices and groups of trees. Because they usually live in woodland and are very shy, retreating to cover as soon as they are disturbed, goshawks are rarely seen. Nevertheless, their numbers have been very much reduced through hunting, because their feeding habits have clashed with the interests of hunters. Over many parts of their original range goshawks are rare or extinct. They probably bred regularly in Britain at one time but by the 19th century breeding pairs were very scattered and eventually died out. Between 1938 and 1951 a few pairs bred in Sussex but they were persecuted by gamekeepers.

Pouncing on its prey

Goshawks take a wide variety of prey. Gamekeepers hate them because they kill pheasants, grouse and other gamebirds, domestic poultry and waterfowl. On the other hand they catch many animals that are the gamekeeper's foes, such as jays, magpies, squirrels, foxes and wildcats. Rabbits, pigeons, mice, thrushes, finches, lizards and snails, even sparrow-hawks and buzzards have been included in the goshawk's diet. Closer studies have revealed, however, that individual goshawks are not so liberal in their diet as this impressive list would suggest. One pair studied in Denmark for 2 years fed almost exclusively on black-headed gulls. Other goshawks nearby hunted crows and ignored the gulls. It is not uncommon for a predator to exploit to the full a readily available source of food; this is often done almost to the exclusion of all other prey once the predator has learned to take advantage of the particular food supply. Poultry-taking, too, appears to be a habit formed by certain

A killer among killers: the golden glare of the goshawk, agile assassin of the air.

individuals, but unfortunately the wrath of the poultry owner is turned against all goshawks.

In a study in Minnesota goshawks were found to account for 30% of all the losses in a population of grouse, while in spring, when the cover was thin, they were responsible for 50% of the losses. Each pair of goshawks was operating in a range of 5 miles radius from their nest.

Goshawks hunt by waiting on a perch for suitable prey to come past, or actively seek it out, flying rapidly through the treetops or along the edges of woods, pouncing suddenly and despatching their prey by gripping with their talons. It is then taken to a perch or patch of open ground and dismembered.

Father does the shopping

Normally silent, goshawks can be heard calling near the nest in the breeding season. They display high above the nest, flying about on slow wingbeats, soaring and diving like other hawks.

The nest is usually in a tree, but goshawks have been known to nest on the ground. Sometimes the same nest is used in consecutive years and occasionally the abandoned nest of a buzzard or other bird is taken over and improved by the addition of extra twigs and boughs.

The female incubates 3 or 4 bluish or white eggs. The male brings all her food, usually leaving it on a nearby perch for her to collect, or calling to her so she comes out to meet him, when he will toss the prey to her. The eggs hatch after 36—38 days. The young goshawks are covered in white down, and the covering of feathers appears at 3 weeks. The male continues to supply his family, the female very rarely bringing any food to the nest. Instead she takes the prey from the male, tearing strips off it and offering them to her chicks. Later, when the chicks are nearly full grown and more active, both parents bring food, and each item of prey is handed to one chick to deal with by itself. When 6 weeks old they leave the nest for nearby branches, and fly soon afterwards.

Warrior hawk

The goshawk has a long history. It was sacred to Apollo, and Attila, the King of the Huns, who was known as the Scourge of God, had a crowned goshawk as his personal emblem which he bore on his shield and helmet. A warrior like Attila was no doubt impressed by the fierce eye and long, sickle-like claws of the goshawk as well as by its swift, death-dealing swoops. When used in hawking, goshawks will take up to a score of rabbits in one day, whereas a peregrine can be flown only twice or three times a day at the most before becoming sated. In mediaeval Japan goshawks were flown at Manchurian cranes or Tanchõs (see p 562) which are several times their size. Any goshawk that caught a crane was entitled to wear purple jesses, the thongs attached to the legs of birds used in falconry. In mediaeval Europe, however, the goshawk was not held in such esteem. There was a rigid hierarchy in the use of hawks. Gyrfalcons and peregrines were the prerogative of royalty and nobility, sparrow-hawks and goshawks were used by yeomen and priests and kestrels, at the bottom of the scale, were used by servants and for instructing children.

class	**Aves**
order	**Falconiformes**
family	**Accipitridae**
genera & species	***Accipiter gentilis*** *northern goshawk* ***A. melanoleucas*** *black goshawk* ***A. novaehollandiae*** *white goshawk* ***A. trivirgatus*** *crested goshawk* ***Melierax musicus*** *chanting goshawk* *others*

G Ronald Austing

△ *Soaring, with fanned primaries and tail. The goshawk is a master of the ambush, killing its prey with deadly, sudden-clutching talons.*

▽ *Pirate and booty: a goshawk, its youth proclaimed by its streaky underplumage, straddles over the lure which has caught its fancy.*

Georg Nystrand

Gouldian finch

The Gouldian finch's gorgeous plumage makes it popular with bird fanciers and gives it the alternative names of rainbow finch or painted finch. It is one of the grassfinches, which are not true finches but weaver-finches related to the avadavat.

Gouldian finches are 5 — 5½ in. long, have a stout, typically finch-like bill and two long central tail feathers that taper to a point. The plumage of the adult male cannot be done justice in a verbal description. The colours appear to be hand-painted as the borders between them are so clear. The back and wings are grass-green, the rump sky blue and the tail black. The head and cheeks are dull scarlet with a black patch on the throat continuing as a ring around the scarlet of the head. The black ring is finely bordered with light blue. The breast is lilac and the belly orange, grading into a rich yellow. Females have rather duller colours which are not so clearly defined. Young birds are wholly green.

As if not satisfied with plumage that would put Joseph's coat to shame, the Gouldian finches have four or more colour phases. The commonest is the black-masked variety in which the scarlet on the head is replaced by black. Rarer varieties are the yellow-masked and the white-breasted Gouldian finches.

Australian nomad

Gouldian finches live in northern Australia, from Derby on the northwest coast to the eastern coast of Queensland. Outside the breeding season they live in flocks, moving southwards in the wet season and returning to the wetter coastlands as the interior dries up, for they are never found far from water. They prefer open plains with scattered groups of tall trees or the edges of thickets and mangrove swamps. Gouldian finches are shy and avoid human settlements.

Feeding above ground

Unlike many other grassfinches the Gouldian finches rarely feed on the ground but climb agilely among vertical grasses eating seeds. During the wet season they eat a large number of insects and at the beginning of the breeding season may be almost entirely insect-eating. They pursue flying insects such as termites, ants and flies and raid webs for both the spiders and their insect prey.

Nests in holes

The song of the Gouldian finch is a very high-pitched hissing and clicking, difficult to hear over a distance of more than a few yards. Courtship takes place high in the trees, where the male displays on a branch, showing off his brilliant colours. He fluffs the feathers of his head and raises his tail to show off the blue rump. At the same time he 'bows' with his body horizontal and waves his bill from side to side as if wiping it against the branch.

The nest is built in a hollow in a tree or termites' nest, sometimes several pairs sharing the same entrance. It is a poor affair made of grass and sometimes the 4 — 8 eggs are merely laid on the floor of the hollow. Both sexes incubate the eggs but the female alone broods them at night. Each year 2 or 3 broods are raised. The chicks have conspicuous markings in the throat together with luminous swellings that shine in the dim light of the nest and enable the parents to put food into the right place.

Inherited colours

The colour varieties of Gouldian finches are not geographical races found in different parts of the species' range. They are simple variations caused by genetic variations, or mutations, and birds of different colours interbreed as readily as humans with different coloured hair. The inheritance of the colours is much simpler than that of human hair colour. It is difficult to predict a baby's hair colour from knowing that of its parents. In Gouldian finches the black-masked variety is dominant, so two black-masked parents produce mainly black-masked offspring. Black-masked Gouldian finches are three times as common in nature as the red variety. Bird fanciers have tried breeding pure strains of the red-masked variety, but linked with the inheritance of the red head is a tendency to throw fits, making it very difficult to build up a breeding stock.

The yellow-masked bird, a variation of the red, is much rarer, occurring only once in every thousand or so birds. Recently, another variety has been bred with dazzling white instead of lilac breasts.

class	**Aves**
order	**Passeriformes**
family	**Estrildidae**
genus & species	***Poephila gouldiae***

Painter's palette plumage: the Gouldian finch is a miniature riot of colour.

Okapia

Grackle

Highly adaptable pests of farmland and suburbs, grackles belong to the family of American orioles that includes the cowbirds (p 542) as well as such diverse birds as the American blackbird, the meadowlarks, oropendolas and caciques. They are songbirds, although their songs are not always very musical, and they have long pointed bills like marlinspikes merging into a flattened forehead. Plumage is dark brown or black with iridescent blue or green on the head and neck, and in a bright light grackles are extremely handsome. The boat-tailed and great-tailed grackles are 17 in. long, with fan-shaped tails.

Grackles range from Canada to Venezuela and Peru. The bronzed grackle can be found in southern and western Canada and the great-tailed grackle is found from Venezuela north to Texas. In recent years it has spread slowly northwards into southern Texas and Louisiana. Other grackles live in the southern USA and central America.

The slender-billed grackle is confined to marshes near Mexico City and may now be extinct, and the Nicaraguan grackle lives only on the shores of two lakes in Nicaragua.

Flocks of thousands

Grackles are attracted to urban areas where they are as much of a nuisance as starlings because they live in large flocks, often numbering many thousands. Like starlings, with which they sometimes associate, they fly into their roosts in trees just before nightfall. They whistle and chatter for a couple of hours before going to sleep, and again in the early morning, making sleep for their human neighbours almost impossible.

The great-tailed grackle is very much a bird of coasts and swamps, rarely being found more than 50 miles inland, when it may be seen near the banks of large rivers. Other species live farther inland, but even the great-tailed grackle is very much terrestrial in habits, stalking about the ground on its long legs. In a heavy wind the tail seems to be a disadvantage and a boat-tailed grackle is hard put to keep on its feet. In flight the grackle is rather like a magpie: it appears to fly laboriously with its long heavy tail dragging it down.

Diving for fish

Grackles are versatile feeders; they eat many kinds of food, taking it in a variety of ways. They are often pests of agriculture where the flocks descend on rice, maize or grain crops to strip the ripening grains or to tear up sprouting seedlings. To offset this damage, however, they take large numbers of noctuid moth caterpillars, known as

A water foray: three common grackles dip at the surface while a fourth shoots up in a startled, Nijinsky-style leap, claws still dripping.

cutworms, Japanese beetles, corn borers and other insect pests. They regularly search for insects, such as beetles and their larvae, among the roots of grasses and capture small lizards, frogs and mice. They will also follow cattle for the insects they disturb, or, by contrast, eat bananas and acorns. The bronzed grackle opens acorns and nuts with the aid of a horny keel on the upper part of the bill which, moved by a special muscle, exerts a great pressure on the shells until they break open.

Grackles have a bad reputation among the general public for killing other birds. They take eggs and nestlings and kill the adults by pecking or crushing their skulls in the bill. Sometimes they seem to destroy nests or kill birds out of sheer devilment, leaving the corpses uneaten.

Grackles also take food from the water. They search in the shallows for tadpoles and newts and can be seen turning over stones to catch fish, scooping them up without getting their plumage wet or plunging in headfirst like terns.

Some grackles take to thieving. They have been seen following ibises as they probe in shallow water for crayfishes. When an ibis catches a crayfish it flies up with it, and is immediately set upon by the grackles who either snatch the crayfish from the ibis's beak or force the ibis to drop it.

Communal nesting

In February and March the great flocks of grackles break up and the males establish small territories where the females will later build their nests. Nesting is colonial, and up to 100 nests may be found in one large tree. The females are attracted to the colonies by the displays and ear-piercing calls of the males. No permanent bond is formed, the females accepting one of the displaying males, mating with him, then building the nest and raising the young by herself. The nest is built of rushes, grasses, and mud, in trees, bushes or rushes and sometimes in holes in trunks or in niches in buildings, the female having to guard continuously against her neighbours stealing nest material.

Incubation of the 3—5 eggs lasts for a fortnight. The young take to the air after 3 weeks, having left the nest a few days previously to climb around the branches. When able, they follow their mother on foraging expeditions and may continue to solicit food from her even when they can feed themselves. There are usually two broods a year.

Keeping apart

For a long time the great-tailed grackle was included in the same species as the boat-tailed grackle, because the two could not be distinguished by plumage. The great-tailed grackle has now spread northwards and overlaps the range of the boat-tailed grackle in a 100-mile wide strip between Houston, Texas and Lake Charles, Louisiana. The boat-tailed grackle tends to breed on farmland and the great-tailed on coastal marshland, yet they sometimes breed in mixed colonies. Interbreeding does not take place, proving that they are separate species.

When two species breed in the same place some mechanism generally prevents interbreeding. In fruit flies, for instance (p 830), the males have a courtship dance that enables the females to tell their own species. Grackles have the same mechanism. A male grackle courts any female but she will accept only a male of her own species, rejecting ones whose song and displays are incorrect.

△ *Boat-tailed grackle at an artificial nestbox. Many grackles are invading towns in the USA.*

▽ *Two's company: a displaying couple of common grackles, with a dour third-party spectator.*

class	**Aves**
order	**Passeriformes**
family	**Icteridae**
genera & species	***Quiscalus quiscula*** *common or bronzed grackle*
	Q. major *boat-tailed grackle*
	Q. mexicanus *great-tailed grackle*
	Q. nicaraguensis *Nicaraguan grackle*
	Q. palustris *slender-billed grackle*

Grasshopper

As their name suggests, most grasshoppers live among grass and herbage on the ground. They are variously coloured—mostly green and brown—and are protected as long as they keep still by blending with their surroundings. Grasshoppers are active by day and if disturbed jump suddenly and powerfully, using their greatly-enlarged hindlegs. They can also crawl slowly by means of the other two pairs of legs.

Nowadays the term 'grasshopper' is applied to the short-horned Acrididae, while the long-horned Tettigoniidae are called 'bush-crickets' because they are more closely allied to the other main family of the order Orthoptera (the Gryllidae or true crickets) than to the Acrididae. In all Orthoptera the forewings are leathery and serve as coverings for the folded, membranous hindwings which, in the flying species, are the sole organs of flight.

Grasshoppers are mainly ground-living insects, while most bush-crickets live in the foliage of trees and bushes. There are 14 known species of grasshoppers in Britain and 10 of bush-crickets. True crickets have been dealt with (p 570) while locusts, which are in fact swarming grasshoppers, will be dealt with under a separate heading.

Fiddlers in the grass

The familiar chirping chorus in the fields and hedgerows of the countryside is the result of grasshopper's stridulation. A row of evenly spaced, minute pegs on the largest joint of the hindlegs is rubbed over the more prominent veins or ribs of the forewings. Usually, but not always, only males can sing. Each species has its own song, and these may be learned, like the songs of birds, and used in identifying the species. The colours of species of grasshoppers vary so much that their song is a better means of recognizing them than their appearance.

Apart from stridulation, both pairs of wings serve their usual function. In all but one of the British species the hindwings are fully developed in both sexes and the insects can fly. The exception is the meadow grasshopper *Chorthippus parallelus* in which the hindwings are vestigial; even in this species there are occasional individuals in which the wings are fully developed and functional. Among Orthoptera it is not uncommon for species to occur in two forms, winged (macropterous) or wings much reduced (brachypterous). The most usual cases are like the one described, in which occasional winged individuals occur in a normally brachypterous population.

The largest British species is the rather uncommon large marsh grasshopper *Stethophyma grossum*. The three commonest are the meadow, common field and common green grasshoppers *Chorthippus parallelus, C. brunneus* and *Omocestus viridulus*. The common groundhopper *Tetrix undulata* is common on moors and in open woodland.

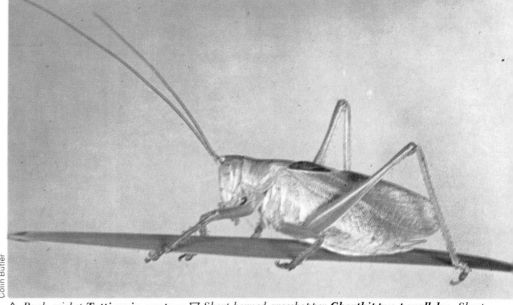

Colin Butler

△ Bush-cricket **Tettigonia cantans**. ▽ Short-horned grasshopper **Chorthippus parallelus**. Short-horned grasshoppers have 3 joints in the end part of the legs, short antennae and egg-laying organ, sing by rubbing hindleg against forewing, and have 'ears' at the abdomen base. Bush-crickets have 4 joints in the end part of the legs, long antennae and egg-laying organ, sing by rubbing forewing against forewing, and have 'ears' on the knees of the forelegs.

Colin Butler

Bush-crickets mating. Male (right) is placing the spermatophore—a package of sperm—at the base of the female's ovipositor. The blade-like structure of this organ is typical of bush-crickets.

Friedel Schox

Rhapsody in purple: an inch-long South African grasshopper of the family Eumastacidae.

Openings to the hearing organs on the foreleg of a bush-cricket—sensitive enough to pick out the calls of different species.

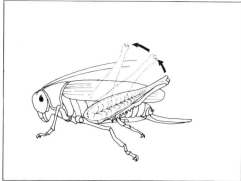

Stridulation—the voice of the grasshoppers. Left: Long-horned grasshopper rubs a hindleg over the ribs of the forewing. Right: Bush-crickets have one of the left wing ribs adapted to form a row of teeth, which is rubbed against the trailing edge of the right forewing to produce the sound.

Bush-cricket crawlers

Although some species live on the ground, most bush-crickets are at home in the foliage of trees and bushes. These tend to be mainly green while the ground-dwelling ones are brown or blackish. Unlike grasshoppers bush-crickets are not lovers of the sun, but become active in the late afternoon, or may be wholly nocturnal. Their hindlegs are adapted for jumping, but they have not the prodigious leaping powers of grasshoppers, moving mainly by climbing and crawling.

Singing a different song

They are also noisy and call by stridulating, but the mechanism is very different from that of grasshoppers. In the left forewing a rib, formed by one of the veins, has a row of minute teeth and this is rubbed against the hind edge of the right forewing. The arrangement is the same as in crickets except that the roles of the left and right forewings are reversed. Here again the species all have distinct songs, and there is good reason for this. In both bush-crickets and grasshoppers the song is mainly a courtship invitation addressed to the female, and it is important that the females should be able to recognise the call of males of their own species.

By far the largest and finest species seen in Britain is the great green bush-cricket *Tettigonia viridissima*. It ranges across Europe, Asia and North Africa. The female is 2 in. long, including the straight, blade-like ovipositor, and is bright green in colour. The male is a little smaller and his song is very loud and sustained, and uttered at night. This bush-cricket is not uncommon along the south and west coasts of England. In the late summer and autumn the speckled bush-cricket *Leptophyes punctatissima* is common in gardens and hedges. It is a plump, soft-looking insect, green with the wings reduced to small vestiges; the female ovipositor is broad and curved.

Two ways of laying eggs

Both grasshoppers and bush-crickets lay eggs. In the former they are enclosed in a tough case called the egg-pod, which the female buries in the ground. Each pod has from 5 to 6 or up to 14 eggs, more or less according to the species. Bush-crickets lay their eggs without any covering and usually singly, some putting them in the ground or crevices of bark, others inserting them in stems or leaves by cutting slits with the ovipositor. In both, the young hatch in the form of tiny worm-like larvae which moult immediately after hatching. They then resemble their parents except that they have no wings. With each moult (ecdysis) their size increases. The wings also appear and grow larger at each moult, becoming fully formed and functional, in the species that fly, at the last moult. All the British species have one generation a year.

Mainly vegetarian

Grasshoppers are entirely herbivorous and can be fed in captivity on bunches of grass tied with string and lowered into their home. The floor of the receptacle should be covered with 1½ in. of slightly damp sand, and in these conditions they will breed readily.

Bush-crickets are at least partly predatory and one species, the oak bush-cricket *Meconema thalassinum,* is entirely carnivorous and hunts caterpillars and other insects in oak trees. The others feed partly on grass and leaves and partly on insects. In captivity they must be given plenty of room; if they are crowded cannibalism will occur. Lettuce leaves seem to suit most of them, but they should have some animal food as well. Small looper caterpillars can usually be found by shaking bushes and branches into an open umbrella held underneath them.

Colour means nothing

Some grasshoppers show an extraordinary range of variation in the colour and markings on both legs and body. In the stripe-winged and common green grasshoppers *Stenobothrus lineatus* and *Omocestus viridulus* there is a small number of well defined colour varieties, but in the common field and mottled grasshoppers *Chorthippus brunneus* and *Myrmeleotettix maculatus* there is almost every shade of colour: green, brown, yellow and red are the main colours and to these must be added extremely varied patterns of stripes, spots and mottling. As a result it is hopeless to try to tell a grasshopper by its colour.

class	**Insecta**
order	**Orthoptera**
family	**Acrididae**
genera	***Chorthippus, Omocestus, Stenobothrus, Myrmelotettix, Tetrix***
family	**Tettigoniidae**
genera	***Tettigonia, Leptophyes, Meconema***

*Standing room only: a crowd of **Phymateus** grasshopper nymphs. Wings show after moulting.*

933

Grass snake

Until the beginning of this century this non-poisonous reptile was known as the ringed snake. A third name, one at least as appropriate although seldom used, is water snake.

Grass snakes are usually 2½—3 ft long but occasionally longer ones are recorded. These are females, which are larger than the males. One from South Wales measured 5 ft 9 in. This was exceeded by one from Southern Europe measuring 6½ ft. The colour is usually olive brown, grey or green along the back with two rows of small black spots arranged alternately. Along the flanks are black vertical bars. The most obvious feature by which the snake can be recognized is the yellowish patch either side of the neck forming an incomplete collar or ring. This may sometimes be orange, pink or white.

The ringed snake ranges from Britain, through Europe (south of latitude 65 degrees). It is absent from Ireland, and although there are reports of it from the Highlands of Scotland none of these has been confirmed. There are 75 related species of water snake, most of them in the Old World, a few in North America, all similar, except for details of colouring.

A master swimmer

The grass snake is usually found near ponds and streams, on marshy ground or in damp woodlands, rarely on sandy heaths or on dry ground. It is active by day and especially in spring can be seen basking on banks or on logs. A good climber, it may go up into shrubs or low trees but never more than a few feet from the ground. It readily enters water, swimming strongly with side-to-side movements of the body, holding the head well clear of the water and moving it from side to side as if searching. One grass snake was watched for 20 minutes swimming underwater without coming to the surface to breathe. Another was found 20 miles from land in the Bay of Biscay, still heading out to sea. Grass snakes hibernate from October to April, but the period varies according to latitude, being shorter in the south. Usually many come together in holes in the ground, but smaller numbers may pass the winter under logs, boulders or piles of brushwood.

Big meals at long intervals

Grass snakes' main food used to be frogs. In Britain at least these are now rare compared with a quarter of a century ago, so presumably most grass snakes must be feeding mainly on other animals. Newts were their second preference, and after this fish and tadpoles. A few eat toads, but the majority, to avoid the toads' poison, refuse them. Lizards and slowworms, shrews, mice, voles, and young birds are also taken occasionally. One grass snake was seen eating honey bees but insects are not in the normal diet. Much of the food is caught in the water, smaller prey being swallowed while the snake is still submerged, larger prey being brought to land to be eaten. The main feeding time seems to be early morning, and when food is plentiful large meals are taken, for example, 17 newts one after the other, a 7in. gudgeon swallowed in the usual way, head-first. Young grass snakes feed on earthworms, slugs, tadpoles, newt larvae and small fish.

Bundles of eggs

Mating takes place in April and May. The male glides up to the female and places his chin on her back near the base of her tail. With his tongue flicking in and out rapidly, he caresses her back with his chin as his head moves towards the back of her head. Then, throwing his body in loops over her, coupling is completed. Eggs are laid in June or July, under heaps of decaying leaves or rotting vegetation, under hayricks or heaps of sawdust in sawmills, in compost or manure heaps. The number of eggs laid at a time is usually 30 – 40 but may vary from 8 to 53, each oval and up to 1 in. long. They

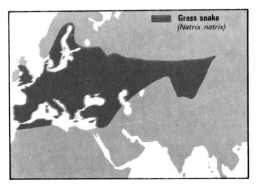

Grass snake
(Natrix natrix)

Prospective diner, apprehensive menu: a grass snake investigates a toad. With body inflated and raised stiffly on all fours, the toad is trying to get the snake to change its mind — unless the snake is really hungry the toad has a good chance of survival.

Friedel Schöx

stick together and as they dry and the 'glue' hardens they lose their glistening appearance and become matt white. Sometimes several females lay in the same place, as in North Wales in 1901 when 40 bundles of eggs totalling well over a thousand were found in a hole in an old wall near a row of cottages.

The eggs hatch in 6—10 weeks, the baby snakes slitting the parchment-like shell with the egg-tooth on the snout. On hatching they measure about 7 in. Grass snakes have lived for 9 years in captivity.

Defence: a nasty taste

There is not a great deal of positive information on enemies. Badgers and hedgehogs have been seen to eat adult grass snakes, and birds of prey have been watched flying up with them. The greatest mortality is among the babies. From 7 in. when first hatched they grow to 10—12 in. at a year old. Many are probably eaten by large and small flesh-eaters, possibly at times because of their worm-like appearance. More precise information is needed, however, because although a toad will seize a baby grass snake in its mouth it quickly rejects it and shows every sign of having a nasty taste in the mouth. Among other things the toad wipes its lips vigorously with first one front foot, then the other. This unpleasant taste may well protect young grass snakes from some other flesh-eaters.

Shamming dead

An adult grass snake uses an unpleasant secretion from its vent as the second line of defence. Its first line is to strike as any poisonous snake would, but the grass snake does so with the mouth shut. At the same time it blows up its body and hisses. This is pure bluff. It is soon followed by the unpleasant secretion, which is evil-smelling as a skunk but not in such quantity. The third line of defence is to sham dead. The grass snake quickly turns onto its back, opens its mouth, lets the tongue loll, and holds itself rigid. It is a realistic performance. The snake looks quite dead. If, at this point, you turn the snake over onto its belly and close its mouth, it turns as soon as you take your hands away onto its back, opens its mouth and lets its tongue loll. You can keep on doing this and each time the snake flips over, goes into what looks like a death posture, as if it were determined to look dead, come what may.

class	**Reptilia**
order	**Squamata**
suborder	**Serpentes**
family	**Colubridae**
genus & species	*Natrix natrix* *others*

△ *Best way to identify a grass snake is by the collar patches — yellow, orange-pink, or white.*

▽ *Grass snakes are expert swimmers, gliding smoothly along with the head raised.*

△ *Shamming dead, with head aslew, jaws loosely gaping, and tongue lolling.*

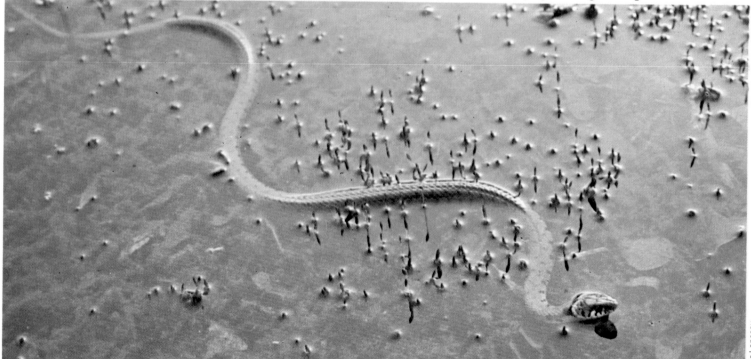

Grayling

Some say the grayling is one of the most beautiful of freshwater fishes, others say it is the most beautiful. It has been called the Lady of the Stream, the Flower of the Water, the Queen of the Water. And it has all the qualities of a superb sporting fish.

The grayling has also been named the umber because its swift swimming makes it disappear like a shadow. A relative of the salmon, it has been switched back and forth from the salmon family to a family of its own, the Thymallidae, and is at the moment back in the salmon family. Like a salmon in shape, it has a large purple dorsal fin which has been compared to a sail and to a butterfly's wing. The resemblance to the second of these is heightened by its 4 rows of dark blue spots. Its colour varies from a back coloured greenish-brown to blue-green, with flanks of silvery grey and a white underside. There are dark spots on the sides of the head and the front half of the body, and the paired anal and tail fins have a varying amount of purple. Dark zig-zag lines run the length of the body marking the boundaries between the rows of scales. Over the whole fish is a greenish-gold sheen.

It is a northern fish, growing up to 5 lb or more, found throughout Europe except in the southwest, but everywhere localised. It is found in Scandinavia, Lapland and Finland, and farther south in the alpine districts of central Europe. In the British Isles it is mainly in the midland and northern counties of England, has been introduced into southern Scotland but is absent from Ireland.

Aromatic beauty

The grayling needs clear, swift-flowing streams with plenty of water and with a stony or rocky bottom. In warm weather shoals are seen in the shallows near the bank. In Scandinavia the grayling leap in the waterfalls of mountain rivers in spring as they make their way up to spawn following the break-up of the ice. Unlike typical members of the salmon family, grayling do not go down to the sea but are wholly freshwater. Trout often live in grayling streams but are less migratory than the grayling.

The large dorsal fin makes the fish look top-heavy but it is a graceful swimmer, swift also, and in the eyes of the fisherman as tough a fighter as the trout. These qualities added to the grayling's coloration account for the eulogies showered on the fish. There is also its taste, some people asserting that its flesh is superior to that of a trout. When freshly caught it has a faint odour of wild thyme, from which its generic name *Thymallus* is derived. Another thing which increases its popularity is that its flesh is best in autumn when trout are not in season.

Two ways of feeding

Although it will take almost any form of insect, mayflies and caddis worms are particularly acceptable. Grayling also take freshwater shrimps and some worms. The fish keeps near the bottom, rising to take its food. Should an insect land on the surface the grayling will slowly float upwards, almost stalking its prey. In contrast, any insect or crustacean passing over the fish will be taken by a swift upward pounce, a movement largely helped by the sail-like dorsal fin.

Spring breeding

Spawning is from early March to mid-May, the female digging shallow troughs in the sandy or gravelly stream bed in which to lay her 5—6 thousand largish eggs. These hatch in a few weeks.

Long-standing favourite

The grayling has been a favourite with the connoisseur for many centuries. It was Ambrose, Bishop of Milan in the 4th century who named it the 'flower of fishes' or 'flower-fish'. Aldrovandus, the 16th-century Italian naturalist, claimed that the fat of the grayling being set a day or two in the sun, with a little honey is 'very excellent against redness or swarthiness or anything that breeds in the eyes'. Apparently no praise was too great for it and no claims for its virtues too extravagant. The fish has, however, been a disappointment in one respect. Attempts to breed it artificially have had little success. The grayling is very particular about the conditions under which it lives, and has become extinct in many rivers because of pollution. It is also highly susceptible to injury from being handled.

In 1961 a writer in *Nature* suggested that two English rivers were named after the grayling, the Humber (=umber) and the Thames (=thyme). There have, however, been other explanations for the origins of the names of the rivers.

class	**Osteichthyes**
order	**Salmoniformes**
family	**Salmonidae**
genus & species	***Thymallus thymallus***

The grayling's beauty lies in the subtle blending of the colours of its back and fins.

Eric Hosking

Soggy home among the reeds: little grebe or dabchick on the nest.

Grebe

Grebes are waterbirds with long necks and short tails that give them a distinct, blunt-ended appearance. Many species have plumes on the head. The feet are set well back on the body, as in the divers. They are not webbed but each toe has a horny fringe that acts as a paddle. The feet are used for steering both in the air and in the water, the vestigial tail being useless for this purpose.

The largest grebe is the 19in. long great crested grebe, whose behaviour has been studied in great detail. It is found in most of Europe except northern Scandinavia, in many parts of Asia, Africa and in Australia and New Zealand. Its upperparts are light brown and the underparts white. The black ear tufts and, in the breeding season, chestnut and black frills on the sides of the head are particularly distinctive. The Slavonian grebe is darker on the upperparts than the great crested grebe. In the breeding season it has a glossy black head with a golden stripe running through the eye, and chestnut neck and flanks. Its range is circumpolar, from Iceland, Faeroes and Scotland through parts of Scandinavia and a broad belt across Asia to North America. Another widespread species is the little grebe or dabchick, the smallest of grebes, which has dark plumage. It breeds in Europe as far north as southern Sweden, in Asia as far as the East Indies and Japan and in most of Africa.

Of the 18 species of grebe, 10 are confined to the New World. In comparison with the wide-ranging species described above, others are extremely restricted. One is restricted to Madagascar, another to New Zealand and a third to the Falkland Islands. In the highlands of South America there are three species tied to single lakes. The flightless Titicaca grebe lives on Lake Titicaca, 2 miles high in the Andes, another lives on Lake Junin in Peru, while the giant pied-billed grebe, also flightless, lives on Lake Atitlan in Guatemala.

Shy stay-at-homes

Grebes live on lakes, reservoirs and flooded gravel pits, only rarely on slow-moving rivers. Some stay in one place all the year round but others, such as the great crested grebe, migrate to the coast in winter. Generally, however, grebes do not fly much and have to run across the water to take off. When disturbed they scutter to safety or dive and, like cormorants and darters, can swim half submerged by flattening their plumage, so squeezing the air out. Grebes are not gregarious, only occasionally are they seen in small parties. More often they live in pairs not straying from their territories, which in great crested grebes are about 2 acres. The great crested grebe can often be seen swimming slowly about in open water and can be watched diving re-

Grebe courtship

Penguin dance: a rare and complicated ceremony in which both male and female come high up out of the water and shake their heads with nesting materials in their bills.

Rearing display: the male, or the female, climbs onto the nest, rears up, and with bent neck moves the head from side to side as an invitation to coupling.

Invitation to coupling: as courtship proceeds the female takes more turns at mounting the nest (often only a copulation platform) and makes this final display.

Mating begins as the male jumps onto the female. This remarkable series of photographs by George Rüppell illustrates the now famous observations of JS Huxley in 1914 and KEL Simmons in 1955

Series by G Rüppell

peatedly for food, but the little grebe lives a very secluded life among reeds and other vegetation surrounding its lake or pond. It can be seen only by accident or by patiently waiting for its occasional trip from one reed bed to another.

Eating fish and feathers

Grebes eat fish, aquatic insects and crustaceans together with a few newts, tadpoles and some plant matter which they find by swimming underwater. A grebe usually stays underwater for $\frac{1}{2}$ minute or less, depending no doubt on the depth of the water, abundance of food and so on. They have been known to stay submerged for as long as 3 minutes. In calm, clear water a grebe can easily spot its prey while swimming with its neck raised, but in ruffled water or if searching for small animals it may swim with its head just underwater, waiting to submerge suddenly and plunge after its prey. Insects are sometimes picked off the surface or snatched out of the air.

Fish are swallowed alive, head-first. They may have to be juggled before being in the right position for swallowing. Grebes usually eat 4–6 in. fish, but larger ones are sometimes caught and the grebe can only gulp them down slowly. It is not unusual for dabchicks, and other waterbirds, to be choked by the spines of bullheads they are attempting to swallow.

A strange habit of grebes is feather eating. They regularly eat their body feathers, or soak them, and give them to their young. In the stomach the feathers break down to a felt-like mush which is thought to make sharp fish bones easier to regurgitate.

Floating nests

Grebes are famed for their spectacular courtship dances. Both sexes have plumes and ear tufts and both take the initiative in courtship. The great crested grebe has several displays with various functions. They vary from simple head-shaking to the penguin dance. Both birds dive, surfacing with weed in their bills, then rise up breast to breast and sway from side to side before relaxing. In the 'cat display' the grebe lowers its head with ear tufts spread and holds its wings out with the forward edges turned downwards. The western grebe of North America performs incredible dashes over the water. The two grebes rear up out of the water and dash across the surface side by side with their necks arched forwards. The dash is ended by both birds diving.

Some of the courtship is carried out on the nest, which is a large pile of waterweed built by both birds among the weeds, or occasionally floating freely. The adults take turns in incubating 3–10 faint white or blue-green eggs. If they are frightened off the nest they will often cover the eggs with nest material before creeping away.

The eggs of large grebes hatch in a month and those of small grebes in 3 weeks. The nest is abandoned as soon as the chicks dry out and the young chicks are carried on the parents' backs for a week or more. They occasionally get carried under when the parent dives or carried aloft when it flies. As they grow older they spend less time on the parent. This behaviour protects them

A great crested grebe cruises slowly in placid water, carrying the young on its back.

from enemies, the worst of which, in Europe, is the pike. In a survey carried out in Britain, pike were the main cause of chick mortality, followed by foxes, otters, herons, trout and eels.

The young begin to dive when 6 weeks old and are independent by 10 weeks. Some species raise two broods in a season, the male guarding the first clutch while the female incubates the second.

Save the grebes

In 1860 the British population of great crested grebes fell to below 50 pairs because their feathers were used in hat-making. Since then, however, their numbers have increased, and now the bird is by no means rare. It is now the turn of another species, the giant pied-billed grebe, to be endangered. It is one of the rarest birds in America, only 100 surviving in 1965 on the 10 by 12 mile Lake Atitlan. The reason for their decrease seems to have been the introduction of largemouth bass as a gamefish. This on the face of it was an admirable scheme designed to enrich the area, but as all too often happens the project backfired. Largemouth bass, which weigh 10–12 lb, are predatory and live on the same small fish and crustaceans that the grebes hunt, and it seems that they also take young grebes. More seriously the bass have upset the delicate balance of the lake animals and the 50 000 people living round the lake are feeling the effects of this on their important fishing industry.

Steps have been taken to save the grebes. A small bay has been isolated from the lake by wire mesh, the bass killed off and grebes introduced. Rigorous patrolling against poaching has allowed the grebe population to increase. This is very encouraging, but expensive and one wonders whether it will be possible to eliminate the bass to allow both grebes and men to continue their fishing in peace.

class	**Aves**
order	**Podicipediformes**
family	**Podicipedidae**
genera & species	***Podiceps auratus*** Slavonian grebe ***P. cristatus*** great crested grebe ***P. ruficollis*** little grebe ***Podilymbus gigas*** giant pied-billed grebe others

Changeover: great crested grebe male takes on the job of incubating the last egg of the clutch while his mate prepares to leave with the chick.

Ronald Thompson

942

Greenfinch

The greenfinch is a typical finch, nearly 6 in. long with a short conical beak, powerful enough to crack hard seeds. Despite its name, the greenfinch or green linnet is only tinged with green, and most of this is olive-green or greenish-brown. Even this is hidden after the autumn moult when the plumage appears brown, the green tints appearing as the ends of the feathers become rubbed off. The more distinctive feature is the bright yellow along the edge of each wing and in a patch on either side at the base of the tail. The young greenfinch has a brownish plumage marked with lines of dark spots and streaks, a pattern found in many young finches, and in the adults of quite a number. The streaks can be indistinctly seen, but only at close quarters, on the head of the hen greenfinch.

The species ranges across Europe and much of Asia.

Hangers-on around houses
Greenfinches are sociable and move about in flocks except during the breeding season. Even then they tend to nest in groups in a hedge or among scrub. When the young are first fledged they keep together with the parents in a fairly compact family group. In areas where houses are few and widely separated greenfinches keep to pinewoods, which may have been their original habitat. Elsewhere they live around houses, gardens and farmhouses and are then absent from the wilder parts of the countryside. At the end of summer they gather in large flocks which scavenge arable land and stockyards for fallen grain or seeds of wild plants, especially those that are weeds on tilled soil. When disturbed they rise as a flock with a whirring of wings and twittering notes. The flight is bounding, as the bird alternates a few rapid wing beats with closing the wings and losing height, rising again on the next wing beats. The male, brighter in colour than the hen and with a grey-brown cap, is especially bright in spring and his yellow patches catch the eye. His twittering song is punctuated by a drawn-out whistle which sounds as if it were being made by an intake of breath. Greenfinches also mimic other birds' songs.

Weed controller
The food is cereal grains taken only when dropped from the ear, small seeds, berries such as yew, bramble and hips, insects including aphids, ants and beetles, spiders and occasionally the buds of fruit trees, but seldom to the point of being a pest.

Going to roost
Before sunset greenfinches begin to assemble, perhaps in a tall tree. They remain perched with only a small amount of flying from twig to twig, after a while dropping into a steep dive to the evergreen bushes below or into a hedge. They come down in ones and twos, diving steeply or following an erratic course like leaves falling in autumn. For a half-hour this goes on, with late arrivals coming in to perch on the tree before diving down. In the fastness of twigs and leaves of the roost itself the 50-odd finches move uneasily from one twig to another until darkness begins to gather and they settle for the night.

Aerobatic courtship
In spring the male alternates his indrawn whistle with flying up from his perch and floating around with slow wing beats in a butterfly- or bat-like flight, twittering. This is the main part of his courtship display. As a rule the nest is built in a hedge, evergreen bush or shrub, of twigs, moss, bents and wool lined with roots, hair and feathers. The 4—6 eggs are laid in May, each ¾ in. by ½ in., dirty-white to greenish-blue with reddish-brown or violet markings. The hen alone incubates for 2 weeks, during which she is

Seed husks surround a feeding greenfinch, clear proof of the 'nutcracker' qualities of its cone-shaped bill. The greenfinch's subfusc plumage has as much yellow in it as green.

fed by the cock, and both parents feed the young by regurgitation for another 2 weeks, on insects and some crushed seeds.

High infant mortality
The enemies of small songbirds such as greenfinches are hawks as well as owls, which will sometimes beat them out of their roosts by flapping with their wings. They may be caught on the ground by small beasts of prey, such as stoats, weasels and domestic cats. The highest mortality is, however, in the first three months of life, including the time they are still in the egg, from nest-robbers such as magpies, jays and squirrels, even rats. Once fledged, the carnage continues and is augmented by accidents due to inexperience. In the several species in which this aspect of the life history has been studied a 60—75% mortality has been recorded in the first 3—6 months of life.

Drug addicts
Writing in *Animal Behaviour* in 1961, M Pettersson reported on a remarkable instance of drug addiction in a species of bird. The bird is the greenfinch, the drug is contained in the berries of an ornamental shrub *Daphne*, a native of Europe that has been widely planted as an ornamental. It was noted over a century ago, in the Pennine district of England, that when the berries of *Daphne* ripened in June the greenfinches descended on it and stripped it of its berries. The habit spread outwards from this centre until the greenfinches over nearly the whole of Britain were eating these berries. The spread was orderly, at a rate of 2½ miles a year. The berries are said to have an intoxicating effect on the greenfinches, which appear to give all their attention to the berries, as if they could not have enough of them. An extensive survey made by Pettersson suggests that this has been a genuine spread of a habit. Perhaps the most interesting feature of all is that the habit has spread at about the same rate as human cultures such as bronze-working and iron-working are known to have spread.

class	**Aves**
order	**Passeriformes**
family	**Fringillidae**
genus & species	***Chloris chloris***

△ *Sociable birds, greenfinches flock in autumn.*   ▽ *Like a Whitsun crowd of holiday-makers: a migrating greenfinch flock.*

Greenhouse frog

The greenhouse frog is so-called because in Florida, where it has been imported from the Caribbean, it is often found in the moist earth of greenhouses. Its maximum length is 1½ in., but average females are ¾—1 in. long and males slightly smaller. There are two colour phases: striped and mottled. Striped greenhouse frogs are pale grey or cream with an orange or tan stripe running from each eye down the back. Across the back there are brown stripes, while the underparts are spotted. The mottled phase is similar to the striped, but the back is dark brown mottled with light brown. Frogs from one clutch of eggs may be either striped or mottled, and very rarely one frog may have a combination of both patterns.

The family Leptodactylidae, to which the greenhouse frog belongs, lives in the West Indies and tropical America, and in Australia, a good example of discontinuous distribution, suggesting that the family is very old and once was more widespread. The members of the family are very varied and include the 2lb 'mountain chicken', the South American 'bullfrog' and the Holy Cross frog of Australia. Closely related to the greenhouse frog is the barking frog of Texas and Mexico. From a distance its calls sound like the yapping of a terrier.

The greenhouse frog originally lived on Cuba and the nearby Isle of Pines, but it has been introduced to many parts of the Caribbean such as Jamaica, Cat Island, the Bahamas and others. It has also been introduced to Florida where it is found as far north as Jackson.

Living on land

Greenhouse frogs live on land, in damp situations where the air is always moist, such as under rocks, fallen trees or piles of decaying plants. Although classed as Amphibia, these frogs like a good many other species spend no more time in water than do land-living reptiles or mammals. They are, however, usually found near the banks of sluggish streams.

In warm weather when the temperature rises above 16°C/60°F, the greenhouse frog becomes quite active and jumps for cover if disturbed. It is nocturnal but will come out during the day if it is raining. If the ground dries out it digs to avoid being dried up. The voice has been described as being like a tiny bell or the cheeping of very young ducklings. Greenhouse frogs can be heard mainly at dawn or dusk, but throughout the day if the weather is overcast.

Feeding in leaf litter

Greenhouse frogs live on the ground or only a few inches up low vegetation. Consequently their food consists of ground-living animals that can be found under leaf litter. Their food is mainly ants and small beetles and cockroaches with a few centipedes, millipedes, spiders and earthworms.

Hatching out as frogs

The greenhouse frog and its very close relatives lay their eggs on land, but breeding takes place during rainy periods and the eggs will not hatch unless the surrounding air is almost saturated with water vapour. Mating usually takes place around sunrise, when the air temperature is low but humidity is at its highest. On average each female lays 16 eggs in one clutch. They are deposited under a stone or log, in a neat pile. The female digs a hole to take them, and if the stone or log is not in direct contact with the ground she scrapes earth over them by kicking with her back legs. Unlike its close relatives, the greenhouse frog does not guard its eggs.

The eggs take 2–3 weeks to hatch depending on the air temperature. The tadpole stage is passed within the egg and the froglet emerges ⅕ in. long with little sign of a tail or external gills. Like other frogs that lay their eggs on land, the young greenhouse froglet has an egg tooth. This is not a chalky knob like that found on the beaks of newly-hatched chicks, but a real tooth placed at the tip of the upper jaw. With it the froglet tears open the egg membrane and climbs out. The egg tooth is soon shed.

Keeping in water

In 1869 Professor Eberth of Zurich described a layer of tissue in the skin of common and edible frogs. He did not know its function and no more was heard about it. It was shown in drawings of frogs' skin that appeared in scientific journals, but it was not even labelled, let alone mentioned in the text. Then a few years ago Dr E Elkan examined 112 species of frogs and toads in search of this mysterious layer of skin. His findings are reported in the *Journal of Zoology* where he shows that, in most cases, amphibians that spend most of their time in water, such as the clawed frog, do not have the layer, but those that spend a certain amount of time on land do have it. The layer is made up of mucopolysaccharides, slimy substances that both hold water and prevent its passage. Thus the layer of this substance in the skin of many frogs and toads enables them to live out of water without drying up. It is not as effective at waterproofing the body as the skin of a reptile or mammal, but is sufficient protection for an amphibian, like a greenhouse frog, living in moist places.

class	**Amphibia**
order	**Salientia**
family	**Leptodactylidae**
genus & species	***Eleutherodactylus planirostris***

*Left: Greenhouse frog **Eleutherodactylus planirostris**.*

▽ *Conserving water: amphibians breathe through their skin, which must be kept moist to allow oxygen to diffuse through—but this works both ways. On land water evaporates, and the frog tends to dry up. The top two sections of frog skin show the Eberth-Kastsch layer—a stained blue line along the middle of the sections—which partially prevents water loss in land-living frogs. The bottom section is from a water-living frog, which does not need it.*

Malcolm McGregor

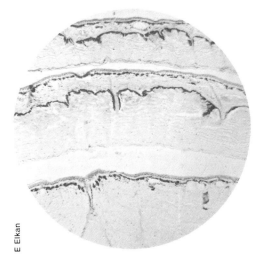

E Elkan

Green lizard

This is the second largest lizard in Europe; the male is 15 in. long, of which 10 in. is tail. Europe's largest lizard is the eyed lizard, 24 in. long of which 16 in. is tail, and there are records of 36 in. total length. The eyed lizard is often dark green spotted with yellow and black. There are blue spots forming rosettes on the flanks.

The head of the green lizard is large, its legs stout and the toes, especially on the hindfeet, long. The length of the toes is most marked in the males although the females are usually slightly larger than the males in total body size. The colour varies and while usually bright green in the male it may be yellowish-green or brown and yellow on the flanks of the female. Males are noticeably thick at the root of the tail.

Green lizards range across southern Europe from northern Spain and the south of France to southwest Russia and northwards to parts of Germany. They are also found in the Channel Islands, but attempts to acclimatize them a few degrees farther north, in southwest England, have failed.

Lovers of dampness

Green lizards live among rocks and on rough ground especially along the margins of woods, where the ground is not too dry. They are particularly found on river banks, but they may also occur in meadows, especially where there are damp ditches. They climb well and are reputed to be good swimmers and to take readily to water when disturbed and seek refuge on the bottom. They are active by day, hunting or basking, but seek the shade when the sun is hot. Hibernation is from October to March, in holes in the ground, under buttress roots of trees or under vegetation litter, the period of hibernation being shorter in the southern than in the northern parts of the range.

Shell-cracker jaws

Green lizards feed on insects, spiders, woodlice, earthworms and other small invertebrates but also eat smaller lizards and small rodents. They sometimes take birds' eggs, cracking the shells with their powerful jaws which can give a strong but non-venomous bite on the hand. They occasionally eat fruit.

Females just give in

The breeding season starts in late April and continues into May. The male's throat goes cobalt blue, and is used as a threat in the many contests that take place between males. He also uses the same intimidating displays towards females and it is the fact that she responds submissively, that is, she does not return his menacing attitude, which tells him she is a female. A short time after mating the female lays 5–21 dull white oval eggs, about ¾ in. long, in soft earth. She stays near her eggs and will come back to them even after being driven off. They hatch 2–3 months later, the newly-hatched young being 2–3½ in. long, brown with one or two rows of yellowish-white spots. They gradually turn

△ Seconds out: green lizards fighting.
▽ The second largest lizard in Europe.

green as they reach maturity. Green lizards may live for 10 years in captivity although their life in the wild is doubtless generally less than this.

Victims of pet-keepers

This lizard is attacked by the usual enemies of lizards, particularly the larger birds of prey, and it has the usual lizard defence of casting its tail and growing a new one. The chief danger to the green lizard, as with several other southern European reptiles, notably the Greek tortoise and the wall lizard, is their export for pet-keeping. Thousands each year find their way northwards to central and northern Europe to be kept in vivaria, to be used in laboratories, or to re-stock the many zoos.

No place like home

Some idea of the traffic in these attractive reptiles can be gained from the attempts to naturalize them in England. In 1899 an unspecified number of green lizards were liberated in the Isle of Wight and for a while they bred there. The last were seen in 1936. In 1931 some were introduced into Caernarvonshire, in North Wales. These did not breed and survived for only 4 years or so. In 1937, 100 green lizards were set free at Paignton, in south Devon. A few were still alive in 1952.

The wall lizard, a medium-sized European lizard, 8 in. long, was also introduced at Paignton in 1937, 200 being set free. They lasted only a few years, yet the wall lizard is a more northerly species than the green lizard, ranging from Jersey, in the Channel Isles, across Holland, Germany and Poland to the southern European mountain ranges.

South Devon is only a few degrees farther north than the Channel Islands, but it seems this is enough to make the difference between survival and extinction for the green lizard. Subtropical plants grow well in south Devon so, while temperature may be important, there must be other factors working against the lizards. An animal set down in a foreign environment must find suitable hiding places, suitable food and other necessities for successful living. Everything around is strange and, far more than for a plant, it is a gamble whether an animal will settle down. Nevertheless, we have the instances in which one group of green lizards survived in the Isle of Wight for at least 37 years and another group in South Devon continued for at least 15 years. The climate of the British Isles is said to be slowly getting warmer. It may well be that future attempts at acclimatization might prove more successful, provided there is then more sunshine than is usual now. Experience with captive green lizards shows that without sufficient sunlight they are prone to skin complaints that shorten their lives.

André Fatras

△ *A meal of a brimstone butterfly.*
▽ *Feeling blue: a male in the mating season.*

Klaus Paysan

class	**Reptilia**
order	**Squamata**
suborder	**Sauria**
family	**Lacertidae**
genus & species	*Lacerta viridis* green lizard *L. lepida* eyed lizard

Green turtle

Once abundant in tropical seas, the green or edible turtle has been wiped out in many parts of its range and made very rare in others because its flesh and eggs are good to eat and easily gathered. The name comes from the green tinged fat. It is one of the true sea turtles, together with the logger-head, the hawksbill and Ridley turtles. The shell of horny shields covering an inner layer of bony plates is made up of two parts, the dorsal carapace on the back and the ventral plastron covering the under-surface. The head is too large to be drawn into the shell. In the adult, the shell is marbled or spotted with yellow on an olive or dark brown background. The young are a uniform brown above and yellow underneath. The shell reaches a maximum length of 4 ft, 3 ft 4 in. on average, and the adults weigh 300 – 400 lb.

A long way to breed

The true sea turtles usually come on land only to lay eggs, but the green turtle will sometimes come on shore to bask. Movement on land is hampered not only by the sheer dragging weight of the shell, but by the necessity to lift the shell to allow the lungs to expand. The turtle stops every few feet and heaves a great sigh as it takes a breath. To complete the melancholy picture the turtle's eyes are continuously running with tears. This is a device used by many sea animals, including reptiles, birds and mammals, to rid the body of the extra salt taken in while eating and drinking.

At sea, the turtle is a complete contrast. It is a good swimmer, rowing itself slowly and gracefully with its front flippers. Dives can last up to five hours, during which time the heart slows down considerably.

Outside the breeding season, green turtles live in shallow parts of the sea, usually in coastal areas, far from the breeding grounds. Results of tagging turtles with metal bands have shown that they migrate regularly between their two homes. Green turtles travel from the coast of Brazil to the little island of Ascension, some 1 400 miles out in the Atlantic Ocean. How they manage this feat of navigation has yet to be discovered. It may be that they are using the angle of the sun in the same way as birds are presumed to do. Preliminary experiments have been made of attaching radio trans-

Russ Kinne: Photo Res.

△ *Long, strong strokes: in its element, the green turtle is a leisurely, graceful oarsman.*

▽ *One of the most exhausting periods of the green turtle's life: scooping out the nest.*

Okapia

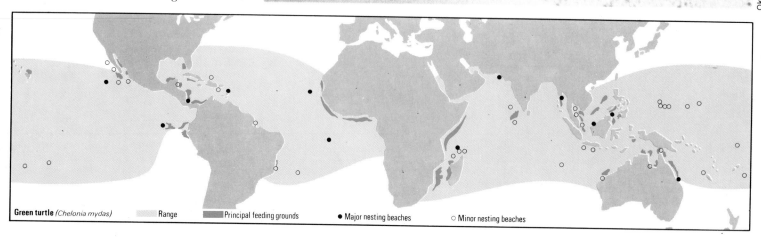

Green turtle *(Chelonia mydas)*   Range   Principal feeding grounds   ● Major nesting beaches   ○ Minor nesting beaches

*After laying its eggs, a green turtle
slowly drags itself back to the sea.*

mitters to green turtles. As they swim slowly and usually near the surface they should be able to tow a float containing the transmitter which could be tracked by satellite.

Grazing sea grass

Adult green turtles are herbivorous, living mainly on 'turtle grass' that grows in sheltered shallow water. During their first year, young green turtles are carnivorous, feeding on practically any kind of animal food.

Hatching en masse

Mating takes place offshore after migration from the feeding grounds. The females come ashore to lay their eggs in the sand, always at night because they will die if exposed to the sun for too long. At a suitable place above the high tide line, after a laborious haul up the beach, they start to dig their

young can crawl out of the eggshells quite easily. The whole clutch hatches at about the same time and the hatchlings fight their way to the surface some days later. They nearly always emerge at night so avoiding the heat of the sun as well as many enemies.

The baby turtles set off for the sea as soon as they reach the surface, 'paddling' wildly with their flippers to reach the water and then swimming out to deep water and comparative safety. They have an almost unerring ability to head for the sea straight after leaving the nest, even on cloudy and moonless nights and when the nest is hidden from the sea by a sandbank. This infallible direction-finding has been tested experimentally and it has been found that the turtles are reacting to the brighter light over the sea, which reflects more light than the land behind them.

sometimes before laying their eggs, and this is another cause of the green turtle' decline.

In several parts of the world attempts are being made to limit the decline by trying to ban the hunting of turtles, which are such an easy quarry as they lie almost helpless on the sand, or by improving the chances of the young turtles' survival. To the latter end, turtle hatcheries have been set up. Eggs are collected from the nests and reburied in fenced compounds where they can develop in safety. On emergence the young turtles are kept in pools until their shells harden, then liberated out at sea, beyond the reach of at least some of their enemies.

Hatcheries are a vital part of any attempt to restore the green turtle's fortunes. A small egg eventually grows into a large valuable turtle which can supply many

Moment of truth: a sand-covered female green turtle lays her eggs.

Breakout of over 100 baby green turtles on the Great Barrier Reef.

nests. A body pit is dug first by sweeping sand away with all four flippers until the turtle is lying in a pit, its back below the surface of the sand. Next an egg hole is dug just under where her tail is, using only the hind-flippers as scoops. When finished this is nearly 2 ft deep and the female is ready to lay her eggs.

Each clutch consists of about 100 round white eggs, about the size of a ping-pong ball and each female lays five or more clutches, returning to the nesting beach at 10 day intervals. After the clutch is laid, a process taking about 10 minutes, the female turtle fills in the nest with sand and leaves the eggs to incubate.

The female does not press the sand down hard over the nest so the eggs are in a cavity with plenty of air. When they hatch, 7–10 weeks later depending on climate, the

Hazardous dash to the sea

Newly hatched turtles have soft shells and are easy prey for many predators. If the nests have not been dug up by dogs or monitor lizards the emerging turtles may be snapped up by ghost crabs, snakes, cats, tigers, dholes and many other predators. If they reach the sea they may fall foul of crocodiles and sharks. Clutches that emerge during daylight are likely to be wiped out by gulls and frigate birds.

Turtle farming

The many enemies, however, are insignificant by comparison with man. Turtle eggs are dug up by the million as it is easy to trace the nests by the tank-like tracks left by the female as she plods up and down the beach. Worse still, the females are also taken,

pounds of meat or, perhaps better, be used as a cash crop before buying other necessities. Whatever the answer, the downfall of the green turtle is that it is only the females that are captured. On page 839, the recovery of the fur seal stocks was described. From near extinction the herds have built up because only the surplus males are now killed. Unfortunately for the green turtle the female is the more vulnerable as she comes ashore, while the males wait in the safety of the sea.

class	**Reptilia**
order	**Chelonia**
family	**Chelonidae**
genus & species	*Chelonia mydas*

Grey fox

Sometimes called the tree fox, the short-legged grey fox is noted for its ability to climb and it uses trees much more than other foxes. Up to 27 in. head and body length and 15 lb weight, the grey fox has a bushy tail up to 17 in. long. The general colour of the fur is grey with underparts white but there is a rusty tinge along the sides of the neck, lower flanks and underside of the tail. There is a black line along the middle of the back, continuing along the tail, and black lines on the face. There is a noticeable ridge of stiff hairs along the top of the tail. Its size and colour vary from one region to another. In the northeast of its range its coat is a dark grey; in the southwest it is paler and slightly redder.

The range is from southern Canada through the United States to Mexico, Central America and northern South America. A smaller animal with shorter ears living on certain islands off southern California is regarded as a second species. It scavenges the beaches and makes its den among the cacti.

Climbing fox

Grey foxes live in forests, especially of southern pines, or brush country in the dry areas of the southwestern United States and Mexico. It is difficult to assess numbers because the animal is not only about mainly at night but is also adept at keeping out of sight at all times. It is therefore comparatively seldom seen and even its yapping bark often passes unrecognized, even if heard, partly because it is somewhat like the call of the coyote. During the day it rests in thick vegetation or among rocks, or in a tree hollow. Much of its food is caught on the ground but the fox will not only go up into trees when pursued but will also do so of its own will, especially to find fruits in season. It will run up a leaning trunk or climb a straight trunk gripping it with its forelimbs and pushing upwards with the hindfeet, the long claws on the toes of the hindfeet acting as climbing irons. Once in the tree it may leap from one branch to another. In descending the fox backs down the tree. It is not a fast runner, nor can it run long distances. The difference between the crude climbing of the red fox and the skill of the grey fox can best be illustrated by an accident. A grey fox was found dead in a tree its tail caught by the tip in a forked twig and further held by having passed through a second fork. From the scarring on the bark of the nearby twigs the fox had made desperate efforts to free itself. The important point is that all the twigs around the fox were no more than $\frac{3}{4}$ in. thick and most were nearer $\frac{2}{5}$ in.

Fox and grapes

Its diet is wide and takes in mice, squirrels, small birds and eggs, as well as insects. It also includes more plant food than is usual in the dog family. Grain and fruits, especially wild grapes and wild cherries, form the bulk of the food at certain seasons and in particular areas. With such a wide diet the grey fox readily takes to farmland and can be a nuisance, especially where there is poultry. It is also established in some built-up areas, for instance, the outskirts of New York City. The actual requirements of grey foxes were worked out by Richard F Dyson, Curator of Large Mammals at the Arizona-Sonora Desert Museum at Tucson. Because some of the mammals were overweight and had shaggy coats he tested grey

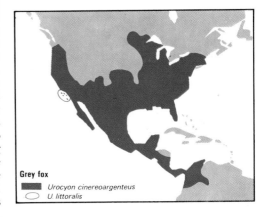

Grey fox
- Urocyon cinereoargenteus
- U. littoralis

The bushy-tailed, forest-dwelling grey fox. Shy and nocturnal, it often passes undetected—and one reason is because its voice resembles the familiar call of the coyote. Unlike many other foxes, it is not a fast runner, nor can it cover long distances at full speed.

foxes for 6 months and found they kept in excellent health on 3·8% of their own body weight of food (flesh and fruit) per day. Later it was shown that this held good for other carnivores.

United families

The cubs are born in spring after a gestation period of about 2 months, the litter averaging 3 or 4, but it may be from 2 to 7. At birth the cubs are black, blind and helpless, about $3\frac{1}{2}$ oz weight. They are weaned at 6 weeks. The male helps in bringing up the family, the cubs finally leaving the parents at the age of 5 months. Grey foxes have lived up to 12 years in captivity.

The grey fox may be killed by wolf, coyote, bobcat and lynx but today its main enemy is man. Because of its habit of going quickly to ground or up into trees it is not hunted but trapped. In this the trapper takes advantage of the regularity with which a grey fox uses a run through the vegetation and sets his traps accordingly. The pelts make only second-rate furs.

Dogs do climb

But for its habit of tree-climbing the grey fox would hardly be noticed by zoologists. Yet tree-climbing foxes are no novelty, even among those whose coats are red. Many a fox has outwitted the hunt by running up the trunk of a leaning tree and hiding among the foliage. Others have ascended by using low branches but at least one red fox in England denned up in the crotch of a large tree and had her cubs there. The crotch was 15 ft from the ground and the vixen reached it, judging by the scratch marks on the bark, by jumping up from a buttress root and scrabbling the last few feet. This is highly unusual, but ordinary tree-climbing by red foxes seems to be more common than we suppose. One thing they never do is cling by the forelegs, as the grey fox does. That is a cat-like action, but it is probably also a result of the grey fox's short legs. Domestic dogs will sometimes climb trees. Those that do this most successfully are the small breeds with short legs.

class	**Mammalia**
order	**Carnivora**
family	**Canidae**
genus & species	*Urocyon cinereoargenteus* grey fox *U. littoralis* beach fox

Bundle of innocence: a grey fox cub. At 5 months, however, when it becomes independent, it will be a wily, hard-to-catch, farmland predator.

A Visage: Jacana

952

Greylag

The greylag goose is the ancestor of the farmyard goose. It is one of five 'grey geese' the others being the bean, white-fronted, lesser white-fronted and pink-footed geese. They are all similar and difficult to tell apart in flight. The greylag is up to 3 ft long and 9 lb in weight. Its plumage is grey-brown with lighter margins to the body feathers, white upper and under tail coverts and a white tipped grey tail largely overlapped by white coverts, so it appears white in flight with a dark rear band. The breast is often spotted or blotched with black. The forewing and rump are grey. The head is heavy and the orange bill is large and stout with a white or brownish nail. The legs are flesh-coloured.

The original breeding ground of the greylag probably extended over the whole of Europe Destruction of its habitat through cultivation has broken this up. Now it breeds in Iceland, Northern Scotland, Scandinavia, in a belt from Denmark to the Balkans and eastwards to the Black Sea. An eastern race breeds throughout central Asia. From these areas there is a southerly migration in winter.

Migrating formation: Greylag geese fly with regular wingbeats, fast and direct in 'V' formations or trailing lines, each bird at a regular distance from its neighbour, except for the odd straggler.

Arthur Christiansen

Formation flying

Wary and suspicious, greylag geese are usually unapproachable, and when feeding there are always a few birds of the flock on the lookout for possible danger. Stories of organized sentries are probably over-statements but as one bird gives up watch another will take over. Greylags never perch. They walk easily, but without the waddle of domestic geese, can run well, swim well but seldom do, and will dive if necessary to escape danger. They fly with regular wing-beats, fast and direct in 'V' formation or trailing lines (skeins) each bird at a regular distance from its neighbour and led, so it is said, by an old bird. The call is a deep 'aahng-ung-ung', but geese use many other notes and are said to be able to recognize each other by their voices. Hissing is used to warn of impending danger.

Greylag geese feed by day on salt and freshwater marshes, fens and bogs, near estuaries or lakes and rivers where there are reeds, rushes or willow thickets. Fields of young grain or stubble and ricefields are also favoured. The night is spent on sand-banks and shoals in rivers or large lakes or on the coast. Outside the breeding season they are in flocks (or gaggles) of half-a-dozen to hundreds, or even thousands.

Grazing geese

Wholly vegetarian, the food is mainly grass but they will eat a variety of grain, tubers and other plants, including potatoes, turnips and acorns.

Good parents

Geese are credited with mating for life. They differ from ducks in that the family unit is close-knit. The nest is in thick heather built of heather twigs, grass and moss mixed with down and small feathers, or it may be in rushes. Floating nests of reeds may be used. The oval creamy-white eggs, $3\frac{1}{4}$ by $2\frac{1}{4}$ in., may become nest-stained yellowish or pale brown. The usual clutch is 4 – 6 but may be 8, and where there has been interbreed-ing with domestic geese it may be up to 15. They are laid in late April, sometimes earlier. Incubation begins when the clutch is completed and lasts 4 weeks, the goose (female) sitting all the time with the gander (male) within range. The young (goslings) can pick up food from birth but are accom-panied by the parents for a further 8 weeks.

Used by man

Geese were probably domesticated as early as Neolithic times. The greylag has a strong tendency to throw up white individuals and these were regarded, especially by the Romans, as being of superior quality. Geese are always ready to over-eat, which makes fattening easy. It also made easy the Roman practice of stuffing them with a mixture of flour, milk and honey to enlarge the liver. The Greeks kept geese for the table and for their eggs and Aesop produced the fable of the goose laying golden eggs. The Romans, however, exploited them most. The nobility ate only the front part of a goose, leaving the rest for the household staff. The Romans plucked their geese twice a year for the down, to stuff cushions, and goose quills were used as pens at least as early as the 5th century AD. Goose lard was used for skin diseases and, taken internally, for colic.

Although geese have been credited with stupidity, the Romans considered them highly intelligent, the result no doubt of honking geese saving the Capitol in 390 BC by raising the alarm when the Gauls were trying to climb in. In pre-Roman Britain the goose was held sacred, according to Caesar, and not eaten. In the days of Pliny, geese were imported from Germany, where very pure white birds were being bred. It is recorded that these geese were herded across the Alps on foot and all the way to Rome in Italy.

Following foster parents

The name of Oscar Heinroth is virtually unknown outside the circle of those who study animal behaviour. He was a pioneer in the early years of this century. He it was who studied the intimate family life of the greylag and described how, in a mated pair, the gander, after driving off an intruder, returned to his goose uttering a triumph note, a resonant note followed by a low cackle, with his neck outstretched and head low to the ground. The goose responds in similar manner, and so will any goslings they may have. ('See that, my dear, I drove him off.' 'How clever of you, darling.') Heinroth was also the first to make a study of imprint-ing, the work being carried on by Konrad Lorenz, famous not only for his scientific work but for crawling on all fours followed by a line of goslings (or ducklings).

Heinroth found that young geese reared from eggs hatched away from the parents would follow the first large moving object, whether a human being or a tractor, as if it were their parents. They become 'im-printed' on it and if this continues for a few hours, or even minutes, the young bird con-tinues to accept a human being—any human being, not just its guardian—as parent, companion and fellow member of the species. Later, it becomes attached to one person, which it treats as a mate. Further studies by a number of people have shown that imprinting can occur in many species of birds, in some fishes, even in some insects. It is the secret behind the pet bird that not only clings, in a social sense, to one person but will pay court to that person; it all came out from Heinroth's study of geese.

class	Aves
order	Anseriformes
family	Anatidae
genus & species	*Anser anser*

Takeoff (above) and touchdown (left). Greylag geese are usually unapproachable. When feeding there are always a few birds on the lookout for possible danger.
Family afloat. Geese are thought to mate for life, the goslings being cared for until 8 weeks old.

Sunset encounter of greylag geese

Grey seal

*The grey seal does not really live up to its name; its colour varies from almost black through brown to silver depending on whether the animal is wet or dry and also on its state of moult. The grey is basically a background colour with irregular blotches or spots. The back is generally darker than the underside. In Canada a few bright green seals have been noticed. This colour results from the growth of a green alga **Enteromorpha groenlandica** among the hairs of the back.*

The sex of a grey seal can often be told by the markings; the bulls have a dark background colour, usually grey, marked with irregular blotches of a paler shade, the females are pale grey or silvery marked with smaller darker spots or patches. Some adult cows, when they float vertically in the water, show spots about the neck very much like a Dalmatian dog. This is very characteristic of the grey seal.

In profile the grey seal has a noticeably convex outline to the head, its so-called 'Roman nose', which has led to the seal being known as the 'horse head' in parts of Canada. This profile is most distinct in the adult males, and it is the best way to distinguish the grey seal from the other resident British seal, the common seal, which has a rather doglike concave profile. The adult male grows up to a maximum length of 9½ ft and just over 600 lb weight, the females being much smaller at about 7 ft long and up to 550 lb weight.

The grey seal is found on both sides of the Atlantic and well into the Arctic, but about three-quarters of the world's population is to be found around Britain, and the great majority of these live around the Scottish coasts.

The range of the grey seal extends from the Gulf of Saint Lawrence, around Newfoundland, south to Sable Island and Cape Breton Island, then across the North Atlantic including Faeroe and Iceland to the British Isles, where the largest colonies are to be found at North Rona, the Orkney Islands, the Hebrides, and on the Farne Islands in the North Sea. Smaller colonies are found in Wales, Scilly Isles, in Ireland, and there is a very small colony off Norfolk. It is also found all around the Baltic coast and some of its islands, then up the Norwegian coast as far as the White Sea.

Protection and destruction

Since earliest times the grey seal of the British coasts has provided sealskin for clothing and oil for lamps, especially around the Northern Isles. At the turn of this century it was feared that it was rapidly being hunted to extinction, and in 1914 the Grey Seal Protection Act was passed in Parliament to give the animal legal protec-

tion during the period October 1–December 15. In 1932 the second Grey Seal Act extended this close season from September 1–December 31, and as a result the numbers of grey seals have increased dramatically in many parts of Britain. The Conservation of Seals Act 1970 allows the rapidly expanding colonies to be managed under supervision.

The Farne Islands' population shows the results of protection. Although grey seals have been known there since about the 12th century they have never been particularly plentiful and have often been killed for oil. During the 12th century the Islands belonged to the Prior of Durham and seals were often sent as gifts from the Prior to

influential people; they were considered a luxury food and the oil was also greatly valued. At the time of the first Grey Seal Act it is thought there were about 100 seals on the islands, whereas today more than 1 900 pups are born every year.

Controlling the numbers

Although the grey seal has been saved from total destruction in Britain, its recovery has not been applauded by everyone. Due to its habit of helping itself to an easy meal of salmon straight from the fishermen's nets there have been several attempts to get its numbers reduced in recent years. In the Farne and Orkney Islands, a number of pups have been culled in an effort to control the population and cut down the damage to nets. To be able to organise protection and culling properly the biology of the grey seals has been studied. During the investigations large numbers of pups have been tagged with metal or plastic tags fastened to the tail or flipper web so their movements can be traced. These pups leave

the breeding ground at the age of about 2 months and some have made quite remarkable trips. One pup tagged on the Farnes turned up some 7 weeks later in the Faeroe Islands. Another was seen on the English coast at Withernsea and again only 4 days later on the Dutch coast about 200 miles away—some journey for an animal less than 2 months old. These wanderings by the newly weaned pups are not a regular migration in the same way as swallows migrate to Africa, but more of a dispersion from the breeding grounds. Tagged pups from Orkney and the Farnes have turned up in Holland, Iceland, Norway and the Faeroes. Adult grey seals do not wander as much as the young ones.

Variations of grey: the grey seal does not really live up to its name; its colour varies from almost black to silver depending on whether the animal is wet or dry and also on its stages of moult.

Fred Bruemmer

Preying on the salmon

Seals are a notable pest of salmon nets. On the Scottish east coast there are a number of salmon stations where the fish are caught in fixed nets, staked out from the shore. These provide an easy source of food for the seal, which can remove fish from the net instead of having to chase them in the open sea. Sometimes fishermen remove from the net salmon with claw marks on the flanks. At other times all the fisherman gets is the head, the seal having taken the rest. Such things have made the grey seal disliked by the salmon men and are the reason behind attempts to control their numbers. Young grey seals feed at first on shrimps and any small fish found in the rock pools, graduating to cod, salmon, saithe, halibut and herring as well as commercially unimportant fish such as congers and lumpsuckers.

White-coated pups

Grey seals in Britain bear most of their pups in September and October, although births have been recorded in almost every month of the year. Those on the western side of the Atlantic, together with the Baltic population, produce their pups in the spring. The breeding season in Britain starts with adult males and pregnant females congregating on the breeding islands. The larger, older bulls take up the best territories and keep the younger bulls away. As with most seals, the pups are born very quickly. They are about 30 in. in length, weigh about 30 lb and are covered with a coat of white hair. This 'whitecoat' is shed at about 3 weeks leaving the fat pup with its valuable 'bluecoat' so prized by hunters. During these first 3 weeks the females suckle their pups, the rich milk rapidly being converted to blubber in the pup, forming a reserve to last it until it is able to feed for itself. By this time the pup should weigh about 90 lb. If not, it does not have much chance of survival, as at weaning the pups are abandoned by their mothers. They spend the next few weeks splashing around rock pools, learning to swim and to feed themselves before eventually taking to the sea. If they lack a good reserve of blubber they will starve during this period.

When the adults leave the breeding beaches they disperse to the open sea to feed and replace all the blubber used up while they were ashore giving birth to their pups and mating. They reappear early in the following year to moult, the females coming ashore in February and the males about a couple of months later. After moulting they go back to sea to feed again and build up their reserves for the following breeding season.

Seal sirens

There are many legends, especially in Celtic countries, of seal-women who can be heard mourning the loss of their children, or trying to lure men to their doom by their songs like the Sirens of the Odyssey. The basis of the stories are most likely the calls of hungry grey seal pups, pathetic bleats that sound almost like a baby crying, to which the cows reply with a mournful howl. Distorted and magnified by echoes from the cliffs around the lonely breeding beaches these calls could be quite enough to give rise to legends. Sometimes these seal-women are said to be the unnatural off-spring of man and seal, but these may be stories of a more political nature put about by one clan to discredit the morals of another.

Other legends tell of seals saving fishermen from drowning, but this was presumably before rivalry grew up between seal and salmon fishers. The basis for these legends is the inquisitive nature of seals. When they are not disturbed too much, they are very curious and will swim over to investigate anything new. Anyone sitting quietly on a rock in the vicinity of seals is likely to come under their scrutiny.

class	**Mammalia**
order	**Pinnipedia**
family	**Phocidae**
genus & species	***Halichoerus grypus***

958

Fred Bruemmer

The Roman nose Brigade

Above left: The 'Roman nose' brigade. Cow grey seal attempts to escape her mate on Sable Island in the Atlantic, 150 miles east of Halifax, Nova Scotia, Canada. The female is identified by the spots about the neck which look very like those of a Dalmatian dog. The bull has a dark background colour, usually grey, marked with irregular blotches or spots. Above right: Plump 'whitecoat' pup is sniffed by its mother. By three weeks this pup will be 90 lb, having increased its weight threefold. It will start to shed its coat at this stage looking rather strange (middle left). An enjoyable snack is eaten by holding it in the front paws and biting off pieces (right). Note the claws and fingers, usually seen as a single unit—the webbed flipper. 'Old men-of-the-sea' (left). Inquisitive but at the same time wary, grey seals watch a photographer on the Farne Islands, off the Northumbrian coast, England. This is one of the largest colonies of grey seals in Britain (which has ¾ of the world's population). About 5 000 seals visit the islands, which are a wildlife sanctuary owned by the National Trust, and give birth to some 1 700 pups, every year.

Geoffrey Kinns: AFA

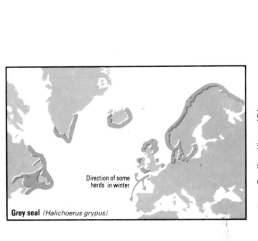

Direction of some herds in winter

Grey seal *(Halichoerus grypus)*

'Whitecoat'. The grey seal pup's protective pelage is shed at about three weeks leaving the fat pup with its valuable 'blue coat' so prized by hunters who will slaughter them relentlessly.

Grey whale *Eschrichtius glaucus*.

Malcolm McGregor

Grey whale

At one time the Californian grey whale lived in the Atlantic Ocean and was hunted by Icelanders in mediaeval times. Now it is confined to the North Pacific where there is a population on the eastern side.

It is a rather unusual whale, having points in common with both the rorqual (family Balaenopteridae) and right whales (family Balaenidae). It is about the size of the right whales, reaching 45 ft long and 20 tons in weight. The flukes of the tail are proportionally longer and more delicate than those of right whales, but more stubby than those of rorquals. The dorsal fin is replaced by 8–10 small humps along the tail just in front of the flukes. On the throat the grey whale has 2–3, rarely 4, grooves extending a short distance as compared with the 40–100 grooves extending to the belly in rorquals and the complete absence of grooves in right whales.

As the name implies, the grey whale is usually dark slate-grey but it may sometimes be blackish. It is lighter on the belly than on the back, as is usual in marine animals. Many grey whales have crescent-shaped marks or patches on the skin, especially on the back. These are caused either by lampreys or by barnacles.

Sluggish swimmers

Grey whales are very slow, usually swimming at 2–3 knots with bursts of 6–7 knots when alarmed, compared with 20 knots of a fin whale. As they also come very close inshore this makes them very vulnerable to hunters. In early spring the grey whales migrate down the west coast of North America. In 1840 there were estimated to be around 15 000 grey whales but soon after this there was very intense hunting all along the coast. By 1875 it was unusual to see more than 50 migrating whales at a time, although they used to be seen by the thousand. While the whales were in the Arctic Ocean they were (and still are) hunted by Eskimos; in

the Bay of Vancouver and around the Queen Charlotte Island they were attacked by Indians from canoes, and farther south the Yankee whalers chased them in sailing boats. The grey whales of the Western Pacific used to calve off Korea but the last one was killed in 1933.

Dog food or tourist bait?

By 1936 the world population was thought to be as low as 100–200. Then the governments of America, Japan and Russia came to an agreement on the future of the grey whale and declared it a protected species. This protection, together with the animal's fairly high rate of reproduction, has resulted in a gradual build-up of the population and it is now thought that they number about 11 000. Each year thousands of tourists gather on the west coast to watch the grey whales come down from the Bering Sea to give birth to their calves in the shallow and sheltered coastal waters of California and Mexico. Unfortunately, the large numbers of boats going out to see the whales cause considerable disturbance.

Straining out their food

Like the blue whale (p 248) the grey whales collect their food by means of rows of baleen plates in their mouths. Various crustaceans and molluscs floating in the sea are eaten in this manner.

Swimming south to breed

The migration of the grey whale is one of the better known aspects of its behaviour. They spend the summer months in the far north, principally in the Bering Sea, where they live in mixed herds. As summer draws to a close they swim slowly southwards and come in close to the coast, particularly so when they approach California where they can be seen swimming only a mile or so offshore. Here the herds segregate; the females stay together and led by an older cow come really close into the bays and lagoons where they get shelter from the weather to give birth to the calves. These are usually born at about the end of January, measuring about 15 ft in length and weighing around 1 500 lb. Normally only a single calf is produced but twin births have been recorded,

the calves suckling for about 9–10 months. As spring approaches the migration is reversed. The males, who have been waiting in deeper water, join the females with their newborn calves and the herds make their way back to the northern oceans to feed again in the colder waters where food is more abundant.

Chivalrous males

It has sometimes been noticed that grey whales show a one-sided faithfulness. If a female is injured or gets into difficulties one or more males may go to her aid, either to keep her at the surface where she can breathe, or to defend her from the attacks of killer whales. But if a male gets into similar difficulties, the females have been seen swimming away from the scene of trouble!

After man, killer whales are the greatest danger to grey whales. It is said that when a small school of grey whales are attacked by a large group of killers they may become so terrified by the attacks that they just float at the surface, belly uppermost, paralysed by fear and making themselves extremely vulnerable to further attack. The grey whales' habit of coming close inshore during the breeding season probably keeps them fairly clear of the attacks of killer whales who prefer deeper water. Sometimes grey whales have come so close inshore that they have practically run aground, and on one occasion a grey whale was seen playing about in the surf like a seal. They have also been found stranded at low tide, apparently without ill effect as they just floated off again at the next high water. This is most unusual since, for almost every other species of whale, stranding means death.

class	**Mammalia**
order	**Cetacea**
family	**Eschrichtidae**
genus & species	*Eschrichtius glaucus*

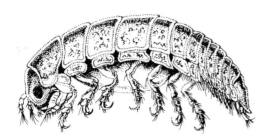

Gribble

*Gribbles belong to the group of crustaceans known as Isopoda (**iso** meaning the same) because all their legs are of equal size. They are related to the land isopods known as woodlice or sowbugs and closely resemble them, and in Australia they have been called timber-boring lice. The fully grown animal is ⅛ in. long but on the coasts of the United States alone it accounts for over 50 million dollars worth of damage each year to pier piles and other wooden structures immersed in sea water. There are enormous numbers of gribbles in wood in coastal waters— perhaps 300–400 in one cubic inch of infested wood.*

There are 21 species of gribble and 14 of them burrow into wood, the rest burrow into the holdfasts of the large seaweeds known as oarweeds. The common gribble is world-wide. Its body is flattened and completely divided into segments. The abdomen is short and the limbs on it are flattened into plates serving as gills. The eyes are set on the sides of the head. The seven pairs of legs, ending in sharp claws, are used for crawling, never for swimming. The jaws form a rasp-and-file. The right-hand jaw ends in a sharp point with a roughened file-like edge and this fits into a groove with a rasp-like surface on the left-hand half of the jaws.

Wreaking havoc

Gribbles attacking wood work in pairs. They first eat away a saucer-shaped depression in its surface, holding on by the hooks on the tips of their legs so they are not swept off by currents. From this they begin to tunnel obliquely downwards but soon level out and tunnel parallel to the surface at a depth of ⅛ in. for a distance of 1 in. As they do so they eat a hole upwards at intervals, like the holes in a flute, to let water in for breathing. The female is at the blind end of the tunnel and she, it appears, does most of the work. The behaviour of the two partners, when disturbed, also differs. The male retreats backwards, the female clings with the hooks at the ends of her legs to the surface of the tunnel, to avoid being pulled out. As a result of large numbers of gribbles eating into a post it begins to crumble and one infested for a long time becomes a rotted stump, pencil-pointed at the top. Creosoted wood has less chance against the gribble than against the shipworm, another marine animal that destroys timber.

Gribble damage
*The gribble (left) burrows into submerged timbers in such numbers that they crumble to rotten pointed stumps (below). It can destroy a wharf pile nearly a foot square in 2 years. Sectioned fragments showing gribble borings in piles from Southampton are seen centre below. **Chelura terebrans** (bottom) an amphipod, cannot burrow itself but lives in the tunnels made by gribbles.*

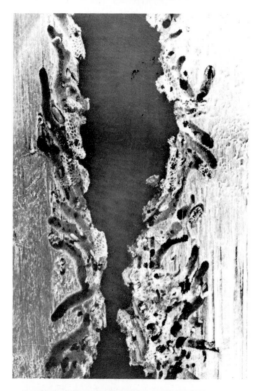

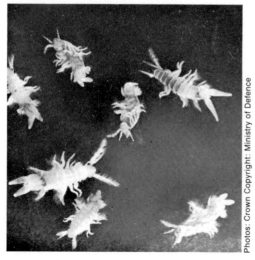

Chewing mainly for shelter

Although they appear to be eating the wood —they are able to digest it to some extent— they will also bore into the insulation of submarine cables, which is not digestible. Experiments, moreover, have shown that gribbles fed on filter paper only, can live twice as long as those kept without food. They feed mainly, however, on fungi that have entered the wood. Tests have shown that a gribble kept in water free of fungus, and given fungus-free wood to eat, dies in about 4 days. On the other hand, they live longer than this without wood if fungi are put into the water for them to eat.

Learning at mother's knee

Mating takes place when two gribbles have made a new burrow. The eggs are carried in a brood-pouch by the female, who lays three broods of 20–30 eggs in one year. The baby gribbles are miniatures of their parents when first hatched, and they soon start to make a burrow in the sides of the parental tunnel. Later, they pair up and move on to start their own burrows, beginning with the saucer-shaped depression in the surface of the wood.

Mighty atoms

Although gribbles must have been a nuisance to mariners and harbour-builders for centuries, they seem to have remained more or less unnoticed until the 19th century. William Dampier, famous English navigator, in the late 17th century, wrote of his wormy ship being attacked by small animals resembling sheep-lice. Not until 1811 was the species described and given a scientific name, and the common name, which seems to mean 'little grub', was not set forth in print until 1838. It has been said that the gribble was not discovered until Robert Stephenson found it was destroying the timber being used in the building of the Bell Rock lighthouse, but as Stephenson was only 8 years old when the animal was given its first scientific description this clearly must be incorrect. How much of a nuisance they are can be judged by the way they will destroy a stout wharf- or pier-pile nearly a foot square in about 2 years. The first attacks do not go deeper than ½ in., but as the outer layer crumbles and flakes off, battered by the waves, the newer surfaces are in turn attacked. All this is the result of multitudes of minute excavators busily biting and rasping, jerking their heads backwards and forwards, at the same time turning them, like so many terriers with an outsize in rats. The fragments of wood torn off are swallowed and each piece passes through the gribble in about 80 minutes, time enough for any fungus growing in the minute interstices of the wood to be digested.

Photos: Crown Copyright: Ministry of Defence

phylum	**Arthropoda**
class	**Crustacea**
order	**Isopoda**
family	**Limnoridae**
genus & species	*Limnoria lignorum*

Grosbeak

This is a collective name for a number of species of the finch family, having in common a stout conical beak. They include the hawfinch, scarlet grosbeak and pine grosbeak of Europe and a number of species in America. Among the latter are the black-headed, blue, blue-black, rose-breasted and evening grosbeaks of North America, as well as the pine grosbeak and the ultramarine grosbeak of South America. At other times birds in Africa and Asia— even the European greenfinch and bullfinch—have been called grosbeaks. Since there is not the space to give all these equal and adequate treatment the choice must be for the first species to be so named, and this seems to have been the hawfinch.

The names 'grosbeak' and 'hawfinch' appear to have come into general use at about the same time, towards the end of the 17th century. From then on writers on natural history in Britain spoke of the hawfinch as the common grosbeak. This probably indicated that the pine and scarlet grosbeaks, common on the continent of Europe, were occasionally and uncommonly seen in Britain. The choice is apt because of all the birds named the hawfinch has the most disproportionately large (or gross) beak.

Hawfinch quenches its thirst at a mossy pool.

The shy hawfinch

Perhaps the most surprising thing is that anyone should have called Britain's grosbeak, the hawfinch, common. It may be that our forebears were more observant than we are or that hawfinches were more numerous or less shy than they are today. The hawfinch is the largest British finch but with only a local distribution. It also ranges across Europe, into northern Africa, and across much of central Asia to Japan. It is 6½ in. long. The male is the more brightly coloured in spring and summer, in winter both sexes look more alike. The male is reddish-brown shading to greyish-white on the belly. The nape is grey, the throat black, the short tail is black and white and there is a white patch on the blue-black

Rose-breasted grosbeak of North America.

wings. The female is paler and less red. In winter hawfinches move about in flocks feeding on seeds. They can crack even cherry and olive stones in their beaks, and seeds and stones on the ground, neatly cracked in halves, tell of hawfinches having been there. In the kitchen garden empty pea pods testify to their visits in summer, but the birds themselves are seldom seen. They nest high up in trees and bushes, especially evergreens; the nest, made of twigs and roots lined with finer roots, hair or fibre, is usually on a horizontal bough. In April or May 4—6 eggs are laid.

Europe's grosbeaks . . .

The scarlet grosbeak, slightly smaller than the hawfinch, but with much the same habitat, ranges from eastern Europe over much of Asia. The male has a carmine head, breast and rump with brown wings and tail. The female lacks the red colouring. The pine grosbeak, a larger bird, 8 in. long, has much the same colouring but looks more like a large crossbill although its beak is straight. It lives in both pine forests and mixed woodlands in northern Europe, across northern Asia, and it is found over most of Canada and down into the western United States.

The scarlet grosbeak builds a nest of dead stalks and grass lined with roots, in bushes and low trees from ground level to a few feet up. For 12 days the hen alone incubates the 4—6 vivid blue eggs marked with chocolate spots, but both parents feed the chicks by regurgitation. The pine grosbeak nests usually in conifers, again at no great height. The hen alone builds a bullfinch-type nest of interlaced twigs and lined with fine roots, wiry grass and some moss. She alone incubates for 2 weeks the 4—5 greenish-blue eggs blotched and spotted with black or purplish-brown.

. . . and their American cousins

Three of the American grosbeaks belong to a subfamily of finches, of which the cardinal is a well known member. The rose-breasted and blue grosbeaks, both about the size of the hawfinch, are tropical species that have spread north into the southern United States. The first of these and the black-headed grosbeak, of western North America, are unusual among finches in that the male does most of the incubating. He often sings while doing so. The nest, built in deciduous

Hawfinch—note its disproportionately large beak.

woods, is a flimsy cup of fine roots in which 3—5 pale-blue eggs blotched with brown are laid. The rose-breasted grosbeak is well known for eating the Colorado beetle, which few other birds will touch. The blue-black grosbeak of Mexico to Bolivia is unusual in that both male and female sing while building their nest. The male ultramarine grosbeak is blue-black, the female a deep brown, and both keep together as a pair, the female singing almost as well as the male. They live at the edges of woodlands from Venezuela to Argentina.

A feature of this American group of grosbeaks is that those nesting in temperate latitudes lay an average of 4 eggs, while those in the tropics lay 2 but may have 3 broods a year.

Nutcracker beak

Although grosbeaks all have stout conical bills their food varies. Hawfinches mainly crack open stout seeds such as cherry and olive which we would need a hammer to break. The scarlet grosbeak eats small seeds, the pine grosbeak berries, small seeds, buds and some insects and the rose-breasted is renowned for eating a particularly noxious beetle. The hawfinch not only has the biggest beak but the accessories to make full use of it. In most birds the upper half of the beak is slightly moveable on the bones of the skull. This is especially noticeable in a parrot. In the hawfinch it is thickened, rigid and firmly fixed to the skull. Powerful muscles work the two halves of the beak, in particular an unusually stout muscle runs from the top of the beak over the top of the skull. Inside the beak, on the roof of the mouth, are horny pads. So although a hawfinch weighs less than 2 oz it can exert a pressure inside the beak of 159 lb.

class	**Aves**
order	**Passeriformes**
family	**Fringillidae**
genera & species	***Coccothraustes coccothraustes*** *hawfinch* ***Pinicola enucleator*** *pine grosbeak* ***Pheucticus ludovicianus*** *rose-breasted grosbeak* ***P. melanocephalus*** *blackheaded grosbeak, others*

Ground beetle

Most ground beetles look like any other beetles, but some are quite the reverse. The fiddle beetles **Mormolyce** of Indonesia and Malaysia are extraordinary looking insects, 4 in. long with the head and thorax long and slender and the elytra flattened and extending out on each side, so the beetle has the general shape of a violin. They are not uncommon in the humid rain forest, but 50 or 60 years ago they were believed to be as rare as they are remarkable, and museums paid high prices for them.

Ground beetles form the Carabidae, a family of beetles of cosmopolitan distribution. They are closely related to the tiger beetles (Cicindelidae) and like them are predators both as larvae and adults, the latter being usually long-legged active runners with large toothed or pointed jaws. Their eyes are normally well developed and the antennae, in which the sense of smell is situated, are long and mobile. They do not usually fly very readily and in many of them the wings are vestigial or absent altogether. The wing-cases (elytra) are usually polished, often grooved or striated, and coloured black or dark metallic green, blue or violet. The end joints of the legs have five segments.

About 340 species of ground beetles are found in Britain. The genera **Carabus** and **Calosoma** include some of the largest species, up to 1 in. long. **Abax** and **Nebria** are medium-sized and small beetles found in ground debris and under stones.

Mainly night hunters

Most of the ground beetles are nocturnal, hiding away by day. The active black beetles so often found under logs or stones are almost all carabids. The nocturnal species most probably hunt by scent, though normally their eyes are well developed. In some of those living in the perpetual darkness of deep caves the eyes are much reduced or absent.

The beautiful bronze-green species of Calosoma are ground beetles only by classification, for they live among the branches and foliage of trees, subsisting largely on caterpillars. They have well-developed wings and can fly.

Larvae work unseen

Like all beetles the carabids undergo complete metamorphosis with larva, pupa and imago stages. The larvae are elongated and active with the legs well developed. They live underground, under loose bark and in such places as compost and manure heaps where there is an abundance of other insect life to provide prey. Nearly all are carnivorous, but a few feed on seeds and cereals or burrow in fungus. The larvae usually make a cavity in the earth in which to pupate. Most ground beetles have one generation a year, but full details of the life cycle are not known in many species. Some of the larger kinds live as adults for several years.

is the gypsy moth, which was introduced from Europe about 1868. One of the means used to control it has been the deliberate introduction of the European beetle *Calosoma sycophanta*. Some success has been achieved, but nothing approaching complete control of the moth.

Some ground beetles are specialised feeders, and there are several groups which prey particularly on snails. These are adapted for probing into the shells of their victims. The British species *Cychrus*

too closely. At least one entomologist has received a squirt of liquid in the eye from this beetle which blinded him for 5 minutes or more. It is interesting that *Cychrus* gives warning by making a creaking sound (stridulating) before it discharges its 'tear gas'.

Most remarkable of all the carabids which defend themselves in this way are the bombardier beetles *Brachinus*, one species of which is quite common in chalky districts in Britain. The spray of liquid which it emits from its hind end is discharged with

Anthony Bannister: NHPA

AB Klots

Night hunters

◁ *Carabus olympiae, Italian version of the common violet ground beetle of Britain and one of a world-wide muster of 20 000 species.*
△ *Jaws of the South African ground beetle* **Anthia thoracica** *(approx 3 times life size).*
△ ▷ *The searcher or caterpillar hunter* **Calosoma scrutator** *destroys great numbers of caterpillars (hence its common name) and other insects.*

Hunting with a sweet tooth

As active predators there is no doubt that ground beetles keep down the numbers of many harmful insects. In continental Europe the handsome *Carabus auratus* (a rarity in Britain) is known to prey largely on the very harmful larvae of cockchafer beetles. The species of *Calosoma*, already mentioned as living among trees, destroy great numbers of caterpillars. One of the most serious insect pests of North America

caraboides has the head and thorax much narrower than the hind part of the body, and in another genus of snail predators *Scaphinotus* the mandibles are elongated and hooked. Not all ground beetles confine themselves entirely to animal food. *Harpalus ruficornis* has been found damaging strawberries, and the large and very common violet ground beetle *Carabus violaceus* is often found by moth collectors who use the 'sugaring' method. The beetles climb the tree trunks that have been daubed with the sweet treacle-and-rum bait and eagerly suck up the drops. They are often there when the lure has failed to attract even one moth.

Chemical warfare

A number of ground beetles are known to defend themselves by emitting ill-smelling or corrosive liquids. The snail-eating *Cychrus caraboides* should never be inspected

explosive force, making an audible 'crack', and instantly vapourises into a tiny cloud. Close study has shown that hydroquinones and hydrogen peroxide are simultaneously secreted in a gland near the beetle's tail, and they react instantly, releasing oxygen with enough force to shoot out the corrosive quinones with a small explosion. A bombardier beetle can fire as many as 20 charges in rapid succession, effectively driving off nearly all predators, from toads to ants, spiders and other carabid beetles.

class	**Insecta**
order	**Coleoptera**
family	**Carabidae**
genera	**Abax, Anthia, Brachinus, Calasoma, Carabus, Cychrus, Harpalus, Mormolyce, Nebria, Scaphinotus,** *others*

Ground squirrel

Ground squirrels include two most remarkable animals, one living in hot desert, the other under arctic conditions.

There are 230 or more species of squirrels: flying, tree and ground squirrels. It is not easy in some instances to draw a line between the last two as some tree squirrels spend a lot of time on the ground and some ground squirrels often take to the trees. In some ground squirrels the tail is bushy but never so much as in tree squirrels, and it is usually not so long.

Ground squirrels are 8—31 in. long of which $\frac{1}{3}-\frac{1}{2}$ is tail, the proportions varying with the species. There are three kinds of colouring: almost uniformly yellowish grey, the same but with the back lightly spotted with light buff or yellowish white, and brownish grey with dark stripes, often with lines of yellowish spots. Their ears are small, their legs short and their feet bigger by comparison with tree squirrels such as the grey and the red. A few of the 32 species live in Africa, but most of the others live in North America, from Mexico to Alaska, where some of them are called gophers. There are seven species ranging from eastern Europe across northern and central Asia, which are usually called susliks and spermophiles.

Life among logs and rocks

Ground squirrels are active by day, alert to danger, sitting up on their haunches or standing on their hindlegs to watch for enemies, giving a twittering or whistling alarm call when an intruder is sighted. Some, like the rock ground squirrel, live in groups, others are more solitary. All either dig their own burrows or find shelter low in hollow trees, under logs, among rocks or in similar sheltered places.

In the southern parts of their range ground squirrels are active throughout the year except during bad weather. Farther north they hibernate, the length of the winter sleep being longer to the northward.

Cheek pouches for carrying food

The diet of ground squirrels includes seeds, nuts, roots, leaves, bulbs, fungi, insects, birds and eggs. They will also eat carrion. The amounts eaten of these foods vary from one species to another. The rock ground squirrel eats mainly plant food with some insects, Franklin's ground squirrel eats mainly plant food, with some insects but adds toads, frogs, mice and birds, and the thirteen-striped ground squirrel eats only a small proportion of vegetable matter. Food is hoarded, quantities of seeds, nuts and grain being carried away in cheek pouches to be stored.

Large families—not always welcome

There is usually one litter a year but there may be two in some species, and litters are usually large, up to 12 or more, born after

Peter Johnson

Joseph Van Wormer

Fred Bruemmer

Active in feverish heat

A remarkable ground squirrel is that known as the antelope ground squirrel, living in the deserts of the southwestern United States. It gets its name from the way it carries its tail high exposing a white rump, like the pronghorn antelope. The antelope ground squirrel runs a fever every day yet is never ill from it. When the air temperature is 43°C/110°F or more and the sand beneath its feet is 66°C/150°F the squirrel dashes about from place to place. It shows no signs of discomfort even when its own body temperature rises above 110°F. It can stand exceptionally high temperatures because it loses little water in its natural functions. Its urine, for example, is almost solid. It does not sweat but loses heat by conduction, convection and radiation. To get rid of heat it retires to a shady spot and flattens itself on the ground or else it dives down into its burrow. Within 3 minutes its temperature drops from 42°C/107°F to 33°C/100°F. If things get bad it can lose heat by panting and it can, as an emergency measure, cool itself another way. It drools and then spreads the saliva over its head with its forepaws, as if washing itself. At a pinch the squirrel can endure several hours of the blazing desert heat by running around with its head soaking wet.

At the other extreme, in Alaska, at Point Barrow, the snow lasts for most of the year and the ground is permanently frozen to a depth of hundreds of feet. During the short summer the earth may thaw for a few inches, at most a few feet. There lives the Barrow ground squirrel, on 'islands' of sandy soil, sleeping 9 months of the year. In May this squirrel looks out, after waking, on a still snow-covered world and feeds on stores of leaves, stems, roots and seeds laid up the previous year. As the air warms slightly the ground squirrels mate, the young are born 25 days later, towards the end of June. Their eyes open at 3 weeks, and 2 days after this they begin foraging. In a little over a month they must grow, dig their own burrow and provision it before going to sleep for 9 months. For the adults things are little better because they have the burden of bringing up a family, feeding to recover their strength, lay in stores for the winter and re-furbish the burrow, all in 3 months. This is why the Barrow ground squirrel works for 17 hours each day, with restless urgency, whatever the weather, undeterred by rain and bitter winds.

*Above left: Who goes there? A South African ground squirrel **Geosciurus inauris** stands erect in typical posture on lookout for danger. Left: White-tailed antelope squirrel gets its name from holding its tail high and exposing a white rump, like the pronghorn antelope. Above: Warm coat for Arctic ground squirrel.*

a gestation of 23–28 days. The babies are born naked, blind and toothless. The eyes open 3–4 weeks later, and soon after this the young leave the nest. When food is plentiful high populations build up and together with other rodents, ground squirrels can cause widespread damage to crops. Some species are suspected of being carriers of diseases, including bubonic plague. The golden-mantled ground squirrel of the Rockies is one. It also tends to cause erosion by burrowing in the mountainside. The numbers of ground squirrels are controlled to a large degree by natural enemies: weasels, lynxes and hawks. In North America the coyote and bobcat are two of their main enemies. The golden-mantled ground squirrel readily forages on crops, where these are available. Elsewhere it visits houses and camp sites searching for food, and as a result is something of a favourite.

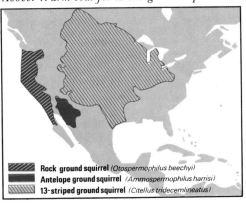

Rock ground squirrel (*Otospermophilus beechyi*)
Antelope ground squirrel (*Ammospermophilus harrisi*)
13-striped ground squirrel (*Citellus tridecemlineatus*)

class	**Mammalia**
order	**Rodentia**
family	**Sciuridae**
genera & species	***Citellus tridecemlineatus*** *13-striped ground squirrel* **C. parryi** *Barrow ground squirrel* **C. harrisi** *antelope ground squirrel* **C. leucurus** *white-tailed antelope ground squirrel* **C. beechyi** *rock ground squirrel* *others*

Grouper

There are 400 species of related fishes forming the family Serranidae which are variously spoken of as groupers, sea bass, sea perch, or rock cod. Some among them have more exclusive names such as wreckfish, jewfish and soapies. The name 'grouper' has nothing to do with living in shoals but is from the Portuguese name for the fish **garupa** which may in turn be derived from a South American Indian name.

Serranids (groupers or sea perches) live mostly in tropical seas, but a few live in temperate waters and some in fresh water. Most of them are similar in appearance, heavy-bodied with large heads, strong jaws and capacious

mouths armed with many strong, needle-sharp, backward-pointing teeth. In some species the teeth are arrow-headed. When the mouth of a large grouper is gaping its interior has the same wicked look as a shark's mouth, and like sharks they snap up any animal food. The fins are typically perch-like, with two dorsal fins, the one in front being spiny, the rear one having soft rays. Serranids range in size from those that are little more than an inch long when fully grown to the Queensland grouper **Epinephelus lanceolatus** of the Indo-Pacific said to grow to 12 ft long and nearly half a ton in weight. It is reported to stalk divers as a cat does a mouse and one has actually rushed a diver in an apparent attack. There are unconfirmed stories about this giant swallowing skin-divers.

Active and passive

The habits of groupers are varied. Some lurk on the bottom and wait for prey to come to them; others swim about, actively searching. An example of the first is a serranid known as the wreckfish or stone bass *Polyprion americanus*, up to 6 ft long, common in the Mediterranean and tropical Atlantic. It takes up position near rocky reefs and is also noted for haunting wrecks where it has at times been caught in large numbers. By contrast, the striped bass *Roccus saxatilis* swims about, and because of its active nature makes a good sporting fish which gives the fisherman something to test his mettle. Its original home was the Atlantic seaboard of North America but it has been taken across the continent and released off the Pacific coast. There, it quickly became established and is now the basis of a commercial fishery. The striped bass ascends rivers to spawn, but several of

968

◁ *Giant swallower—the Queensland grouper may grow to 12 ft long and weigh nearly half a ton. There are unconfirmed reports that this giant has swallowed skin-divers.*

△ *An inquisitive 30lb brown spotted grouper swims unafraid by cameraman and comrade.*
▽ *Golden striped grouper, small by comparison, being only 5 in. long, frequents rock pools.*

through a period when they were both female and male—or neither female nor male—and incapable of breeding. Once they have turned into males there are still the remains of egg-producing tissues in their reproductive organs, but for all practical purposes they are males. This unusual situation has not been fully explored in any one species of grouper, and it has been studied in only a few species, but it is suspected that all groupers show this unusual reproductive change to a greater or lesser extent.

Quick-change artistes

As well as their unusual sex behaviour groupers are noted for their remarkable colours and changes in colour. Many of them are covered all over with hexagonal reddish-brown spots bordered with white or blue, a pattern reminiscent of the colouring of a giraffe. The hamlet *Hypoplectrus* of the Caribbean is generally orange with black spots or blotches and with blue lines, the fins being checkered with orange and blue. A complete list of the colour changes it can undergo becomes, however, almost a catalogue of rainbow hues: deep indigo blue with bands and bars of black and dark blue; pink-brown or violet-black body with yellow or black fins; orange with blue, black or violet spots; yellow and black body with a blue head. The Nassau grouper *Epinephelus striatus* has 8 colour phases, including uniformly dark, creamy-white, dark above white below, back banded and belly white, light brown all over, pale with faint dark markings, light-coloured body with dark bands and mottlings and blue with vertical brown bands. None of these can be called normal and a collection of groupers in an aquarium may show all these colours and each fish may pass from one to the other. No two photographs of Nassau groupers ever show the same colours, and the individual fish may pass through several of these phases in a few minutes. Whatever the meaning of these colour changes, and we are not certain what it may be, all the vari-coloured Nassau groupers in an aquarium will become light coloured with dark bands and mottlings when they are alarmed and dash for security among the crevices in rocks. A fisherman who speared a grouper in the Indian Ocean saw the fish take shelter in a clump of coral and refuse to leave it. As it lay there the red spots on its body exactly matched the coral polyps. Perhaps the biggest surprise came to someone who watched a grouper, blue with brown bands, swim into a clump of coral. When it came out a few minutes later it was brilliant yellow with black dots.

its relatives in North America are wholly freshwater. These include the yellow bass *Morone mississipiensis* and the white bass *R. chrysops*, each 1 ft or more long.

Another grouper with a commercial value is the 10in. golden-striped grouper *Grammistes sexlineatus*, of the Indo-Pacific seas, that is a favourite with some aquarists. The name 'jewfish' has been given to several different fishes but really belongs to a grouper *Epinephelus itajara*, which also has a commercial value of sorts. It grows to 6 ft long and 600 lb weight and is a dark green, heavy-headed and sluggish fish with rough scales, living in fairly deep waters of the Caribbean and Mexican coasts. Its flesh is not highly valued but it is prized by the sports fisherman. The name 'jewfish' is believed to have been given because the fish has very obvious fins and scales and therefore qualifies as a clean fish according to Levitical law. Around Bermuda groupers

make up three-quarters of the commercial fish catch.

Unusual members of the family are the soapfishes *Rypticus* living on both sides of the Atlantic. When alarmed they give out a slime from the skin and also thresh about, the slime becoming beaten up into foam like soapsuds.

Male and female in one
The family Serranidae is remarkable for having several members that are hermaphrodite. A true hermaphrodite is an individual that has both male and female reproductive organs. The young groupers mature at 2–5 years of age, depending upon the species. They then are females, able to lay eggs, but they also have the beginnings of organs that will later produce sperm. For all practical purposes, however, they are females. At 7–10 years the females finally turn into males, having passed

class	**Osteichthyes**
order	**Perciformes**
family	**Serranidae**
genera & species	***Epinephelus lanceolatus*** Queensland grouper ***Grammistes sexlineatus*** golden striped grouper ***Epinephelus* sp.** spotted groupers others

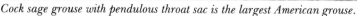

Cock sage grouse with pendulous throat sac is the largest American grouse.

Camouflaged red grouse hen with her brood on Scottish upland moor.

Grouse

The name grouse, originally used in the 16th century for the red grouse and black grouse, has been taken across the Atlantic and given to a number of North American birds, such as the ruffed, spruce, sage, blue and sharptailed grouse. All these belong to a single family of game-birds, which includes the capercaillie (p 365), the prairie chicken and the ptarmigan, which receive special treatment elsewhere.

The 18 species of the family Tetraonidae range in size from a domestic hen to a turkey. They live mainly in the northern parts of the Northern Hemisphere. In all the male is markedly larger than the female. Their legs are partly or completely feathered, the toes are edged with comb-like filaments or are covered with feathers, their nostrils are covered with feathers and there is usually a bare patch of skin over each eye. Their food is mainly vegetarian, buds, leaves, shoots, seeds and berries, but they also eat insects. Grouse will burrow into snow to feed.

Game bird of the heather
The red grouse lives on upland moors or low-lying peaty bogs and in places where heather is the main plant. The male grows to 15½ in. long, the female to 14 in. The summer plumage of the male is reddish brown marked with black and buff bars, the female being similar but more yellow. The winter plumage of the male is more red and the bars less marked, the female in winter having a plumage like that of the male in summer. Essentially ground birds, they rise when flushed with a whirring of wings, to travel for a short distance alternating rapid wing beats with long glides on bowed wings. At the approach of the breeding season the males take up territories which they defend from rival or neighbouring males. Males display at each other by stretching up,

fanning the tail, and blowing out the red wattle over each eye. In courtship displays the male takes up position on a rock or a hummock and from it jumps into the air and descends on down-curved wings which it beats rapidly just before touchdown. Monogamous, the red grouse makes scrapes in the ground as part of the courtship and eventually the female uses one of these, lined with dried grass or twigs, for her 6–11 yellowish eggs blotched with dark or reddish brown. She alone incubates them for 3 weeks and leads the chicks away when hatched, brooding them from time to time, the male being in attendance all the time.

Red grouse or willow grouse?
The red grouse lives in Wales, the northern half of England and Scotland, and there is a separate subspecies in Ireland, but it has been introduced into other parts of England. Some ornithologists take the view that it belongs to the same species as the willow grouse, differing from it in not having a distinct change of plumage, from brown in summer to white in winter. The willow grouse ranges across northern Europe, northern Asia and northern Canada.

Blackcock and greyhen
The black grouse has a similar geographical range to the willow grouse except that it is absent from North America and is found in central and parts of southern Europe. Their habitats differ, however, the black grouse living on the fringes of moors among heather, scrub or rushes, up to 1400 ft. The male or blackcock is a glossy black with a lyre-shaped tail, white wing bar and under tail coverts and a red wattle above the eye. The female or greyhen is brown freckled and barred with black. The main difference from the red grouse is that blackcock are polygamous, with special display grounds or leks. The males indulge in communal dances, bowing with fanned tails, strutting, stretching up their necks, jumping into the air, engaging in ritualized fighting and at times behaving as if in a frenzy. This is accompanied by crowing, wheezing, sneezing and other loud notes. The female is attracted to the leks to choose her mate,

who continues disporting while she goes away to make a nest and raise a family.

The North American scene
The ruffed grouse, ranging from Alaska to Newfoundland, is monogamous. The male is a rich brown with a barred tail. He performs his dances on a log, spreading his wings to beat them with a drumming sound which carries long distances through the woods. When the female, drawn by the sounds, comes near he raises the black tufts of feathers on his neck, raises his tail feathers and struts before her. The female builds the nest and raises the family of 11 or more, with the male in attendance. The spruce grouse is monogamous also and his courtship is similar to that of the ruffed grouse but carried out in pine forests rather than deciduous woodland. The blue grouse of the Rockies is another monogamous species. The male also displays to the tune of loud bubbling hoots.

Blowing out his chest
The sharptailed grouse is polygamous, like the black grouse, and in and around the pine forests of western North America the males find flat grassland to perform their communal dances. Each postures and poses, with neck stretchings and tail fannings, and wings spread and drooping with shuffles and dances, calling loudly. The hens pay for this show by shouldering the family burdens unaided. The largest of the North American grouse, and the most spectacular, is the polygamous sage grouse. The males may weigh up to 8 lb, against 1½ lb for a red grouse, and measure 2¼ ft including a long tail. In display this tail is erected in a spiky fan and two air-sacs on the throat are inflated, the size and colour of oranges. He struts and bows deeply, booming and groaning and vibrating his stiffly spread wings.

Enemies all around
The enemies of grouse can be best understood from a study made of those attacking red grouse. They include fox, cat, stoat, weasel and rat on the ground. From the air come short-eared owls, carrion crows,

Arthur Christiansen

Territory discussion: beautiful black grouse encounter one another in defence of their territories.

Cyr Color Agency

Springtime booming: Prairie chicken in display.

Charles W Schwartz

peregrine, merlin, harriers, goshawks and golden eagles. Of these, grouse seem to fear eagles most and their reaction to the others can vary with the age of the bird and especially with the season. A hen with eggs or chicks has been seen to repel a pair of crows and a cock on his territory drove off a harrier.

Turning the tables

The reactions to man vary also. On windy or on winter days with snow, red grouse may flush at over half a mile but on calm days a man may get within 150 ft of them. In spring and summer he may almost tread on them before they will fly up, and he may be able to stroke a sitting hen. So far as the cock is concerned, his display to repel rivals or to attract a hen have something more in them than mere show. He may threaten men or vehicles venturing near him and exceptionally he may attack and peck people with unexpected fury, like the capercaillie.

class	**Aves**
order	**Galliformes**
family	**Tetraonidae**
genera & species	**Lagopus scoticus** *red grouse*
	Tetrao tetrix *black grouse*
	Bonasa umbellus *ruffed grouse*
	Dendrophagus canadensis *spruce grouse*
	Dendrophagus obscurus *blue grouse*
	Centrocercus urophasianus *sage grouse*
	Tympanuchus phasianellus *sharptailed grouse*
	others

Bird of the brush: courtship display of the sage grouse. A strutting male begins his display by fanning out his tail feathers and then puffs out a pouch in his neck, exposing the inflatable air sacs. At the height of his display to attract the much smaller hen, his pouch and sacs are so large that his head disappears in a roll of flesh and feathers.

971

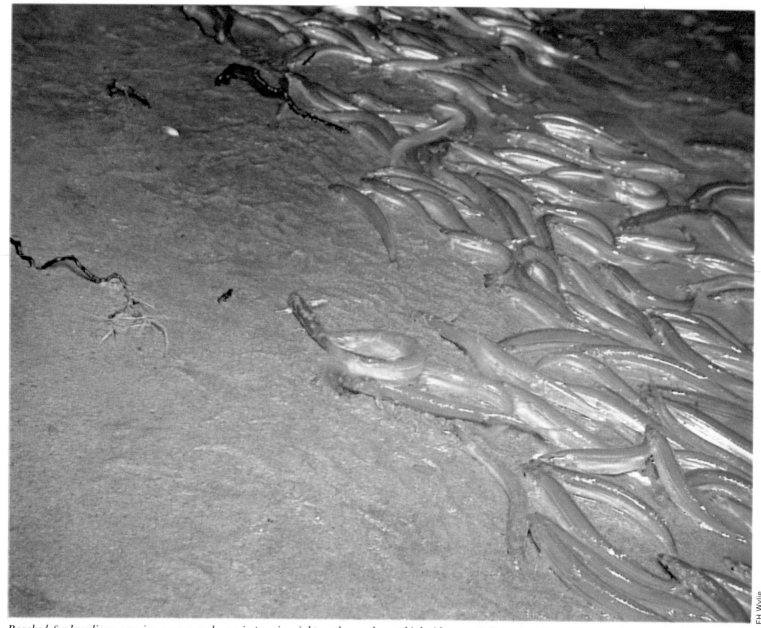

Beached for breeding: grunion masses make an impressive sight as they gather at high tide on a Californian shore. These fascinating scenes occur from late February to early September following a new or full moon. The certainty of large numbers makes for an easy harvest for seabirds and humans.

FH Wylie

Grunion

A fish with most spectacular breeding habits that attract hordes of visitors to the coast of California, the grunion belongs to the family Atherinidae, related to the mullets. The members of this family are also known in Britain as sand smelts, and in the United States as silversides.

The 150 species of atherinids are not true smelts and the name 'silversides' is more descriptive of them. They are mainly marine fishes of tropical and temperate seas. They differ from true smelts in having two dorsal fins, the front one spiny, in lacking a lateral line, and in having a broad silver band along each flank. Some silversides live in the brackish waters of estuaries, others in rivers or lakes. Freshwater species in Central America are important food-fishes.

Best known of the family, the grunion is 5—7 in. long, and lives in the inshore waters of southern and Lower California.

Beaching themselves to spawn
For 3—4 nights following a new or a full moon, when high tides occur, grunions can be seen from Californian beaches, riding in on the surf at extreme high tide. For 1—3 hours, until the tide begins to ebb, the females leap from the surf onto the beach, wriggle into the sand and lay their eggs at a depth of 2 in. Each is accompanied by a male, sometimes two or three. They wrap themselves around her and fertilise her eggs as they are laid. Having spawned they flop back into the water.

With the next tide, and for days following, the water does not reach so high up on the beach. The eggs are ready to hatch a week later but nothing happens until, at the next spring tide, a fortnight later, the surf goes into the sand and washes the eggs. These then hatch in about 3 minutes. Succeeding waves wash the young grunion out of the sand and carry them down the beach and away into the sea.

This happens from late February to early September. One species spawns only at night and they seem to have an uncanny knowledge of the state of the tides. A second

species, living along the coasts farther north, spawns by day, also on extreme high tides, and in doing so is exposed to attacks by seabirds.

Legendary dancing fishes
Bruce Arthur Woodling, in *Sea Frontiers*, the journal of the International Oceanographic Foundation at Miami, has described how at the stroke of midnight, under a full moon, thousands of silvery fishes leave the sea to perform a mysterious dance on the beach. They sparkle like diamonds on the beach, from Point Conception in the north to Baja California in Mexico, to the south, a distance of several hundred miles. At its highest intensity there may be more fish visible than sand, creating an illusion of a silver canopy over the beach. This is the sight that regularly draws large numbers of visitors, some to watch the sight for the first time, but most of them to gather an easy harvest of fish. If the scene is fascinating the biological facts associated with it are hardly less impressive.

Just before the spawning run, the shallow waters just beyond the edge of the tide are crowded with jostling fishes awaiting their opportunity. At first a few throw themselves onto the beach singly. These are males; there is a popular belief they are scouts, and that if they are prevented from returning to the sea the rest will not venture out. Experience suggests this may be so because when these first fishes are picked up by over-eager visitors the spawning run may fail on that part of the beach. It is believed also that the light from hundreds of fires along the more popular beaches, lighted to cook the fish, may inhibit the run.

Each female grunion is out of the water for several minutes but the actual spawning takes less than a minute. During that time she thrusts her tail into the sand, anchors herself by her pectoral fins, arches her body and waggles her tail in a drilling action so she is finally half-buried. At this point she lays her 1 000 – 3 000 eggs, according to her age, a process each female repeats 4 – 8 times in a season.

Far from being chaotic, as the poetic account of sparkling dancing fishes suggests, for each individual fish it is a matter of precise timing. Not only must it be aware of the day and time of extreme high tide, it must not be too early. As the waves of a flowing tide tend to remove sand from the beach and the ebb tide throws up sand the eggs must be laid after the tide has turned. Otherwise the eggs would be uncovered and washed away. Full advantage must be taken of the ebbing tide before it has receded too far down the beach, so spawning should start as early as the ebb, and here also the fishes need an awareness of what is happening.

Shaken awake

If the eggs were washed out of the sand without time to develop, they would not survive. Experiment has shown that grunion eggs develop normally when embedded in sand and die when floating free in water. What makes them hatch on the next high tide? If allowed a week in which to develop the eggs will hatch as soon as they are shaken. This, in nature, is what happens when the next high spring tide stirs up the sand. The eggs are shaken and hatch, and the young escape to the sea before the first females come out to lay their fresh batch of eggs. It is all so beautifully and automatically timed, with adequate safeguards all along (except against the human marauders!) in a rhythm that fully justifies the comparison with a dance. And any eggs the waters may not reach on one tide will almost certainly be shaken by another a fortnight later or by one a fortnight after that. In the meantime growth of the baby fish within is suspended, but is ready to be resumed and the eggs hatched as soon as they are shaken. The advantage of this complex spawning is that the eggs develop safe from the many hungry mouths in the sea.

class	**Osteichthyes**
order	**Atheriniformes**
family	**Atherinidae**
genera & species	**Leuresthes tenuis** *spawns at night* **Hubbsiella sardina** *spawns by day*

Fertility rites

Grunions riding in on the surf at extreme high tide on a Californian beach. This occurs for 3 – 4 nights following a new or full moon when high tides occur. Until the tide begins to ebb, the females wriggle into the sand to lay their eggs at a depth of 2 in. (above). Each female is accompanied by a male who wraps himself around her and fertilises the eggs as they are laid (right). After the rigours of spawning, a female grunion issues a final burst of energy and wriggles out of the sand, returning to the sea until she is ready to spawn again. During her spawning activity, a female may, however, be surrounded by as many as nine males. This is seen below, the female's head poking out from the mass of males.

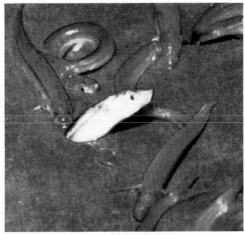

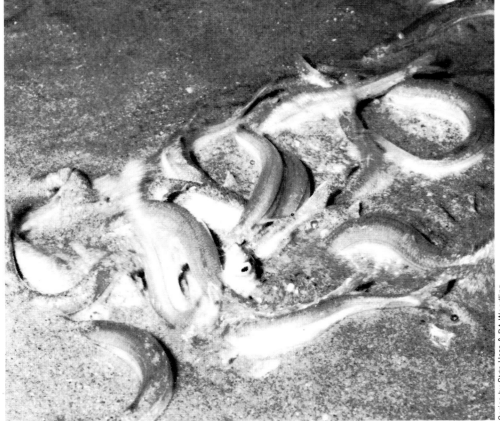

Gudgeon

The gudgeon is a small member of the carp family, rarely longer than 6 in. or 5 oz weight. It is grey-green to blackish-grey on the back, lighter on the flanks but silvery with dark spots underneath. Its scales are large and there is a barbel at each corner of the mouth. The gudgeon is found in streams, rivers and lakes across Europe except in Spain and Greece.

The bronze to green gudgeon has been described as a smaller and prettier edition of the barbel, which grows up to 3 ft in length and 20 lb weight in England, although in continental Europe it grows up to 33 lb, and even 50 lb fish have been reported from the Rhine and Danube. Conversely, the barbel has been called a giant gudgeon. In England it was once common in the rivers Thames and Trent, but is generally much smaller in size in the first and has disappeared from the second. It was introduced into the Stour 50 years ago and has from there reached the Hampshire Avon, while other barbels were introduced into the Severn.

Moustachioed bottom-dwellers

The gudgeon lives in slow waters, often keeping near the bank in large shoals near the bottom. Sand or gravel beds are preferred. The barbel keeps at the bottom, also in shoals, but in deeper water, being found especially in weir pools, in early summer. It favours especially well-aerated waters. In winter it lies torpid in deep water, and tends to hide away by day.

Both fishes, as the shape of the snout and mouth, as well as the presence of barbels indicate, are bottom feeders. The gudgeon is wholly carnivorous. The barbel feeds mostly at night, on insects and their larvae, snails, worms, sometimes small fry. It also eats plant food, rooting for this in the mud of the banks or in the bottom with its pointed snout. It will also eat the roots of water plants. Its method of feeding and the wide diet taken caused Frank Buckland to speak of it as a 'regular fresh-water pig'.

Spawning over gravel

The gudgeon spawns in running water in May and June. Each female lays 1 000 – 3 000 transparent eggs that stick together in small clumps on the bottom, only a few eggs being laid at a time. These hatch in 10 days, the baby fishes carrying at first a large yolk-sac. Barbel spawn at the same time of year but on gravel beds in deep water. Each female lays on average 9 000 eggs which she covers with gravel, and these hatch in about a fortnight.

Fighting fish

Although so similar, except in size, there is a marked contrast between the two fishes in the fisherman's eyes. Gudgeon are described as fish that are caught by accident, or with a red worm or even bread paste. The barbel has fighting qualities that make it a splendid fish, which may in the end break quite strong line if care is not taken. Partly this comes from its larger size but it is more due to its lightning rushes, its rolling tactics and dogged persistence, and to some extent to its living where there are underwater snags. It has been credited with trying, when hooked, to saw through the line with its dorsal fin or break it with blows of its tail.

Tasty dishes

The opinions expressed about the palatability of the two fishes have been conflicting. At various times, and by various writers, gudgeon have been described as fit only for bait to catch better fishes. Another writer thinks they make a delightful dish when cooked in hot fat, and garnished with red pepper and lemon juice, while a third writer recommends cooking them on the river bank. This last is sound advice if only because the more quickly fish are cooked after being landed the better (by far) is the flavour. This may also explain the popularity of gudgeon in former times — and there used to be a regular fishery — because it was a fish easy to keep alive in fresh water until it was required. This may also account for the various descriptions of it: sweet, tender, delicate flavour, delightful, tasty, wholesome.

Its larger relative, the barbel, has been called all manner of names, from evil fish to uninteresting, a fish of medium quality flesh only to be tolerated if made palatable by elaborate cooking. It is true that the hard roe is poisonous and may affect the flesh adjacent to it. Yet in the days of Elizabeth I the barbel was of sufficient value as a fish to be protected by special statute.

R Boardman

△ Barbel searches for food using its barbels.

Geoffrey Kinns: AFA

▽ Gudgeons frequent slow freshwaters of Europe.

class	Osteichthyes
order	Cypriniformes
family	Cyprinidae
genera	*Gobio gobio* gudgeon
& species	*Barbus barbus* barbel

Guenon

*The term 'guenon' is used for any member of the monkey genus **Cerco-pithecus**. There are some 10—20 species forming a very mixed company with a gay assortment of colours, some of which probably help the monkeys to recognize their fellows quickly. Their interrelationships are poorly known. All are medium-sized or small monkeys 28—70 in. long including the tail, which forms from ½—⅔ of the total length. They have dexterous grasping hands and feet, short faces and very brightly coloured fur.*

Monkeys with fine colour-schemes

Guenons are some of the best known and most colourful monkeys. The green monkey, also known as grivet or vervet in different parts of its range, is greenish with a black face, white throat and white whiskers. The male has a bright blue or turquoise scrotum. It lives in the open savannah areas of most of Africa south of the Sahara. The blue monkey is blue-grey with black arms and legs and bushy cheek-whiskers. It lives in the forests of East and Central Africa. Some races have a golden-hued back. The red-tailed monkey is olive-green with a red tail, white nose, and white cheeks crossed by a black line. It lives in the forests of East Africa. It is closely related to a West African species known as the putty-nosed monkey. The Diana monkey is a deep blackish-purple with a red area on the back, a white thigh-stripe, white crescent on the forehead and long white back-curving beard. It is restricted to West Africa. The De Brazza monkey, a very robust, thickset species of East and Central Africa, greyish-speckled—with a white beard and chestnut forehead stripe. Hamlyn's monkey, a rare species from the eastern Congo, has a white stripe running down the nose, and a cape of hair covering the ears. The moustached monkey, distinguished by its blue and white moustache, is a small species from the swampy forests of western Equatorial Africa (Gabon, Cameroun). The talapoin is the smallest of all Old World monkeys. Green, with white hairs radiating fanlike from the cheeks, it lives in swampy forests of Gabon, and in the eastern Congo.

Pacifist societies

The easiest to study is the green monkey because it lives in fairly open country. JS Gartlan studied those living on Lolui island, in Lake Victoria, where there are about 1 500 of them. Green monkeys live in groups of 6—20, with an average of 12, the groups having home ranges which overlap and have trees or clumps of bushes at their centres. Each such clump is the base for at least one group, and some of the larger clumps contain up to four groups. All green monkeys belong to a group. The solitary individuals and all-male groups found in other monkeys are not found in green monkeys, although some individuals may be somewhat on the outskirts of their groups. All ages and both sexes are represented in a group but there are slightly

Born a jockey: for the first few weeks a baby vervet hangs upside down clinging to its mother's hair.

Jane Burton: Photo Res

fewer males than females, in a ratio of one to 1·4. When two groups meet there are no threats or fights although there may be some chasing. The group sleeps at the top of the tree or bush, which is at the centre of the home range, and feeds there in the early morning and in the evening. Towards midday it begins to move down into the undergrowth and out on to the open ground. The group may scatter widely while foraging, with as much as 300 yd between the most distant members.

Although their habitat is very different, blue monkeys and red-tailed monkeys seem to have a very similar type of social organisation, although they only rarely come to the ground.

Crop-raiding guenons

Green monkeys and red-tailed monkeys feed mainly on leaves but eat some fruit and flowers. Diana monkeys are said to be entirely fruit-eaters. Some guenons eat insects, birds' eggs and young birds, but this seems to be rare. They rarely drink, getting most of their moisture from the rain which clings to vegetation. They have been seen running their fingers along a rain-wet leaf and licking off the water. Some guenons raid gardens and are regarded as pests. Every year drives are held in Sierra Leone and other parts of Africa when hundreds of monkeys are slaughtered; unfortunately the tree-top dwellers as well as the crop raiders.

Arboreal amble: a distinctive spot-nosed monkey moves with a high degree of finesse through a canopy of foliage in Ghana.

Monkeys save the children

Like other monkeys, guenons breed through-out the year, the females coming into heat about once a month. In red-tailed monkeys babies tend to be born early in the year. The gestation is about 7 months. Courtship is perfunctory, to say the least: the male merely mounts the female from behind and clings onto her legs with his feet. The young are coloured very differently from the adults, but the baby coat is shed quite early on, except in De Brazza's monkey where the young remain differently coloured from the adult until they reach maturity. There is no doubt that the infant guenon arouses a protective response in the other animals. If it cries out in distress the others come rushing over at once. The infant's dis-tinctive coat also causes a response by the adults. Guenons have been known to live as much as 30 years in captivity.

Making faces at enemies

In the forest, the only serious predator is the crowned eagle, which glides silently among the treetops ready to grab unsus-pecting monkeys. It usually seizes its prey by the head. On the savannah there are many more potential predators, and the monkeys there are correspondingly more wary. In the air there are the martial eagle and various other birds of prey and on the ground leopards are the main predators. The monkeys have separate alarm calls for aerial and ground predators. Guenons rarely defend themselves, but they make threats both to other monkeys and to other intruders such as man. The males display by bouncing up and down on branches or in the crowns of trees; or they may drop into the undergrowth making sure they are seen, trying to lure the intruder away. Meanwhile, the females and young of the green monkey sit looking at the intruder, swaying the upper part of the body toward it, so that the arms go forward along the branch. The head and shoulders may be moved from side to side, but the eyes are kept fixed. The body is then swayed back and the animal sits upright with its arms held straight down. Moustached monkeys wag their heads from side to side, so emphasising the white lip-stripe, while redtails bob their heads up and down, emphasising the white streak on the nose. When really frightened the adults honk and the young chitter. And when frightened they often yawn, which is a way of releasing tension and not a sign of tiredness as one might think.

Layers of monkeys

Guenons live in a variety of habitats. Green monkeys live on the savannah and in the savannah woodland. Others live in forests, but these may be primary or secondary forest, mountain or swamp forest. Moreover, within a certain type of forest different species live at different levels. Four or five species may share the same part of the forest, in what is called arboreal stratification. Tropical rain forests grow extremely tall but not all the trees grow equally tall. So they can be conveniently divided into four layers. The lowest, the shrub layer, consists of a tangle of woody and herbaceous vegetation near the ground. Next up is the first layer of trees forming the lower canopy, at 25–50 ft. The third is the middle canopy, 50–120 ft high, and at the top is the upper canopy, made up of the highest crowns with considerable gaps between them. This is 120–150 ft high. Many guenons tend to sleep at higher levels, coming down lower during the daytime. The Diana monkey, in primary forest, lives in the upper canopy and comes down to the middle canopy. Blue monkeys also live at high levels, coming down into the lower canopy but only rarely, if ever, into the shrub layer. Redtails go up at night into the middle canopy and come down onto the ground by day, so they tend to be at different levels from blue monkeys at any given time of day. De Brazza's monkey lives at low levels and is often to be found on the forest floor, searching for food or just sitting surveying its surroundings.

class	**Mammalia**
order	**Primates**
family	**Cercopithecidae**
genus & species	***Cercopithecus aethiops*** *green monkey*
	C. mitis *blue monkey*
	C. ascanius *red-tailed monkey*
	C. diana *Diana monkey*
	C. neglectus *De Brazza monkey*
	C. hamlyni *Hamlyn's monkey*
	C. cephus *moustached monkey*
	C. talapoin *talapoin*

▽ *Monkey layers: a tropical rain forest can be divided into various layers. Three strata are recognised: the higher canopy of trees with broad umbrella-like crowns, the middle canopy whose tree tops usually meet, and the lower canopy whose trees are closely bound with creepers. From studies guenons have been found to prefer certain levels as shown in the illustration below.*

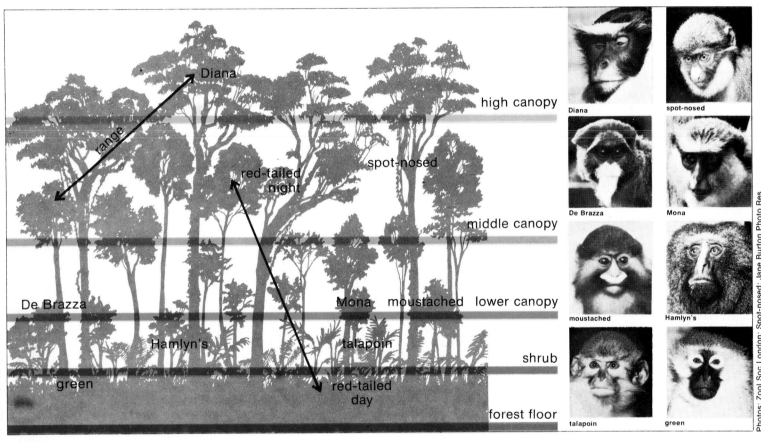

Photos: Zool Soc London; Spot-nosed: Jane Burton Photo Res

▽ *Guenons live in a variety of habitats in suitable parts of Africa south of the Sahara desert.*

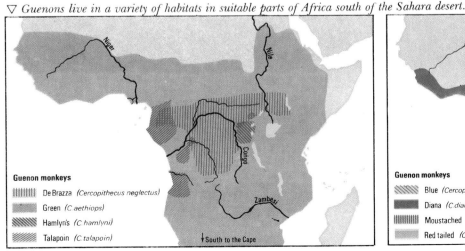

Guenon monkeys
- De Brazza *(Cercopithecus neglectus)*
- Green *(C. aethiops)*
- Hamlyn's *(C. hamlyni)*
- Talapoin *(C. talapoin)*

↓ South to the Cape

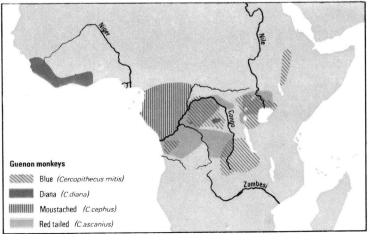

Guenon monkeys
- Blue *(Cercopithecus mitis)*
- Diana *(C. diana)*
- Moustached *(C. cephus)*
- Red tailed *(C. ascanius)*

Guillemot

Guillemots are duck-like on the water; in the air they fly on rapidly-whirring wings and on land they stand upright like small penguins, with their long paddle-like feet stuck out in front of them. They are auks, birds like diving petrels and penguins: committed to the sea except for breeding. In America they are called murres, a name which originated in southwest England.

The common guillemot is 16 in. long, black or dark brown on the upperparts and white underneath with a white stripe on the wings. In the winter the neck and throat turn from black to white leaving a black stripe behind the eye. There is a common 'bridled' form with a white eye ring and white line extending back from it. Brünnich's guillemot is very similar. It has a thicker bill, which at close quarters can be seen to have a pale line on the sides, and in winter plumage it lacks the black stripe behind the eye. The black guillemot, also called the tystie, is smaller, 13 in. long. The plumage is black, or bottle green in a good light, with large white patches on the wings and bright red feet. In winter the underparts become white and the head, neck and back mottled with white.

Guillemots are birds of the northern seas. The common guillemot breeds as far south as Portugal in the Atlantic and North Korea and San Francisco in the Pacific. In Europe it is found on the coasts of Scandinavia, the British Isles and Brittany, and elsewhere in Iceland, Alaska, the Kuriles and Kamchatka, Newfoundland and in one isolated part of the Greenland coast. Brünnich's guillemot lives farther north. It breeds nowhere in Europe but is found on Baffin Island, Spitzbergen, Franz Josef Land and other islands in the Arctic Sea. The black guillemot's range combines the ranges of its two relatives. In Europe, it breeds along the coasts of Scandinavia and the British Isles.

Within the British Isles, the common and black guillemots have decreased in numbers over the past centuries, especially in the south of England. The original cause may have been the warming of the sea that has altered the fish populations so affecting the birds' food, but nowadays oil pollution is serious. The wreck of the oil-tanker **Torrey Canyon** in 1967 and the subsequent mass pollution of the western Channel had a very serious effect, but it is not known yet whether this is permanent. Auks suffer badly from oil because their reaction to it is to dive, thus becoming even more polluted, whereas other seabirds such as gulls take off and so escape.

◁ Common guillemots braving the wind. The white eye-ring and white line from the eye corner identifies the 'bridled' form, which used to be thought of as a separate species.

▽ Distinctive white wing patches identify the black guillemot. In winter or spring it has a complete body moult producing a black nuptial plumage with white wing or cheek patches. It tends to be less gregarious than other auks in the breeding season.

△ Diving success: black guillemots grip their captive fish. The prey is usually obtained by underwater pursuit, the birds submerging with a kick of the feet while partially spreading their wings. Under water the wings are used for propulsion, whereas the feet are used in steering.

◁ 'The ugly duckling': rather an uninspiring chick will emerge to be a fully-fledged striking adult in a few weeks.

▷ Brünnich's guillemots preen and stretch. Very like common guillemot, they are distinguished at all seasons by noticeably shorter and thicker bills. The breeding ledges on the steep cliff shows signs of years of use from the droppings.

DW Hatton

Rewards of a crowded life: common guillemots need to be stimulated by a noisy crowd to mate successfully. They pack tightly together on rocks and pinnacles, the lower ledges being used by kittiwakes and shags.

A babble of guillemots

In the breeding season the air round the cliffs where the guillemots nest is thick with thousands of birds, not only guillemots but other auks such as razorbills and puffins. They are continually flying in and out, coming in to land with feet hanging down for stability or taking off with rapidly beating wings that seem too small to hold the bird in the air. The air is also full of their muttered growls, like the babble of schoolchildren let out to play. At the end of the breeding season all this activity ceases and the ledges and rocks empty as the guillemots migrate southwards and seawards for the winter. Brünnich's guillemot winters off Scandinavia and is only rarely seen off British coasts, although this may be due to the difficulty of distinguishing it from the common guillemot. Indeed, identification of auks is always very difficult unless they have some distinctive feature such as the coloured bills of puffins or the white wing patches of black guillemots. The common guillemot migrates south to winter off southern England, France and Spain in late July or early August, but the black guille-

mot is more sedentary, especially in the southern parts of its range where it spends the winter not far from the shore. Guillemots moult shortly after leaving the breeding grounds. Like many other water birds all the flight feathers are shed at once and the guillemots are incapable of flying until the new set grows.

Eating eels and butterfish

Like diving petrels and penguins, guillemots swim underwater with their wings. They feed on marine animals caught while diving. Fish, such as sand eels and butterfish, make up the major part of their diet. Some shrimps, prawns, crabs, molluscs and worms are also eaten, especially by the black guillemot which feeds closer inshore.

Cliff-hanging nests

Common and Brünnich's guillemots nest on narrow, often very inaccessible ledges on cliffs and only very rarely in crevices or between boulders. They can be seen jammed together on the ledges with hardly room to move, and eggs and chicks are often lost by being kicked off the ledge by

the jostling parents. Black guillemots breed at the bottom of cliffs, in crevices or under boulders and they are less sociable than the other guillemots. Courtship takes place in the water with one bird swimming around the other which spins to face it. Black guillemots utter a wheezy sigh, rather like a gate being slowly opened on a rusty hinge, showing the red insides of their mouths. Sometimes guillemots indulge in communal displays in which several pairs come together, circling and bobbing or standing up and flapping their wings. They also play 'follow-the-leader', swimming, or occasionally flying, in line ahead following the leading bird as it dives and leaps.

Black guillemots usually lay 2 eggs, the others lay one egg which is incubated for 4 weeks. Both sexes share incubation.

Black guillemot chicks leave the nest when they are fully able to look after themselves at the age of about 40 days. The other guillemots leave the nest before their flight feathers have fully grown and are only $\frac{1}{3}$ of the adult weight. The chicks leave the nesting ledges in the evening, leaping off and plummeting down despite rapid wing beats. On hitting the water they call and are joined by their parents who escort them out to sea where they are fed until they can fend for themselves.

The bridled guillemot was once thought to be a distinct species but it is now known that it is a colour phase of the common guillemot, the two existing side by side like red- and black-masked Gouldian finches (p 927) or the crossbills (p 581).

British bird census

In 1938 and 1939 censuses were made of the guillemot colonies in the British Isles and in several other parts of the North Atlantic, mainly by members of the British Trust for Ornithology. The results showed that the proportion of bridled guillemots varied from place to place. In the British Isles it was lowest in the south and east and highest in the north and west, from less than 1% on the south coast to 25% in the Shetlands. In Iceland the change is reversed, from 7–9% in the north to 50% in the south. Over the whole of the North Atlantic there is a general increase of bridled guillemots as one goes farther north. The survey was repeated in 1948–50 and again in 1959–60, and over 20 years the proportions had varied very little. It seems that the bridled form of the guillemot has some advantage in cold climates and this idea is supported by the increased proportion of bridled guillemots in eastern Canada as compared with Britain or Scandinavia. Due to the Gulf Stream, arctic conditions do not extend so far south on the eastern side of the Atlantic as they do in Canada. What advantage bridled guillemots could have over their normal relatives is not known.

class	**Aves**
order	**Charadriiformes**
family	**Alcidae**
genera & species	***Uria aalge*** *common guillemot* ***U. lomvia*** *Brünnich's guillemot* ***Cepphus grylle*** *black guillemot*